Endorsement

I honor my dear friend who calls me "papa"–what a tremendous gift in multiple dimensions. We are forever grateful that Father allowed us to assemble a company of minstrels and psalmists to give legs to the vision Ray Hughes has carried for so long: To release the sound of the blood-redeemed into locations that have been seedbeds of the blues.

The "Blue Journey" changed all of our lives. One of my favorite things about land assignments and prayer journeys are the orchestrated moments that are far beyond what any man could plan. In city after city, the Lord met us and we waded deep in the eternal waters of "blue sound." I said many times on the trip that the blues may bring you relief for a moment, but they can't get you to your destiny; however, the sound of the fullness of the color blue (that Father created) can.

Our Blue Journey team participated in a tiny part of praying for all people to awaken now to the fullness of eternal purpose and original intent, preparing the way for the King of Kings, and oh, what a journey it was.

Our "Blue Journey" was filled with revelation and surprises, which Jonathan has chronicled so very, very well. Read on, dear friend, may your heart be filled with joy, insight, and new dimensions of understanding as you read Jonathan's wonderful account of this life-changing *Glory in the Blues!*

— James Nesbit, prophetic artist, psalmist, and minister
Prophetic Art of James Nesbit (jnesbit.com)
Prepare the Way Ministries International (ptwministries.com)

Glory in the Blues

A Worship Journey

Jonathan Fitt

KAIROS PUBLISHING

Ordering Information:
Quantity sales. Special discounts are available on quantity purchases by corporations, associations, and others. For details, contact Jonathan Fitt at the address below.

jfitt@me.com
www.jonathanfitt.com

Cover art and design by James Nesbit and Pixel Studio
Editing by Inksnatcher.com
Book Layout ©2013 BookDesignTemplates.com

Glory in the Blues: A Worship Journey/Jonathan Fitt. —1st ed.
ISBN 978-0-9818864-6-6

For Ashley, the love of my life and my best friend. I can't imagine my world without you.

Contents

About the Author

Acknowledgements

I am thankful for the inspiration and empowerment of men of God like Ray Hughes and James Nesbit, and for spiritual fathers and mothers everywhere—on whose shoulders we all stand.

I would also like to thank my amazing wife, Ashley, and our four kids: Gabriel, Grace, Liev, and Nora, who have willingly shared their husband/daddy with so many others. You have been my constant source of purpose, joy, and strength.

Last but not least, a huge thanks to everyone that made this journey such a success. Your sacrifices are recorded in heaven! I couldn't possibly begin to list every person who opened doors to us or worshipped and prayed with us in each region, but below are the men and women who drove or flew across the country, far from their homes and families, to be a part of releasing the glory of the blue note.

Blue Journey Team Members

Michael Bartulla

Byron Bishop

Saundra Corner

Doug Dietsch

Jonathan Fitt

Jamie Fitt

Sylvia Prescott Gast

David Munoz

James Nesbit

Isaac Nesbit

Steve Shoaf

Keith Stone

Chuck Thurston

Therese Thurston

Randy Webb

Charles Williams

Foreword

It could be said that in music, all that is present has come out of the past. All of our melodies, rhythms, lyrics, and tones came to us from "once upon a time." Man attempts to define and describe music with words like pitch, meter, form, duration, vibration, and intensity. And, of course, that list has been expanded into a library of terms and a terminology that has filled the educational, religious, and secular halls of the world. I, for one, have great respect for the systems of the world given to helping us understand music and all of its complexities and wonderful contributions to life.

However, when music ceases to be a subject for the inquiring mind and becomes an experience rather than an experiment, the journey becomes music and music becomes the journey. So beware, this journal is not about journalism, it really is about the journey. A journey for a small group of dedicated men and women moved to carry water and wind to some dry places and do something musical that felt a bit like chasing a wind that was chasing them.

One of the most beautiful aspects of the whole thing was knowing that the water was needed and the breezes were appreciated. In communities where people felt lost and forgotten, many felt loved and celebrated. The sounds and songs were like refreshing winds that carried sacred seeds filled with lyrics of truth and awakening hope.

Music is able to reach back and honor the past on one hand while reaching forward and to honor the promise for the future as a powerful force. Jonathan has respectfully portrayed the "once upon a time" and at the same time announced the beauty of the new day.

This writing is a chronicling of that sometimes overlooked quality in music. It has the ability to reproduce itself in the hearts of people. It reminds us once again that where much was sown, much will be reaped, even in dry thirsty places.

And I propose that one of these days, people will look back at the Blue Journey of 2015 and say,

Once upon a time . . .

— Ray Hughes, D.D., speaker, singer/songwriter
founder of Selah Ministries (selahministries.org)
author of multiple books, including the Saunterers series

Many places have laid claim to being the land
where the blues were born.
The blues weren't born anywhere.
The blues became, and went, and they keep going
but they never get gone. They move
like a slow and weary wind across time and space. They love
to linger in places that know and feel song. They long
to live in places where they're not just sung.

They are meant to be heard and seen
and smelled and touched
and tasted,
and they refuse to be limited to only five senses.
Blues are tone poems with a temperature, sweated out
in twelve bars of time. They hang
like a hot mist over sun-fried deltas and creep
through foggy hollers and echo
across ragged mountains.

And they always speak up when a back door opens
in a rainy alley.
Once they are heard, they are old enough to walk.
Once they start walking, they never stop going,
but they never get gone.
And if you think you've got'em, you are dead wrong.

They've got you.

— Ray Hughes
rayhughes.org

Introduction

My family has always been a musical one. Both of my parents were public school music teachers, and both their families and the generations before them were musical as well. You might say it's in the genes. To me, music was more of a hobby than a means of worshipping God while growing up, the only exception being when I occasionally sang in the church choir, but even that felt more like a performance (albeit in church) than worship.

When I was a teenager, I attended a youth conference in Toronto where several things happened. First, I was exposed to Charismatic Christianity in a profound way. Secondly, I was exposed to the use of multiple instruments in worship. I was raised in church, but my paradigm for worship instruments included little more than a pipe organ, a piano, and perhaps a choir of handbells on a special Sunday. The worship band of this conference, however, was made up of electric guitars and basses, drums, synthesizers, etc., and they were playing music that sounded an awful lot like rock and roll! I remember being rather amazed by all this, and thinking we needed it at our church. As a result, we made a decision to start a family worship band to lead this new type of worship at our church. It was a learning process, but a glorious one.

This all happened for me at a time when I was beginning to become much more serious about my faith, and wondering if God had a plan for my life and what that might be. Fast forward almost twenty years: My brother Jamie and I are the directors of a regional worship and prayer ministry called Philadelphia Tabernacle of David. Our family continues to lead worship all over the region, and various parts of the nation. We do our best to serve the body of Christ in this capacity, and we have been raising up a community of worship and prayer warriors for the kingdom.

A Change of Course—Meeting James Nesbit

In 2011, we found out that a man named James Nesbit was on an assignment from the Lord to hold forty days of worship and prayer in Washington, D.C. We were invited to go lead some worship there, and we got to meet James and his team for the first time. After the forty days were over, they came to stay with us for eleven days of meetings in Philadelphia, and a beautiful and lasting relationship was born. The Lord knitted our hearts together. I honor James because he challenged us as a worship ministry, calling us to a whole new level in a way no one else had in quite some time. He was moving in some things that were new to him as well, so in some ways we were growing and maturing together. James is gifted at a lot of things, but to me his most precious gift is the grace to help people break out of whatever box they might be in. As I have gotten to know James better and traveled with him more extensively, I have seen this gift operating in him over and over. He calls it "throwing people out of the boat." Being thrown out of a boat might be a traumatic experience, but discovering that you know how to swim, or even fly, makes it all worthwhile. We all just need a loving father who cares deeply enough about us to guide us through those experiences—to push us out of the boat, pick us up when we stumble, and cheer wildly when we succeed. This is what I have observed James do so many times with so many people, and it is one of the reasons why I call him a "papa."

Chronicling the Blue Journey

In late 2014 James started talking about a "Blue Journey." I was sold on it immediately. Throughout the course of 2015, we would go on about eight trips together, one per month, and visit many of the places where the blues were birthed to release what we carry. I can remember being on the first leg of the trip to Charleston, South Carolina. We had stopped off at a southern BBQ restaurant aptly named "Sticky Fingers." I had heard James's stories from some of his longer prayer journeys before, so I asked him who was in charge of taking notes on the journey—so we could remember all the amazing places we were in and the things the Lord showed us. What I didn't realize was that by asking that, I was basically nominating myself! I started to take the best notes I could along the way, and between how captivated I was with the music history we got to relive and all the things the Lord did along the way, I started to realize I was writing a book.

My purpose in writing this was twofold. First, I wanted to chronicle a journey I believe really shifted some things—not just for us personally, but also for others, and even for our nation. The second reason was to cast some vision for those who might be called to similar assignments. I feel so privileged to be in the company of men like Ray Hughes and James Nesbit, who are forerunners of so much for the body of Christ. I realize, though, there are many who have no paradigm for what we are doing, much less why or how we do it. There's no right or wrong way to go on a journey like this. It is, after all, simply a matter of doing whatever the Lord shows you to do. My hope, though, is that this story might help some to be open to things they hadn't considered before, or to see their own assignments in a different light. My heart is particularly for artists and creative types, that we would all learn how to break out of whatever boxes we are in and use our gifts to effectively bring heaven to earth.

Jonathan Fitt

1

The Vision

The concept for the Blue Journey was birthed by an amazing visionary named Ray Hughes. Ray is a singer, songwriter, musician, historian, speaker, author, and all-around pioneer. He has been inspiring and ministering to the body of Christ in the areas of worship, creativity, and the arts for several decades, and he is a spiritual father to many. One of Ray's particular areas of expertise lies at the intersection of music history and church or revival history. In other words, he researches the sounds and songs that have shaped history and how they pertain to the kingdom of God. It is from this vantage point that the vision for Blue Journey begins to come into focus.

Ray identified a number of strategic locations where a sound known as the blues had either been birthed, or experienced, some major development in its evolution. These places were "seedbeds" where a sound was birthed that undeniably shifted our nation. Unfortunately, the roots and some of the effects of the blues were not altogether positive. The blues became a sound closely associated with suffering, injustice, heartache, and loss, and its purveyors were generally found in the dens of iniquity of their time. Ray's vision was that if the people of God would go to these birthplaces of the blues and release pure worship as redeemed sons, there would once again arise a sound that would shift and impact our nation for the kingdom of God.

Because Ray was and is in such demand as an itinerant minister and speaker, he hadn't had the opportunity to turn this vision into reality, so James Nesbit, a good friend of Ray's, decided to assemble a team of prophetic musicians and intercessors to give legs to Ray's vision. It was this team, which we started calling "The Blue Journey Team," that I was honored to be a part of. We honor you, Ray Hughes, and the incredible vision and inspiration you have brought to us and so many others in the body.

The Power of Sound

To understand what this journey was really all about, I feel you must understand some of the principles behind what we do and why we do it. The first principle is the power of sound. I believe sound is a primary creative force. Here is what I mean by that: When God created the universe and everything in it, the Bible says he spoke or released a sound. This is confirmed many times in Scripture in places like Romans 4:17, where it says "God, who gives life to the dead and calls those things which do not exist as though they did," and also in Hebrews 11:3, where we see that "the worlds were framed by the word of God," or by his sound. When God creates, the vehicle he seems to use is sound.

Not only does he create with sound, but it is through sound that he sustains his creation. Hebrews 1:3 says he is "upholding all things by the word of His power." The universe is suspended in time and space by God's sound. If he were to stop singing his song, our universe would cease to exist. Some scientists say there is observable evidence the universe was created by sound (although obviously we disagree on the source of this sound), and quantum theory suggests that at the most basic level, all matter is basically a frequency or a vibration. This all makes perfect sense, since the Bible clearly tells us that all things were created and are being held together by his sound.

So God creates and sustains with sound, and then everything he has created releases the sound he has placed in it back to him. Scripture is filled with references to creation releasing its sound. The heavens, seas, trees, angels, stars, oceans, rocks, etc. all praise him, and are constantly vibrating at the frequency God created them with. All of creation is joining in the giant symphony of praise to its Creator! We can release the sound he has placed in us too—as praise and worship to our Creator. However, unlike most of the rest of creation, we have free will, and we can choose to honor God or to dishonor him with our sound.

In fact, beyond using our sound to praise him, we are invited to use our sound to become co-creators with him! Ever since God asked Adam to name the animals in the Garden, he has shown an earnest desire for us to partner with him in accomplishing his purposes. I believe that a big part of what it means to be made in his image is that we have been given an imagination, free will, and an incredible ability to be like our Creator when we shape sound. These things give us the ability to see or imagine something and then use sound to create what we have seen in our mind. If we have our minds submitted to the Lord, and what we see in our minds is his truth and his reality, then we can cause that reality to manifest in the earth. But if what we see in our minds is there by our own flesh or, worse, demonic activity, then we can cause this reality to manifest as well. The sound we release is no less powerful if we do it with bad intentions. This was made clear at the Tower of Babel, where God felt it necessary to confuse the sounds of the people so they could not fulfill their evil intent. Perhaps this is why there are so many warnings throughout Scripture about our release of sound. Proverbs 18:21 says "Death and life are in the power of the tongue." James 3 says that while the tongue is a small member, like that of a ship's rudder, it can steer the entire ship.

God has invited us to partner with him, and indeed has given us dominion and authority in this realm to call things forth. But we know it is only out of the abundance of the heart that the mouth speaks, so we are not just releasing sound, we are releasing sound with intent behind it. The intent of our heart is paramount when we release our sound, and this leads into the next principle.

Original Intent

There are no accidents or mistakes when God creates. He infuses everything he creates with divine destiny. There is nothing he makes that is void of purpose or plan. This applies to humanity, as well as the rest of creation. All the earth, including the very ground we walk on, geographic regions, cities, and nations are infused with his purposes. Proverbs 16:4

says "The Lord has made everything for its own purpose" (NASB). Acts 17:26 says "He has made from one blood every nation of men to dwell on all the face of the earth, and has determined their pre-appointed times and the boundaries of their dwellings." We are generally aware that God has plans and purposes for people, but sometimes we don't consider that he has plans and purposes for the rest of the created order; but it should come as no surprise to us, since humans are simply animated dirt with the breath of God in us.

Not only does God have a plan for you, but he has appointed this time—before the foundation of the world—to be the exact moment in history when you would walk the earth. He has predetermined the bounds of your habitation, the places for you to dwell and live, and he even has plans and purposes for that very ground he has called you to live on. All of creation is brimming with his divine purpose and original intent.

Previously I wrote about the intent of our hearts and how important it is. I believe the responsibility and privilege of every believer is to co-labor with Father God through the release of our sound, calling forth his original intent over all of creation. In order to do this, our intent must be aligned with his. Of course, to call forth his original intent we must first know what it is. Sometimes this is fairly obvious and sometimes it takes some real discernment, but one thing we have found is that the Devil is oftentimes very busy trying to get a person, city, or even a nation to operate in the exact opposite calling of its divine purpose. Many times the area of greatest weakness is the area God intends to be the greatest strength.

Jeremiah 29:11 is a great example of the Lord calling forth his original intent: "For I know the thoughts that I think toward you, says the Lord, thoughts of peace and not of evil, to give you a future and a hope." When we see a person, city, or even a nation not fulfilling its God-given purpose, it is our absolute right and privilege as believers to align our intent with his and release our sound over it, say, "That's not what God made you for," and call for the original intent of the Father to be released for that person or that ground.

The original intent of the Lord for many of the places we visited on this journey was for them to be sound portals. In other words, part of the dream of God's heart for these regions was that they would release new sounds and new songs that shift and shape the culture. In some cases, the sounds that have come from these places and the dramatic impact they have had on our nation is nearly inexplicable in the natural. It becomes quite easy to understand, though, once you know it was part of God's divine purpose in creating that land.

Just because something is graced with a gift from the Lord does not mean the gift will always be used for his glory, but this is where the sons of God come into play. Our job is to call everything back to its divine purpose—darkness that's been on the land or on the people, purposes of God that have been abandoned, aborted, or perverted—we call it all back to become everything the Father created it to be.

Eternal Language

This topic deserves an entire book of its own, but suffice to say that as we endeavor to call forth God's purposes in the earth, not only must the intent of our hearts align with his, but so must our language. Since the eternal realm is outside of space and time, there is no here or there. There is no before or after. Everything exists right here, right now. Eternal truths are "right here, right now" truths, no matter where or when we find ourselves in space and time. A great example of this is the atoning work of Christ on the cross. There was a point in time and space when Jesus was crucified, but the reality of his crucifixion is an eternal one. That is why several times in the New Testament, Jesus is referred to as the lamb slain before the foundation of the world. Even though the crucifixion was manifested in the earth realm in 33 A.D., the power of it extends to all of time and space. It is an eternal NOW reality. This is also why John says he saw a freshly slain lamb, even though he saw this many years after the cross (see Revelation 5:6). The reality of the freshly slain lamb is for right now, it is not just an event that happened 2,000 years ago and thousands of miles away. It is an eternal reality we can access as though it were happening right here, right now. This is the nature of eternal reality, and we must let this truth infiltrate how we worship and how we pray.

The purposes of God for people, cities, and even nations are also *now* realities. We must be careful not to declare future possibilities when God wants us to declare now realities. James is famous for saying "God's not about to . . . he's not getting ready to . . . he's not fixing to . . . he is doing it right now!" Remember, the power of life and death are in the tongue—in the sounds we release. We can unintentionally put off into the future what God is trying to do right now. If we perpetually prophesy that something is "coming," we may never see it manifest. God is calling us to prophesy his "right here, right now" realities.

This concept is critical to walking out our faith each and every day. Who you are in Christ is not what you *could* become, it is who you are right now in the eternal realm. It is a now reality. That is why we can claim verses like Philippians 4:13, Romans 8:37, and 1 Corinthians 2:16, even though it seems they haven't manifested in us yet. This is how faith operates. It is accessing and calling forth into the earth the things which already exist in the Spirit.

Perspectives Are Reflected

Of course, our language is also connected to our identity. We can't begin to call forth God's purposes in the earth until we begin to understand that we have been positioned and commissioned to do exactly that. If we see ourselves as merely sinners saved by grace, making petitions before a lofty distant king, our perspective will be reflected in our worship and prayer. Alternatively, if we see ourselves as saints that have been raised up and seated together with Christ, sent forth into the world by the one with all the authority in heaven and earth, as his governing ambassadors, our language will look very different. I believe that mature sons who know who they are and what they are called to do can release a governmental sound in the earth—one all of creation has been eagerly awaiting (see Romans 8:19).

The songs, prayers, worship, and declarations we released on this journey (and that you will be reading about) might seem strange or unfamiliar to you. It was not traditional praise or worship in the sense that we were not simply communicating our adoration to God, nor was it traditional prayer, in that we were not entreating the Lord. Our assignment on this journey was to travel through the land and, through our sound and song, declare the eternal realities of God's divine purpose and original intent over these regions, and all those people connected with these regions.

Hopefully these principles that guided us help put in context the vision of the Blue Journey. The vision was to do something that would shift the sound of our nation by traveling to these sound portals—places where blues music had been birthed—and agree with Father God's original purpose for the region and the people in it. We believed that as we traveled the land on this assignment, there would be a shift in the atmosphere that would cause new sounds and songs to be birthed—sounds that would shift our nation for the kingdom of God, pervading every aspect of culture just as the blues had so many years ago.

Exactly What Are the Blues?

The blues is a genre or style of music that originated in the Deep South during the late nineteenth and early twentieth centuries. It is the meeting of traditional African music—with its roots extending to the transatlantic slave trade—and European folk songs. The blues were used as a sort of coping mechanism of a people born into a segregated society—one in which they experienced incredible abuse and mistreatment. The music carries in it the cries for freedom, justice, and equality, making the history of the blues as much an insight into the inner conflict and turmoil within American society as a musical genre.

From the earliest days of slavery, the songs of the slaves took the call and response format of field "hollers" and "shouts." As the widespread conversion of African slaves to Christianity took place, the "spirituals" were born. Blues music as we know it probably started to develop shortly after the Civil War during the Reconstruction Era. But, the earliest chronicling of blues music didn't happen until the turn of the century. As blacks transitioned from slavery to paid work in lumber, mining, or sharecropping, they began to have time and money to spend on things like leisure and entertainment. Juke joints began to spring up—places where many would gather to dance, sing, drink, and gamble. It was in these juke joints that the music that had primarily been played for self-expression or as work songs became a form of entertainment. The expansion of railroads, another industry many freed slaves began working in, also played a large part in the propagation of the musical genre. As travel became quicker and cheaper for both musicians and audiences, so did the demand for the musical entertainment. The blues did not reach a broader or more integrated audience until decades later, when many blacks began migrating north to larger cities for non-agricultural jobs.

Today, blues music is somewhat difficult to define. Most descriptions either feel far too broad or too narrow. Blues has been so pervasive and so influential on so many other genres and styles that it is difficult to categorically separate them. Rhythm and blues, jazz, rock and roll, swing, soul, hip-hop, and many other styles have a discernible connection to the sound of the blues. Since at least as far back as the 1950s, most definitions of blues music are also definitions for large portions of popular music, and stricter definitions of the blues simply don't encompass all of the music that the earliest and most well-known blues musicians played. The blues became the foundation for countless artists of a multitude of styles, and yet the music itself is much more than a stepping-stone to more advanced expressions. If it were not, it would have become obsolete decades ago. It persists today as a genre widely recognized for spawning much of our most beloved American music, but it's still enjoyed in its rawest, most primitive forms. One can't help but be struck by the irony that some of our nation's most treasured musical art was birthed primarily from the sounds of a people many deemed worthless, except for their value as cheap labor.

From a technical standpoint, the blues could be defined as a cyclical music form with a repeating chord progression, generally 12 measures in length and in 4/4 time, although 8- and 16-measure patterns and 3/4 time are not all that rare. Generally, the progression consists of three chords: The tonic, the subdominant, and the dominant, with the dominant generally being the final chord sounded before repeating back to the beginning of the progression. Of course, many examples from the earliest recordings of proto-blues music defy these conventions.

Melodically, blues is distinguished by "blue notes" which are the flatted versions of the third, fifth, and seventh notes of the scale. These notes could be played purely, but were more often the result of "bent" notes either sung or played on the guitar, and were actually tones that were "between the cracks," or in between the other notes in the scale. These "bent" and "between the cracks" notes are a hallmark of the blues' melodic structure. These tones are easily achievable with the human voice or on a guitar by either bending the strings or using a slide, whereas they are not playable on an instrument like a piano.

Lyrically, the blues have a three-line verse structure, with the second line repeating the first and a different third line. The lyrics were oftentimes improvised, and one theory as to why the first two lines repeat is that it gave the singer extra time to think up what the third line would be.

While a straightforward technical description of the blues would say they consist of flattened notes, twelve-bar patterns, and three-line stanzas, the blues have always been much more than what that description can capture. The blues deliver a sheer emotional impact that simply belies technical explanation. The blues are both a vehicle for self-expression and the song of a community. Like many great art forms, they give voice to a state of mind, but can mean many things to different people. To many, the blues are a compelling and inspiring art form, while to others they are nothing more than the last vestiges of oppression and racial inequality. For some, the blues are any song delivered by a black performer, a view born out of an ideology that the blues pervade every aspect of the black American experience. Blues is generally thought to be the music of sadness and self-pity, but it is also the music of passion and protest. In short, the blues can refer to a long list of things that are as varied as the people who project their meanings onto it.

The Sound and Song

For our journey, we were thinking of the blues primarily as the sound and song of a people who had suffered immeasurable pain, loss, and trauma. It was the sound of a land defiled and covered with innocent blood from slavery, discrimination, and many other injustices. The Devil, the true enemy of all our souls, had used morally blind black folks (in Africa) and white folks (in America and Europe) to steal the song and kill the destiny of millions. The authentic expression of true worship that God places in every person and people group had been stolen and silenced, only to reemerge generations later as a sound of frustration, betrayal, agony, and despair.

But blues singers were much more than the sum total of their injustices. Even the earliest blues performers were one-of-a-kind artists, not merely the voices of an angry or depressed people. The pioneers of the blues sound, and the lands on which they released their art form, were not accidental, nor is anything with God. The destiny of these minstrels and psalmists was to release a sound that would sweep across our nation, permanently changing our culture. And they did that, though there was tremendous darkness mixed into the sound because of the trauma they had experienced.

A Prophetic Prayer Journey

Many would ask us to explain exactly what we were doing on this journey, because it didn't fit their normal paradigms. We aren't exactly what people think of as a typical itinerant Christian ministry; we don't hold conferences, crusades or typical church meetings, nor do we fit into the category of a performance group on tour. We weren't traveling to perform for large crowds or lead them in worship; in fact, in many cases we hadn't been invited into the region by anyone in particular. We didn't make a concerted effort to be in any typical venues— either church related or otherwise. We certainly weren't there to make money, although we did accept donations. We were never sure we would even recoup our travel expenses. We just didn't seem to check any of the normal boxes.

The best way I could describe this journey to people was to call it a prophetic prayer journey. As recently as twenty years ago, prophetic prayer journeys (or land assignments, as some might call them) were something barely anyone in the body of Christ had heard of, including myself. Today you hear about this all the time, at least, you do in certain circles. At the risk of oversimplifying this concept, a prophetic prayer journey is going to a place the Lord tells you, and doing whatever he shows you to do once you get there. I suppose that since we were releasing our prayers set to music, a *prophetic worship journey* might be an even better description. Scripture is replete with examples of God asking ordinary people to unusual things like throwing a hunk of wood into poisonous waters to make them drinkable, shouting down the walls of a city, or striking the ground with arrows to have victory over an enemy army. While unusual, simple acts of obedience can unlock the purposes of God in the earth. I believe the Lord is awakening his body to these truths and assignments in this hour because he is preparing the earth for a great harvest of souls, and he alone will have the glory.

A principle in Scripture is that if God is going to bless a people group and its land, then the high places and the altars to things other than God must be torn down. The kings of ancient Israel were blessed in part by their choice to remove idolatry and defilements from the land. When under righteous kings that removed defilements from the land, Israel enjoyed victory and prosperity. Under wicked kings that allowed the altars to stand or even promoted idolatrous worship, Israel experienced the judgement of God in the form of droughts, famines, and defeats.

Today it is not just the king's job, it is the job of every believer to tear down the high places and remove the defilements from the land God has called us to. We are all his kings and priests. There are a number of things that bring defilement on our land, like idolatry, immorality, innocent bloodshed, and broken covenants. Jesus's work on the cross broke the curse of sin and of death, completely disarmed the Devil, and restored dominion over the earth to mankind, just as it was in the Garden before the fall. The enemy has no authority on earth except that which has been granted to him through human agency. If we want the blessings of God on our land, then it is our responsibility to gain discernment into what the strategy of the enemy has been, and to find out where he has been given legal access (by man) to block the blessings of God and bring darkness on the land. Then, we must close these loopholes through spiritual warfare, praise, worship, prayer, repentance, or a prophetic act, and release the light of the kingdom in place of that darkness. Many are rising up and being released into this kind of ministry, and this was a significant part of our focus on the Blue Journey.

Our assignment on this journey was to go back to these sound portals where the blues had been birthed and release the pure worship of redeemed sons of God. We would do that the best way we knew how: We'd intercede for every bloodline and every family tree connected to the sound of the blues—that they would come out of whatever darkness they were in and into God's glorious light, releasing a sound that would once again shift our nation.

2

Gearing Up

Before the formal part of the Blue Journey began, the team ended up coming together twice—once in New Orleans and once in Philadelphia. We didn't plan it this way, but the Lord was putting us right where we needed to be, as always. Both of these gatherings ended up being times when Ray Hughes ministered and sowed much into those of us who would be traveling through the land. Even though Ray wouldn't be traveling with us on the Blue Journey, we took him with us in the Spirit—through what he carried and released over (and into) us.

In New Orleans, the gathering was called "Releasing the Musical Militia" and was hosted by Keith Stone. It was my first time meeting Keith and Cindi, but they welcomed us all so warmly, we quickly became family. And who wouldn't when there is fresh catfish, jambalaya, cornbread, and gumbo involved?

The gathering was at the time of the two-hundredth anniversary of the Battle of New Orleans (part of the War of 1812), and the Lord had put it on Keith's heart to gather the worshippers in that area, and have Ray come and release what he carries so that a musical militia of worshipping warriors would be raised up in that region. Not only was the timing of the gathering strategic, but the location was as well. Being at the mouth of the Mississippi River, New Orleans is a strategic place in our country. During the War of 1812, Britain knew that control over New Orleans would mean control over the river, and therefore the ability to divide our nation. I believe this is prophetically significant because we still have an enemy who is looking for any opportunity to divide our nation, and certain geographic regions become targets for his schemes.

There were a few things Ray shared with us about the heart attitude of this musical militia that weekend that I know really impacted the team, and became anthems we released as we traveled through the Blue Journey. The Lord was raising us up as a company of those who know how to do battle with weapons of praise—not against flesh and blood, but against the powers and principalities that would seek to steal, kill, and destroy our nation.

Musical Militia

Andrew Jackson was a key figure in the War of 1812, and he led our forces to victory in the Battle of New Orleans. Jackson was hot-headed and ill-tempered. He was a violent man known to prefer dueling as a means of settling disputes. He was also a hard man, earning himself the nickname "Old Hickory." While he may have been out of control in many ways, his brutality and explosiveness served him well as a leader of our troops, and it was this same passion that allowed him to eventually become the leader of our nation. Jackson knew who his enemies were (he was abused by the British as a boy), he loved the land, and he was willing to fight and die rather than let the enemy have his land. There is a huge lesson in that for us as we seek to advance the kingdom. What if we fought the way Jackson did for the destiny of our bloodlines? What if we had the same fiery passion he had and contended for the covenant promises of God over our cities?

An example of Jackson's resolve and toughness occurred when a longtime rival and bitter enemy of Jackson's insulted both him and his wife. In 1806, Charles Dickinson accused Jackson of reneging on a horse race bet, calling him a coward and a scoundrel, and then went on to insult Jackson's wife, Rachel, by calling her a bigamist. She had married Jackson without realizing her previous husband had not finalized his divorce papers. As was typical for Jackson, wanting to defend the honor of his wife and himself, he challenged Dickinson to a duel. Jackson's problem was that Dickinson was a renowned duelist and an accurate shot, and Jackson was said to be a terrible marksman. When the morning of the duel came, Jackson strategized that he would allow Dickinson to shoot first, figuring he stood no chance of killing Dickinson if he tried to fire too quickly. He had to hope that Dickinson's shot would either miss or be non-fatal, and then take his time firing so as to make sure to kill Dickinson. Dickinson's shot hit Jackson right near his heart. Jackson put his hand over the wound, raised his pistol, and shot Dickinson dead. The bullet in Jackson proved to be non-fatal, but it was so close to his heart that they were never able to remove it.

The lesson for us is that there is a certain level of resolve we must start to take on in order to see the kingdom advance. Jackson was willing to lay his life down in order to defend the honor of his wife. He didn't mind taking a bullet, but he wasn't about to allow the lies of his enemy to go unchallenged. Andrew Jackson was by some accounts a terrible president, and he did a lot of very regrettable things, particularly his policies regarding slavery and his forced relocation of Native people—known as the Trail of Tears. In some ways Jackson's presidency contributed to the scars and blood on our land that inspired the sound of the blues, pain we need to bring healing to; but his courage, resolve, and toughness can still serve as an inspiration as we try to get the heart of God for our land.

What if there was a musical militia that had courage and resolve that went beyond having nice church services, that contended for the promises of God in our spheres of influence? What if we began to move in the power of the Spirit, released the sound and the song of the purposes of God over our regions, and drowned out every lie of the enemy in our land? Jesus and almost all of the early disciples laid down their lives for the advancement of the kingdom in their time. While many of us will not be called to physically lay down our lives, it is that kind of resolve and determination the people of God need to grab hold of if we want to see the enemy removed from our land and our families, and see the kingdom advance.

Army of the Thankful

King David was another example of what the musical militia is all about. David was a man after God's own heart, and because of that, God gave David his heart for the people and the land of

Israel. When a giant named Goliath began mocking God and his people, David knew exactly what to do. He charged into battle, silenced the voice of the enemy, and delivered the people of God from the oppression of the Philistines. Because David had the heart of God for the land and people of Israel, he was willing to attack any enemy that stood in between them and the covenant promises of God. David walked in this reality so powerfully that all the men who would surround him—although they were initially in debt, distressed, and discontent—would eventually catch his heart and become mighty men and giant killers themselves.

When David became king, he appointed thousands of musicians and singers to stand before the ark of the covenant, the symbol of God's presence and glory, and release continuous praise and worship. The song of the Lord was released by people who understood the covenant of God for their land; they were part of a musical militia. They developed a vocabulary for the mighty acts and the wondrous works of God in their midst, and the release was so powerful that no other voices could rise up against this sound. Israel enjoyed a level of fulfillment of God's promises that was unprecedented until that time. They moved in the reality that no enemies can stand in the manifest presence of God.

In 1 Chronicles 16:4 we see that David appointed his musical militia "to commemorate, to thank, and to praise the Lord God of Israel." (Imagine having hundreds and thousands of full-time church staff whose only job is to praise and thank the Lord.) All they did all day was sing of the awesomeness of their God. This represents a drastically different set of values than we have today, but this was what David did.

What if there were thousands of those that would carry the presence of God into every city in every corner of society?

What if there was an army raised up that would thank the Lord for who he is and what he is doing every day, and who would take the sound of thanksgiving to a faithful God throughout all the land? What if there was a musical militia that would learn to displace dark atmospheres with the sound of thanksgiving? I believe every hopeless person and every hopeless situation would be drawn to the sound and transformed by it.

What we need is not political activism or emotion-driven church services. God is returning the purpose and power of song to our lives. What we need is a thankful army to arise and drown out the voice of every enemy of God. We need to create atmospheres so charged with the presence of God that every other sound bends its knee, and every lost soul is unable to resist the mercy and the love of the Father.

> *"The LORD is my strength and song, and He has become my salvation."* — Exodus 15:2

The blues were the sound betrayal and abandonment produced; the sound of the blood on the land. Pure worship is the song and the sound of God's covenant with his people and the land. It only takes a small militia to move a lot of things in the spiritual realm and see God's covenant promises established. These concepts of a musical militia and an army of the thankful were keys Ray released, which we carried with us and began to call forth on our journey.

Releasing the Sound of Jubilee

The second of these pre-gatherings was in Philadelphia, again with Ray Hughes. We called this gathering, "Releasing the Sound of Jubilee." Not only were we entering into the actual year of Jubilee on the Jewish calendar (according to many), but also we had been feeling prophetically for several years that our nation had been in an extended season of Jubilee. There is a sound associated with the declaration of Jubilee in the land, and our focus was on releasing that sound over our nation.

God commanded the Israelites to observe the Jubilee every fifty years (see Leviticus 25). You could almost think of it as hitting a reset button. Every fifty years all debts were cancelled, all land was returned to its original owners, and all slaves were set free. The slate was wiped clean for everyone. God did this to remind Israel that the earth was his, and everything in it.

But Jubilee is more than just freedom from debts and bondages. One of the points Ray made so powerfully that weekend was that there is freedom *from* and freedom *to*. Coming out of Egypt is only half of the plan; the other half is to enter into the Promised Land! Deuteronomy 6:23 says "He brought us *out* from there, that He might bring us *in*, to give us the land of which He swore to our fathers" (emphasis mine). Jubilee is about coming out of that which has ensnared you for the express purpose of being free to enter into the inheritance he has prepared for you. This revelation tied in directly to our purpose for this journey—to call forth God's original intent for every bloodline and family tree: that people would come out of whatever darkness they had been in, come forth into the light and walk in the fullness of what the Lord ordained for them.

There is an obvious spiritual application for us regarding Jubilee, in the sense that God has brought us out of the bondage of our sins and brought us into the inheritance of his promises for us. In some sense we live in a state of perpetual Jubilee because of Christ's work on the cross, but in this season of heightened awareness to Jubilee, I believe many people are coming out of slave mindsets and the captivity of old wounds, and stepping into eternal truth.

There is also a natural reality to Jubilee in that sometimes the Lord needs to relocate us to the place he wants us planted in. We already looked at Acts 17:26, which says he has predetermined the time and place in which we are to live. In other words, God has a plan for each and every one of us, and that includes not only our assignments on the earth, but the exact times we are to carry them out and the exact places on the earth where we are to be planted. We can only bear the fruit he desires us to bear, and can only experience him in fullness when we are planted in the ground he has set apart for us, our inheritance. During this season of Jubilee, the Lord is relocating and repositioning many of his saints, and empowering them to walk in the fullness of their destinies.

Our nation has come to the end of a number of fifty-year cycles, particularly as it related to sound. The period of time from 1962 to 1967 was a formative and defining season in our country: there were sounds that were released that have profoundly affected the path our nation has been on for the last fifty years. One sound was the civil rights movement, a sound that cried out for love to triumph over hate. Another sound released was the "shot heard around the world" —the assassination of JFK—a sound that many say signaled a loss of innocence in our country. Prayer was removed from schools, another dramatic shift in sound. The British invasion of pop and rock bands, most notably the Beatles, occurred during this time, permanently altering the sound of popular music. The list goes on. The sounds released during this period in our history represented a huge shift in our nation that has greatly affected the trajectory of our culture for the last fifty years, and it was primarily not a shift for the better.

During this season of Jubilee, as we arrive at the end of many fifty-year cycles, the Lord is calling us out of mindsets that are not of him, and inviting us to step into a new season of walking in the destiny he has for us. It is Jubilee time for those who have been in any kind of bondage. It's time to step into the new day. Releasing the sound of Jubilee was another main theme we would be carrying with us on the Blue Journey.

The Glory of the Blue Note

One of the descriptive taglines James gave this journey early on was "releasing the glory of the blue note." Throughout the book, you may see references to this. Here's why:

The first thing God did when he created the world was create light (see Genesis 1). (Notice, he did not create the sun. That was not until day four.) Out of the entire electromagnetic spectrum that we are aware of, there is only a tiny sliver humans can perceive as visible light. Within that tiny sliver, there is a wide variety of frequencies and wavelengths, and these different wavelengths are what we perceive as colors. God is light, and colors—the frequency of light he has given us eyes to see—represent aspects of his nature and of eternal truth.

Throughout Scripture colors are used symbolically, and certain consistencies seem to develop. For instance, the color red speaks to us of sin and redemption. Isaiah 1:18 is a great example of red referring to sin: "Though your sins are like scarlet, they shall be as white as snow; though they are red like crimson, they shall be as wool." We know that red is the color of blood, which is needed for the forgiveness of sins, both in the Old and New Testaments. Jesus even used wine, another red color, to symbolize his blood, which he said was for the forgiveness of sins. We might also pull on that same verse in Isaiah (as well as many others) to come to the conclusion that white symbolizes purity or righteousness. Green might represent fruitfulness or growth, and so on.

The color blue in the Bible can mean quite a few different things, depending on your interpretation. One meaning most seem to agree on is that it refers to royalty. The color blue in nature (outside of the sky) is actually somewhat rare, as there aren't many blue animals, plants, etc. One of the only ways to make a blue dye in biblical times was to use the secretions of a certain sea snail, which obviously made it difficult and expensive to produce. Only people of great importance or royalty would have had clothes made with this dye, which is why it might symbolize royalty. God instructed that many of the temple furnishings and priestly garments were to include the color of blue, adding further to the idea of a special set-apart item. Blue is also something we associate with the sky and large bodies of water, so it can speak to us of peace or tranquility. According to some who have studied the topic more than me, blue might refer to any of the following: royalty, loyalty, trust, justice, order, peace, righteousness, and revelation.

Somewhere along the line, blue has come to represent the exact opposite of these characteristics in many ways, especially in how it directly applies to the blues as music and as a state of mind. The blues are a sound of sadness, heartache, and loss. Instead of royalty, the blues were the sound of a subjugated people. Instead of justice, the blues were a sound born out of great injustice. They were a sound of no peace and no order. Instead of righteousness, the blues became closely associated with wickedness and darkness. Far from being a special set-apart thing, the blues were labeled by many as the Devil's music.

Blues music as we know it today was not what gave the color blue its current meaning and connotation, but it certainly helped cement it into our language and culture. There are many theories on why the color blue has become associated with sadness and pain, and all of them go back several hundred years. One of the possibilities comes from a seventeenth century English expression "blue devils," a term used to describe the intense visual hallucinations associated with alcohol withdrawal, and that was later shortened to "the blues."

I wrote earlier about how a big part of our focus on this journey was to call forth God's original intent. Part of this included calling forth his original intent for the color blue. We want to restore, redeem, and call into order whatever the enemy has stolen or perverted. James said many times on the trip: "The sound of the blues might bring temporary comfort, but it won't bring you into your destiny". The true glory of the color blue, however, is all about bringing you into your destiny. There is a new blue sound being birthed—the sound of royalty, loyalty, trust, justice, order, peace, righteousness, and revelation—and it's being released in every heart.

Bloodlines and Family Trees

One of the ways we prayed a lot on this journey, as James taught, was to pray for bloodlines and family trees. Every single one of us is part of a bloodline that we can trace straight back to the garden of Eden. The DNA that makes you who you are was carried through all those generations so it could be manifest in you for such a time as this. And you are carrying the DNA of all the future generations to come in your bloodline.

Likewise, we are all part of family trees that connect us with those the Lord has also chosen for this time. You are the current day expression of everything your bloodline and family was designed to be at creation. There is a certain fruit your family tree has been purposed to produce that is different than that of every other tree. There is a certain fragrance only your family tree can release. The Lord has planted your tree where it is because that is where he wants you to blossom and produce the fruit he intends you to produce.

Why are bloodlines and family trees so important? Because they are the basic building blocks of cities. The vision for our journey was to cause a shift in the sound of our nation. Well, the best way to affect a nation is to affect each city. The way to affect a city is to affect the bloodlines and family trees that make it up. We should never underestimate the power of ministering to one person. He or she is the current expression of a bloodline going all the way back to the garden. What if a shift in one person caused a shift in the whole family tree, which then started to produce fruit and fragrance like never before? Family trees can shift cities, and cities can shift nations.

There is divine purpose and original intent on every bloodline and family tree. So what happens when that destiny becomes aborted in some way? What happens when a tree is uprooted and replanted in another area where the Lord did not intend it to be? What happens when a member of a bloodline suffers a severe enough trauma that it affects it generation to generation?

The men and women that started to release the sound of the blues in our nation were members of bloodlines and family trees that had suffered incredible trauma, and were perhaps no longer planted where the Lord intended they flourish. The sound they released was a reflection of this trauma, and perhaps a type of coping mechanism. The West African slave trade uprooted the lives of millions—millions of destines aborted, dreams stolen, and family trees splintered. That kind of trauma can echo down for many generations. And it doesn't echo simply by word of mouth. Scientists have started to confirm that it may be possible for our experiences and memories (particularly traumatic ones) to be passed down to our children through our DNA.

Every bloodline and family tree that is still to this day lost in darkness: We call you into the light. We break off every curse, every trauma, and release the power of the Father's healing love.

We unlock and call forth the divine purpose and original intent of each and every one. We call every tree to produce the fruit and the fragrance it has been created to produce.

CHAPTER 3

Charleston

It's impossible to say exactly where the blues started. Many places lay claim to the title of "birthplace of the blues." For most Mississippi residents, for instance, it is unfathomable to think that the blues were born anywhere else besides the Delta. But if we understand the blues as being influenced by the work songs of slaves, or even by African folk music, calling the Delta the birthplace of the blues creates an issue, as it was largely unsettled land prior to the Civil War.

Musical styles are evolutionary in nature, which makes it difficult to pinpoint "firsts." For every man who was titled "father of the blues" or something similar, you can always point to a predecessor who had a profound impact on his music. Ironically, despite the macho image of the bluesman, it was women like "Ma" Rainey and Bessie Smith who dominated the first few years of blues music recording, not men at all. Still, the evidence suggests that blues music was being sung long before it was ever recorded.

We can point to *defining* moments for the blues, but rarely *primary* ones. Unfortunately for us, there was no one that really documented the earliest blues sounds being released, and that is likely because at the time, it seemed rather unremarkable to those who heard it.

Paul Oliver writes, "When blues singers could be heard in any Southern courthouse square on a Saturday afternoon, and the porches of country stores and plantation cabins were alive to the sound of idly-picked guitars, there were few who stopped to consider the nature of the music. Blues singers were part of the total scene, no more to be remarked on than were the mules that drew the wagons to the cotton gin, or the watermelons ripening on the vines in the spreading patches. There's a certain appropriateness in this, for folk music is the creation of the people and not separate from the whole fabric of living." [1]

The reality is that the blues didn't begin with one man or woman, one show, or one city, and if it had, there was no one to document such an event. There was almost no one at all to chronicle the earliest blues music, save for the artists themselves.

Charlotte Forten

One of the earliest written references to the blues as a state of mind is in the writings of Charlotte Forten. Charlotte was a free black woman from Philadelphia who moved to South Carolina in 1862 to educate slave children, as part of the Port Royal Experiment. In her journal, she wrote about having "the blues" after having heard the cries of slaves as they were being beaten and mistreated. Charlotte certainly did not coin the term

---

[1] Paul Oliver, *The Story of the Blues* (London: Barrie & Jenkins, 1978).

"blues," but her reference to it, and her additional observations about the "strange" and "wild" music she heard coming from the slaves as they worked, predates what are considered to be some of the earliest blues performers by several decades.

Charlotte captured some of the song lyrics she heard coming from the slaves, but she found it difficult to describe their manner of singing:

> *"I wonder where my mudder gone, sing oh graveyard*
>
> *Graveyard ought to know me, sing Jerusalem*
>
> *Oh carry my mudder in de graveyard . . . ."*

While the concept of the blues may have already been commonly known, it is possible that her writings helped connect the term and the state of mind to the style of music being birthed. Since Charlotte was living and teaching in Charleston, SC, during this time, we decided to begin our journey there.

The Journey Begins

The Blues Journey team arrived in Charleston on a blustery Thursday afternoon in February. It was a historically cold day in Charleston's history, setting the record by four degrees. Our hosts Frank, Charlotte, and Judy greeted us warmly, but it was quickly time to head to that night's venue. I remember the excitement of being on our first leg of this journey. I wanted to come prepared, yet I had little idea what to expect. I imagine most of the team felt similarly. We were in unchartered waters in more ways than one, but that's when things can get exciting.

On our first night in Charleston, we gathered to worship at a church but also invited some local musicians to come and jam with us. We were open to any musicians that would come, but we were praying in particular for a drummer, because we did not have one with us. One of the things we had been discussing was that slave owners would ban their slaves from playing drums because they knew it could be used for communication purposes and had the potential to incite an insurrection. James felt as though our difficulty in finding drummers might have been prophetically significant and related to the fact that drums were outlawed on these plantations for all those years.

We were also looking out for any horn players, after James shared the story about the Jenkins Orphanage Bands. Daniel Jenkins was a Baptist minister who started an orphanage for African-American youth and hired music teachers to tutor all the children. Eventually a brass band formed that toured the nation, and even some other countries, raising money for the orphanage. We really wanted to honor that ministry and release a sound over anyone carrying an orphan spirit in that region, but felt we needed to have some horns to do so.

To our delight, we were joined by a number of musicians with various instruments, including several guitars, a harmonica, a violin, and (praise God!) a drummer. Unfortunately, there were no horn players. Some of the musicians were believers, others weren't. It was an amazing time of worshipping together with these local artists, and we believe they were deeply touched as we honored the sound they were carrying. We sang and prayed over the city of Charleston, and over every bloodline and family tree.

At one point in the evening, a rabbi who was playing guitar with us prophesied, "God says he has given you a gift to release rivers of life!" What followed was a powerful time of the one new man, Jew and Gentile together, releasing rivers of life over the region. Afterwards we asked Clay, one of the local musicians with us, to release his heart to the Lord on the violin. Clay released his heart beautifully and took the meeting to an entirely different level.

> *This is a new day! There is a new sound rising in the whirlwind for Charleston. It's a blood-bought sound. We release the sound of holy love! The color blue is opening tonight. The sound of holy order, eternal decree, and blood-bought justice is being released. This is the sound heard around the world. It's the sound of the one new man.*

Another highlight of the evening for us was the pastor of the church dancing with his son and grandson, moving in the sound and in a new level of freedom. He said, "I've gotta have more of this!" We knew what we were there to do was probably outside of some people's comfort zones, so we were happy to have this level of agreement and acceptance from the leadership. I am blessed to be a part of a worship ministry in which three generations worship the Lord together. I realize this is a rare thing, so it blesses me when I see it. We had a great night at the church, and the Blue Journey was off to a fast start.

Edisto Island

The following morning was bright and sunny but still cold as we drove out to Edisto Island. Never having driven around this area before, I was struck by the scenery, particularly the trees. The palmetto trees, which give South Carolina its nickname–the Palmetto state—are beautiful. To a northerner like myself, they give the landscape an almost tropical look, but the real showstoppers are the live oaks that line the sides of the roads. In some places these majestic trees arch over the roads, with Spanish moss hanging overhead. Even in the winter the natural beauty of the area was stunning. The photos I tried to take through the windshield with my phone couldn't possibly do it justice.

Edisto Island

Edisto Island is the place where Charlotte Forten lived and worked for at least part of her time in Charleston, and it is also the location of some of the earliest plantations in America. Once we arrived on Edisto, we connected with Pastor Wey, who graciously opened the doors of his church, Trinity Anglican, to allow us to worship there. In the garden outside the church entrance was a fountain of water that looked like it had frozen midstream. Jamie couldn't resist taking a picture with his tongue stuck to it. We were happy to get inside and out of the cold.

Worshiping with James Nesbit can be quite an adventure. We hardly ever have any songs or set lists; it is all about playing and singing what we see and hear in the moment. During most of our worship sessions, we simply allowed the Lord to lead us in spontaneous worship. There were some times, however, when we wanted to be intentional about releasing our sound in the blues style. At Edisto Island, with David leading out, we released a sound based off of B.B. King's classic, "The Thrill Is Gone," but instead of singing "The thrill is gone," we declared "Joy has come." We declared that fire was going forth from Edisto to the entire east coast, and that signs, wonders, and miracles were breaking out.

> *Joy has come and driven the blues away. We don't sing the blues; our lips were made for praise. You were created for purpose, Edisto. The wounds of the past are healed through the blood of the Son.*
>
> *We agree with Wey's prayers. Wey is making a way. We thank you for the angels of Edisto watching over the eternal intercessions. Signs and wonders are breaking out on Edisto. We bless every bloodline to find its way home today.*

We didn't have a drummer with us at Edisto, so I actually ended up using an iPad app to give us some drum loops to play with. Keith remembers hearing a sound in his spirit as we were driving out onto the island, and he said the drum loops on the iPad captured it perfectly. So, praise God, he was even moving through our technology. After completing our time of worship with Pastor Wey, we bundled up and journeyed out to the beach to put our feet on the land and release the sound of the shofar.

Later that night and the following morning, we held open meetings again at Seacoast Church. James did some teaching, but mostly we released our sound to the Lord. These were powerful times of worship, and we were blessed to be joined by two powerful singers, Barbara and Deborah. The Lord provided us with a fantastic drummer named John. Isaac and Clay played over a woman named Georgeanne who was battling cancer. We also had the opportunity to bless and honor Lilian, a long-time intercessor for the region.

> *It is finished! It's finishing time in Charleston's history; its Jubilee. Father, in your mercy prune every tree. The warmth of Father's love is here.*
>
> *The awakening train is here setting bloodlines free. It's not the year of the blues, it's the year of Jubilee. Charleston is joined with heaven. We release the joy of our song.*

A City of Firsts

Charleston is a city of firsts: The first independent government in America, the first Masonic temple, the first major slave rebellion, the first major naval battle in the Revolutionary War, the first state to secede, and the first shots fired in the Civil War all happened here. Part of God's original intent for Charleston was to be a city that leads and sets trends. Additionally, there have been several sounds or dance movements that have originated here. One was a dance movement called the Charleston, popular in the 1920s, and another was a dance movement called the twist, made popular by Chubby Checker in the 1960s. It seems that Charleston, South Carolina, has the redemptive gift to set trends and release movements that sweep the nation, so while we were there, we declared that a new movement of the Spirit would come forth from Charleston that would sweep our nation.

That evening our hosts were gracious enough to take us for an incredible meal on the waterfront and join us in prayer walking and releasing our sound in historic downtown Charleston. Being on a prayer assignment, we didn't want to spend too much time just sightseeing, but we did want to take at least some time to see and hear the sights and sounds of the land. Sometimes it is difficult to really carry love for a city in your heart if you don't take any time to look around while you are there. It's all too easy to minister in a city and barely see anything outside of the hotel and the church where your meetings are. Our walk made it easier to carry the land and region in our hearts as we journeyed on to the other cities.

Charleston has a long and diverse history, being one of the earliest and most successful settlements in the English colonies. As we explored downtown Charleston, we came to a place called the Four Corners of Law. At the intersection of Broad and Meeting Street stand St. Michael's Episcopal Church, Charleston City Hall, Charleston County Courthouse, and the Federal courthouse. It is called the Four Corners of Law because four buildings represent local, state, federal, and ecclesiastical law at one intersection. James blew the shofar on each of the four corners, and we declared the government of God to all four corners. Nearby, we were also able to pray and make declarations over the birthplace of the Scottish Rite of Free Masonry.

Second Line

As we were praying through Charleston, we heard a wedding taking place about a block away, so we went to investigate. It turned out to be a New Orleans-style wedding, complete with a second line parade and Dixieland band. I think Keith Stone, being from New Orleans, was particularly drawn to this second line sound, so we wandered down to the reception hall—where the procession was entering—and found the band continuing to play outside.

Keith recalled the scene: "When the band played the last note, they were left alone outside the reception hall. James turned and said to all of us, 'Let's honor these musicians and give them a round of applause.' We did, and they all took a bow. We then had the opportunity to speak with the band leader, Fred. James asked Fred to close his eyes and play whatever he had in his heart. Fred said he couldn't recall ever doing that or being asked to do such a thing. He then played a short motif which included a blue note or two."

We couldn't help but feel as though the Lord was intentionally crossing our paths with the horn player we had been praying for. We prayed a blessing over Fred before continuing our journey.

On our way back to where our cars were parked, we passed by the old slave market. Directly next to the slave market was Philadelphia Alley, an alley the people of Philadelphia had generously sent money to help rebuild after it had been decimated by fires. They decided to name the alley after Philadelphia, a strong abolitionist city, which now stands right next to the slave market.

Because our journey had really started before we knew it, in both New Orleans and Philadelphia, we felt that both the New Orleans style wedding and Philadelphia Alley were signs of the hand of the Father blessing our journey. While we come to cities to connect and release the heart of God, we also carry with us our home territory and home sound, so it is a confirmation when God connects us back to our home cities in this way. As we concluded our time in historic Charleston, we drove past several other churches and James blew the shofar over each one. All of us felt a powerful release. We felt much was accomplished as we walked the streets of Charleston.

Sullivan's Island

The following day we ventured to Sullivan's Island. There were several reasons why we felt Sullivan's Island was strategic. The first was that it was the location of a very strategic, pivotal point in a Revolutionary War battle. As the story goes, approximately 435 colonists were able to repel several thousand soldiers in the British Army's Infantry and the most sophisticated navy of that era. They did this by building a fort out of the palmetto trees. The palmetto trees are so fibrous that the cannon shells from the British ships were absorbed into the trees and did not explode. This was also instrumental in South Carolina becoming known as the Palmetto State.

Another major point of significance with Sullivan's Island is that it was the location of the first shots fired in the Civil War. As part of God's divine setup, a member of our team, Keith Stone, grew up in the same hometown as the man who ordered the shot, and Keith's wife is a direct descendent of the man who made the first shot. So we were able to do some identification(al) repentance.

The most significant aspect of Sullivan's Island predates any of this war history: the island was the largest slave port in North America. Scholars disagree on the exact percentages, ranging anywhere from 40 to 80 percent, but it is not in dispute that Sullivan's Island was the single largest point of disembarkation for slaves coming from West Africa into what would become the United States of America. Under extreme conditions of human bondage and degradation, tens of thousands of West Africans arrived between 1700 and 1775, and those who passed through Sullivan's Island account for a significant portion of African Americans now in our country.

As we walked across the island toward the beach, the weight of what this island represented hit me like a ton of bricks. It was palpable. I felt as though I experienced the depravity and cruelty of what slavery represented in a way I never had before. I imagined the island full of thousands of West Africans who had been plucked by their own people out of their homes and forced onto slave ships. The journey itself would have been torturous, being chained in a ship for weeks at sea. And now here they stood on Sullivan's Island. There was no shelter, no bathrooms. The hopes and dreams they once had for themselves and their families were completely shattered. There they mourned the loss of those who didn't survive the trip and were simply thrown overboard, and of those who survived but were driven to insanity by the trauma. Families were intentionally separated, processed, moved around like animals, and prepared for sale to a plantation owner that would force them into hard labor. This was their future, not only for the rest of their lives, but for generations to come. It is no wonder the trauma of this injustice still echoes through the bloodlines and descendants of those who disembarked here. We pondered the fact that large portions of the African-American population, even those from our home cities much farther north, could likely trace their ancestry to this exact spot. In many ways, this was it: Ground Zero, the epicenter of bloodlines and family trees traumatized by slavery and racial injustice.

"Hope deferred makes the heart sick, but desire fulfilled is a tree of life." — Proverbs 13:12 NASB

A big part of what made blues music what it was, was the hopelessness and trauma of slavery. It is the sound of broken dreams and shattered lives. Music was a way of coping with this trauma when nothing else seemed to help, and the earliest sounds and lyrics born out of it reflected this. I knew that a big part of our assignment was to root out and cancel hope deferred off every bloodline that was still experiencing the trauma and injustice of slavery, and replace it with a tree of life.

We were only on Sullivan's Island for a brief time, but I know for many of us it was a life-changing one. It continues to be one of the most prominent moments for me, as I look back on the entirety of the journey. It was a holy moment. We marked the time by sharing communion, blessing the land, and driving a stake in the ground.

We proclaim Jubilee over every bloodline that can connect itself to Sullivan's Island. It is time to come out of every form of bondage and step into the destiny that Father has for you. Hopelessness is broken off. It is time to dream again.

Our final stop in the Charleston area was at Christ's Church, which has over 300 years of history. It was originally built in

1707 and has been destroyed and rebuilt several times—being burnt in both the Revolutionary and Civil Wars, but the original walls still stand. It is located on what was called the King's Highway, a highway from colonial times that connected Charleston to Boston. We set up to play right on the road outside, underneath a large live oak. It had been discerned by some of the intercessors there that this very same tree was used to lynch black slaves, so once again we were confronted head on with the trauma of slavery and general mistreatment of blacks in this region. Having been powerfully impacted on Sullivan's Island, the worship time at Christ Church was intense. We might have worshipped there for longer, but when the rainclouds started to gather and a few drops fell, we knew it was time to pack up and get our gear out of the rain. We prayed a special blessing on our hosts and those who had helped make a way for us before concluding our first leg of the Blue Journey.

> *The lights are on and darkness is fleeing. Bloodlines are singing the awakening song. It's the shot heard around the world. Winds of worship are blowing through the land. Every bloodline is holy rolling on the King's highway. Holy is the sound of the blue note in Charleston. We bless the ground, release your sound. The leaves on the trees are singing.*

4

The Shoals

Florence and Muscle Shoals are on opposite sides of the Tennessee River in Alabama. Together with two other cities (Tuscumbia and Sheffield), they make up the quad-city area, which is collectively referred to by the locals as "The Shoals." It is a land rich with history, particularly musical history, which brings all kinds of music-loving tourists to the area year after year.

There are quite a few logistics to be considered and handled with journeys like these. Flights, hotels, host churches, land assignments, permits, meals, transportation, sound gear, generators, to name a few. Sometimes all the pieces seem to fall in place without extraordinary effort, while other times it seems to be, well, more challenging. Something the Lord has made clear to me, through James and others, is that we are absolutely connected to the prayers of all those who have gone before us. It may not be this way all the time, but the overall ease or difficulty of a prophetic prayer journey can certainly be a sign of the prayers (or lack thereof) of the saints and the overall spiritual climate of a region. If the soil is loose and easy to plant in, it is probably because someone else already paid the price and plowed the ground. If the ground is hard, then there is spiritual plowing that still needs to be done before the land is ready to receive the seed. Florence and Muscle Shoals felt like one of these harder places to us. Very few doors opened to us, and even one of the places we thought was welcoming us closed the doors to us at the last minute. Members of our team had all kinds of challenges with sickness, traffic, and weather.

James had discerned that one of the reasons for the hard ground was religious fear, the type of sentiment that led people to call for the crucifixion of Jesus. It is the fear of disrupting the status quo, fear that our nice tidy religious structures and paradigms will get all messy. Jesus wasn't afraid to disrupt the status quo or to make a mess of the religious structures of his day, and neither should we be. Sometimes a holy disruption is exactly what is needed when the Lord wants to plant something new or uncover something that has been there all along. When Jesus cursed the fig tree and it died, it was a metaphor for the disrupting of the status quo and the coming of the kingdom. His mission, like ours, was to uproot every religious structure of man that doesn't bear fruit and in its place plant the seeds of the true kingdom, which bears much fruit. Religious fear will fight this disruption tooth and nail.

Another thought concerning the "hardness" we were experiencing is that we were being tempted by the powers and principalities in that region. As we began to read between the lines of the history of the region, we knew there was a great deal of lingering bitterness and disappointment. The color blue can represent trust and loyalty, but a root of bitterness can grow where trust has been broken and dishonor sown. It would have been very easy for our team to allow a root of bitterness to grow where dishonor had been sown, especially when a church closed its doors to us at the last minute. The enemy would have liked nothing more than for us to be carrying the same root of bitterness many people in that region seemed to be carrying. Fortunately, Satan is predictable in his methods, and we spotted this temptation and chose to move in the opposite spirit. I honor James for his leadership in that capacity.

The Singing River

With nowhere else to go, we ended up worshipping in a pavilion right on the banks of the Tennessee "singing" River. Jamie and I were experiencing a lot of travel delays and difficulties, so we arrived at the pavilion later than the rest of the group, and they were already set up and worshipping by the time we got there. I'm not sure if James started singing about this because he saw us arriving or if it was a God thing, but as we opened the doors of our car, we could hear the group singing about brotherly love. Since Jamie and I are brothers and hail from Philadelphia, "the City of Brotherly Love," this is a theme close to our hearts. We couldn't wait to get our gear out of the car, plug in, and join the worship that was rising from this little pavilion on the river. It was already raining when we got there, but the rest of the team told us the rain started at the exact moment they had begun to worship.

The worship that night was intense, but the conditions were less than desirable. The only relief from the cold damp wind blowing through the pavilion was a small fire in the hearth that we all warmed our hands at periodically. Only a small crowd of us gathered there, but somehow it consisted of folks from nine different states. I really felt like we were tapping into something ancient as we released our song over bloodlines by the singing river. Our intent was that every bloodline and family tree connected to that land would be awakened, regardless of what kind of condition they found themselves in in that moment.

We sensed there had previously been a sound of mourning in the land, but that night the Lord was giving beauty for ashes as part of his divine exchange. Mike Curtis, our host in the land, played drums with us most of the evening, but toward the end of the evening he got out his guitar and began to sing. Mike is a very gifted songwriter, but we enjoyed hearing him sing spontaneously from his heart just as much as with his well-crafted songs. Our worship that night at the pavilion concluded with us taking communion on the land. Afterwards, as we were putting out the fire, we found two half-burnt objects in the ashes that spoke to us prophetically: a guitar pick and a small spiral notebook. We sensed these items in the ashes spoke of all the musicians and songwriters whose dreams had been stolen or turned to ashes, and whose songs and lyrics had fallen to the ground because of strife and competition.

Brotherly love is here—brotherly love, born from above—brotherly love is here.

The Tennessee River is singing again, releasing the destinies of men, releasing the destinies of men.

The Shoals are awakening to eternal love. The Shoals are rising to the "It is finished" sound.

We bless every psalmist and minstrel in the Shoals with eyes to see and ears to hear. We declare that where there once were ashes, the beauty of the Lord is being seen and heard. Every song and lyric that has been stolen, discarded, or twisted is being redeemed through the blood of Jesus.

There were a number of visions seen that night during the worship. One that really impacted me was shared by David Munoz. He saw the Native people of that land in their canoes, but he realized they were actually rowing their canoes through a river of clouds far above the actual river below. To understand why this was so significant, you need to know what the history of the land is, particularly that of the Native people of the land, the Yuchi.

The Yuchi people lived in this region during the sixteenth, seventeenth, and eighteenth centuries. They were mound builders. Their origins are unclear, as their language doesn't resemble any other known language, but the existence of the tribe was documented as far back as 1541 by Hernando de Soto, an explorer from Spain. Their numbers dwindled due to wars and diseases until the early nineteenth century, when their numbers were quite few. Those survivors were forcibly removed from their land as part of the Indian Removal Act in the 1830s. The Trail of Tears, named for its devastating effects on the people it affected, forced Native people that lived east of the Mississippi to be relocated, mostly to present-day Oklahoma. Torn from their native lands, they were literally force-marched to their destinations. Thousands suffered and died from disease, starvation, and exposure. Similar to the West African slave trade, an entire people group was uprooted from everything it knew and forced into deplorable conditions. Dreams were shattered and all hope was lost. Bloodlines and family trees were traumatized for generations, and there was blood on the land.

One story of the Yuchi people particularly captivated our team. Teh-La-Nay, a young Yuchi girl, was fourteen years old when the soldiers came and made her and her sister, Whana-le, orphans and forced them to start marching west. Stripped of their identities in exchange for a numbered tag, they traveled by foot or wagon over 1,000 miles to the Indian territory that was to be their new home. But after one winter on the reservation, Teh-La-Nay knew she must try to return home. "If I stay here, I'll die" she said. She needed to return to the land she resonated with and loved. Over the next five years, she slowly but surely walked her way back to the banks of the Tennessee River, which the Yuchi had nicknamed the "singing river," because they said the river sounded like the voice of a woman singing. Along the way she broke her leg and suffered immeasurable hardships, and also underwent the risks of being captured or killed. She made it back to her land, though, and married and had three children before dying at a young age.

Tom Hendrix is the great-great grandson of Teh-La-Nay, and today he lives in the area where his great-great grandmother might have resettled. Over thirty years ago, Tom decided to honor his ancestor with a monument of stone, and so for the next thirty years or so he slowly but surely built two stone walls, placing a stone for every step Teh-La-Nay took on her forced journey west to Oklahoma in one, and a stone for every step she took to come back home in the other. The monument is estimated to be made of over eight million pounds of stone. "I wore out three trucks, twenty-two wheelbarrows, 3,700 pairs of gloves, three dogs, and one old man," Tom said. It is an amazing picture of honor to those who have gone before him and what they endured.

David's vision of the Native people rowing their canoes through the clouds spoke of our worship bringing healing to the land. The land of the singing river had been defiled through innocent bloodshed and broken covenants, but the land was being healed, and bloodlines and family trees were being restored and made whole in the sound that was released from the pavilion that night.

> *We release clouds of worship that bloodlines can move in. There is rowing in the clouds, bloodlines are moving. We bless the river of worship and the river under the river. We remove everything that sows darkness in the sound and shut down every false system.*

So what's this all got to do with the blues? The mistreatment of the Native people is directly connected to the mistreatment of the African people. In many cases, the Native tribes were forcibly removed from their land in order to make space for white plantation owners, who then farmed that land with African slave labor. One people group was subjugated and removed to make room for the subjugation of another people group. The net result of all of this was that the land was defiled and the people of the land were left traumatized. The sounds and songs that came forth simply represented the blood on the land and the desperate condition of the people.

The next morning, after our night at the pavilion, we went back to the Tennessee River, which I had not yet seen in the daylight. There on the banks we had another short time of worship with a few acoustic instruments. Steve Shoaf played his Native flutes, and it seemed like the ground was really resonating with that sound. Chuck Thurston was playing his saw (you have to see it to believe it), and Mike Curtis brought out his acoustic guitar.

A placard by the river states that Native tribes may have lived in that area since as long ago as 8000 B.C. Their main food source would have been freshwater mollusks from the river, which is the inspiration for the name Muscle Shoals. As intercessors, we need to understand that the history of the USA is a short blip compared to the full history of this land. Our culture is just the top layer of soil on a very deep mound. If we are going to deal with land issues, we must be aware that the problems experienced by previous cultures will grow up through our culture unless they are cut off at the root. You don't kill weeds by throwing more topsoil on them. Slavery, for instance, was a problem in our land long before the European colonists came or the West African slave trade began.

Native tribes were known to enslave and force neighboring tribes to build their mounds and their monuments. There is a place we have worshipped at many times called Cahokia near St. Louis. It was the capital of North America for close to a thousand years. There are mounds there that took hundreds of years to build and were built entirely through slave labor. There they also practiced human sacrifice and many other wicked things. Dealing with defilement on our land is far beyond the scope of this book, but the point is that when we're examining something like the birth of the blues sound in our nation, we need to be aware of what has happened before us on the land—not just with American history—and that these very issues can still be present and affect our culture today.

Muscle Shoals

Muscle Shoals became well known in the 1960s as a place where musicians could go to find their sound and record hit albums. It started with FAME Studios, where founder Rick Hall assembled a team of musicians that would eventually be known as "The Swampers." Rick started bringing in acts to record, and what they produced there was a signature sound that became known as "the Muscle Shoals sound." Many household names like Percy Sledge, Otis Redding, Wilson Pickett, and Aretha Franklin were some of the earlier artists to record hit records at FAME. When other popular artists heard the sounds coming out of Muscle Shoals, they wanted to record there as well. The Swampers eventually separated from Rick Hall and started another studio, but between the two studios, the list of artists who have recorded in Muscle Shoals is mind boggling. Consider Bob Dylan, Paul Simon, The Rolling Stones, Rod Stewart, Eric Clapton, Lynyrd Skynyrd, U2, The Allman Brothers, and The Staple Singers . . . and that is just getting started.

The important thing to realize about Muscle Shoals is that it is a place that gave birth to sounds that resonated with and shaped a generation of artists. If you've listened to popular music at all from the last few decades, you've undoubtedly heard songs that were recorded there—sounds that went forth and influenced countless other artists all around the world. An estimated 350 million records were produced from what was recorded in this little town. The folks making music here were tapping into something beyond what they could have worked up on their own.

When God created this little patch of ground, the dream of his heart was for it to be (among other things) a place that would produce sounds that would resonate with and shift culture. The Yuchi had recognized it long before, and in the 1960s, the rest of the world started to take notice. In a PBS documentary, Bono, lead singer for the band U2, said, "It was like the songs came right up out of the mud." In a way, the land itself was giving birth to something, and Rick Hall, The Swampers, and all these artists happened to tap into it while the tape was rolling. As with anything else, the sound is released through imperfect vessels. They weren't necessarily trying to shift a generation toward the Lord; they were trying to make a living and maybe become famous.

While in Muscle Shoals, the Blue Journey team was blessed to be able to visit both of the studios where all these influential songs and sounds were birthed. One of the original Swampers, Jimmy Johnson, came to give us a tour of the Muscle Shoals Studio on Jackson Highway. The studio has been restored to its 1960's condition after having been closed for quite a while. A few vintage pieces of equipment give you an idea of what it might have felt like to be in the room when the magic was happening all those years ago. The walls are covered with penned messages, signatures, and framed pictures from all the artists who have been there over the years. Jimmy is such a nice guy, and he was extremely gracious with us, giving us a tour around the inside of the studio and allowing several of us to take unashamed selfies with a living legend in the music business. He even took us out to his car and blasted us some cuts from the most recent project he had been working on up in Nashville.

After our brief visit there, we drove over to FAME Studios, the place that started it all. Our host had arranged for the Blue Journey team to have a few hours of recording time in this historic studio, but really we weren't going there to have a recording session. We were going there to worship and release the sound we carry in that place, but we needed to call it a recording session and pay the money for the opportunity to worship there. FAME Studio is a portal, a place where sounds have been released that have changed and influenced this nation and many others for several decades. Intent is a powerful force, and ours was to bring righteous alignment to that portal, thereby changing the sound released from there and impacting every person who has been touched by the Muscle Shoals Sound Studio. Whereas just about every other person who has released sound in that studio has had the intent of recording a hit song, our intent was simply to worship the Father and sing what we saw—whatever he showed us—in the moment. We couldn't help but wonder if we were possibly the first group to release that kind of worship into this environment.

The engineers who were there to help us greeted us warmly. The pictures of famous artists covered the walls, just like the other studio, and there were rooms filled with decades' worth of recording technology. We were excited to get set up, yet it quickly became clear something was awry. Apparently they were not expecting anything close to the number of musicians we were bringing. Generally, a recording session would have about four to six musicians playing, but . . . well . . . we had twelve with us that day! Still, John, Tyler, and Spencer were incredibly professional, and though it was a bit stressful, they managed to get us all squeezed in and mic'd up. Once we started to release our sound in that place, they were coming out of the booth to take pictures and videos with their phones, and one of them kept saying, "This is friggin' awesome!" I think it's safe to say they hadn't experienced much like that before and were blessed by it. They were particularly enamored with Chuck Thurston who had joined us and brought along his saw. Chuck plays a typical hand tree saw with a violin bow. It makes a high-pitched sound not terribly different than that of a theremin, and the pitch can be controlled by bending the saw. It really is quite a sight and sound if you've not been exposed to it before. Our intent as we worshipped was to change the sound of the region by aligning the portals, of which FAME Studios is certainly one.

> *We release Father's light into Muscle Shoals, so much light that everyone can see it. Everyone that has been touched by the Muscle Shoals Sound, we release light. We break off the orphan spirit and release the spirit of adoption over every singer and musician who records here, and every bloodline and family tree in Muscle Shoals.*

Our worship/recording time was powerful, and we all felt honored to have had the privilege. In addition to its being a fruitful kingdom time, we got to connect with the incredibly rich musical history of that building. For music aficionados, it was a bit surreal. I got to play my guitar through the same amp Duane Allman used. Isaac got to play a keyboard that had been used on some of Aretha Franklin's records. We got to stand and record in the same room that many of our musical heroes had cut their most well-known albums in and then go listen to it in the sound booth, like so many incredible artists have for so many decades. It truly was an honor.

Our initial plan for that Friday evening was to head back to the pavilion we had been in the night before, but due to the cold weather and the fact that a church had opened its doors to us, we decided to scrap the pavilion and stay inside. Pastors Tommy and Theresa opened the doors of Grace Christian Baptist to us, for which we were very thankful. We worshipped there Friday night and again Saturday morning, and we believed and declared blessings over these precious saints who had opened their doors to us in a region where many other doors were closed. At Grace Christian we were also joined by a man named Miles who played guitar with us.

As we worshipped there, we felt a great freedom to release the Spirit's declarations over the entire region, and even the state of Alabama.

> *Alabama is moving in great grace and freedom. Keys of worship are being revealed in Alabama. The fire of God is burning up religion and the religious spirit. Darkness is broken off of the church and true worship is arising. Psalm 24—We welcome the King of Glory! There is a grace storm being released! Grace, grace, grace, triple grace!*

The Lord continued to speak through us about an orphan spirit in the region and the need for the spirit of adoption and the Father's blessings and love. James shared that at FAME we had spoken into the history of the region, but now we were to sing into its future; that yesterday we had worshipped in a building that had seen much, but today we were to worship over buildings that had not yet been seen.

> *We release the rest of the Father's blessing that drives out every orphan spirit, to all lost souls who have been wandering around trying to figure out who they are. We call forth the visionary architects that will build and plant in this area according to the plumb line pattern. This is the company of those the Father has sent.*

One of the final things we did at Grace Christian was to pray and release blessings over Mike Curtis, who had been our main host in the region. We prayed that the Lord would continue to use him and move him into the fullness of his destiny. Mike is a gifted and accomplished singer/songwriter and performer, and we were so grateful to have been with him on this leg of our journey.

The Handy House

As incredible as FAME Studios, Muscle Shoals Sound Studio, and all the history of the '50s and '60s was to experience and engage with, it wasn't the main reason we had initially planned to come to the region. Decades before all that, around the turn of the century, there was a bandmaster, educator, and composer who lived in the Florence/Muscle Shoals area named W.C. Handy. Handy became known as the "father of the blues," but not because he was the first blues musician. Far from it. In fact, Handy wasn't really a blues musician at all, but he was one of the first to write down the blues sound. Handy was intrigued by the sounds he heard, and he wrote about it in his 1941 autobiography:[2]

> "A lean, loose-jointed Negro had commenced plunking a guitar beside me while I slept. His clothes were rags; his feet peeped out of his shoes. His face had on it some of the sadness of the ages. As he played, he pressed a knife on the strings of a guitar in a manner popularized by Hawaiian guitarists who used steel bars. The effect was unforgettable. His song, too, struck me instantly. 'Goin' Where the Southern Cross' the Dog.' The singer repeated the line three times, accompanying himself on the guitar with the weirdest music I ever heard."

Handy was struck by the sound and adapted the blues into a number of compositions that sparked America's first blues

---

[2] W.C. Handy, *Father of the Blues: An Autobiography* (New York: Macmillan, 1941).

craze, earning him his nickname. Some of his most famous
compositions from that time included: "Memphis Blues,"
"Yellow Dog Blues," "Beale Street Blues," and "St. Louis Blues."
Some of these were titular blues – blues in name only. Despite
not really being a bluesman himself, by writing it down and
causing it to be spread, he may have done as much as anyone in
helping to propagate the genre.

Handy's home

The Handy family lived in a very simple house that today
has been preserved and turned into a museum. The curator of
the museum was kind enough to give us a quick tour. The house
is a tiny two-room structure that has been restored to appear as
it might have around the turn of the century. Rudimentary
furnishings and some oil lamps completed the scene.

In looking through the museum part, we learned several key
pieces of information that would direct our worship and
intercession. First, we learned Handy had strife with his
preacher father. When Handy brought home a guitar at the age
of ten or eleven, his father told him, "Son, you need to get that

Devil music out of here," and made him return the guitar. The two were apparently estranged for most of his life. The second thing we learned was that Handy was involved in Free Masonry. Free Masonry is in many ways a system of false sonship. And lastly, we learned Handy was apparently very promiscuous and fathered many illegitimate children. He only had three legitimate kids, but the curator explained that there is a fairly constant flow of people who come into the museum claiming to be a descendant of his, and that the allegations of his promiscuity seem to be well-founded. The curator began to joke with us, "You know how those traveling musicians can be," and then he looked very embarrassed as he realized he was talking to a group of traveling musicians. We all had a very good laugh about it. All of these discoveries about Handy (his contention with his father, his involvement with Free Masonry or false sonship, and his illegitimate children) seemed to point back to an issue of fatherlessness and orphanhood. We began to see why the Spirit had been prompting us to pray and worship in that direction already.

James had gotten permission from the museum for us to set up our sound system and worship in the parking lot, but when we got set up and started to play our instruments, something very strange happened. All of our instruments were out of tune—all the guitars, bass, flutes, and even the sax—and abnormally so. Sometimes changes in temperature and humidity can cause this to happen, especially to instruments made of wood, but generally not to this degree. The guitars we had with us were carbon fiber as opposed to wood, which means they should not have been affected like that at all. Not only that, but our setup seemed to be plagued by cables and other gear not cooperating, and it seemed very difficult to get a good mix on the sound. In general, there seemed to be tremendous warfare over the sound being released in that location. Regardless of whether there were natural explanations for some of this resistance or not, we believed it was a prophetic sign we were in the right spot. Some breaking through needed to occur here, because the enemy had twisted some things right from this very spot.

Many times on this journey we would find ourselves out on the land and mostly by ourselves, but somehow the local newspaper had gotten wind of the fact that we were going to be playing, and it put an ad out to let people know. Consequently, we were joined by a number of folks from the neighborhood. Some seemed to be believers and joined us in worship; others seemed to have come just to see what was going on, since we were right outside a housing development. We sang over Florence, Muscle Shoals, and all of Alabama from this location. One dear sister from the area named Ronita came and sang with us and helped us release the sound of freedom.

We release divine alignment and holy order to every corrupted sound. We release holy fidelity. We bless every bloodline and family tree. This is the new sound of the Shoals, it's the bloodline song.

We're singing a city free, we're singing a nation free. We release the joyful sound—we plant it in the ground—five layers down.

After we worshipped there we drove a stake into the property, which the museum had given us permission to do. Afterwards we all felt drained and agreed it was because we were really moving some things in the Spirit.

Before leaving the Shoals area, we had one more evening of worship with Grace Christian Baptist, and it was yet another time of powerful release over the region. We sensed a level of breakthrough achieved from our time in the land.

> *I hear the sound of pounding nails. Finishing nails. It is finished—Jubilee is here!*
>
> *The wild horses of Alabama are now holy war horses running free. We call out to all those in a "wild" state to awaken to the light, love, and touch of the Father.*

On our last day in Alabama, we drove down to Selma. Selma was the sight of several very important marches during the Civil Rights Movement and where Bloody Sunday occurred. In fact, we had just passed the fiftieth anniversary of these events—another Jubilee. Our assignment there was to connect with a group of folks hosting a twenty-one-day worship and prayer event in a tent. Their worship related to the reconciliation and healing of these racial wounds.

What we didn't know until we were going there was that the rain falling all around us in the pavilion up in Florence had flooded their tent down in Selma. Because of the flooding, they had to abandon the tent and move the meetings to a nearby church. The church they relocated to was a charismatic Episcopalian church (something I hadn't experienced before) called Christ the King. The interior of the church was ornate with banners everywhere, a representation of the ark of the covenant with cherubim, and a large representation of the risen Christ flying overhead. Paintings depicting the stations of the cross were on display all around the room.

Liturgy and priests in collars is not the typical environment for what we do, but these folks were radical worshippers. In fact, the priest removed his collar and was dancing with us, getting totally sweaty in worship. It was really refreshing to see a group that knows how to celebrate the traditions of their denominations without compromising the radical spontaneity of their worship to God. There's probably a lesson in there somewhere for all of us.

Christ the King is also the home church of the archbishop over the southeastern Episcopalian Church of the USA, so it is indeed a governmental house. We thought it was an interesting prophetic picture that the tent had flooded and forced the worship and prayer gathering into this governmental house. Sometimes in our worship we need to come up to a higher place and release a governmental sound over the land, and that is exactly what we felt our assignment was there.

Everything is moving to higher ground. The floodwaters are rising. The governmental sound is being released!

Another amazing prophetic picture was actually outside the church: In front of the entranceway is a big wooden structure, and at the top of it is a large bell with a rope hanging down for ringing it. When we asked the priest about it, he told us that this bell used to be on a slave plantation. When the bell rang out, the slaves knew it was time to come in for a meal. Now, the bell rings twelve times at noon and calls everyone together to come receive the Lords Supper. What a redemption of sound! The very sound that used to remind slaves of their bondage now rings out to rally folks around the very thing that breaks their bondage—Christ's sacrifice on the cross. It is a Jubilee bell!

Being from Philadelphia, where the Liberty Bell (another Jubilee Bell) is located, we couldn't help but give it a couple of good rings and make some declarations from that spot.

From Philadelphia to Selma, we declare that Jubilee is here!
Debts are cancelled, prisoners and slaves are free. Return to
the land of your inheritance and walk in Father's original
intent for you. He is truly making all things new.

After worshipping at the church, we drove down to
Edmund Pettus Bridge, where the marches and Bloody Sunday
occurred. At the foot of this bridge spanning the Alabama River
is a memorial to the leaders of the Civil Rights Movement
before and after the marches. Part of the memorial is a stone
garden, with the largest of the stones having Joshua 4:21-22
inscribed on it: "When your children shall ask you in time to
come saying 'what mean these twelve stones?' you shall tell
them how you made it over." From the center of the bridge, we
prayed and released the sound of shofars.

We declare a whole new Bloody Sunday through the shed
blood of Christ the King.

5

New Orleans

W hen planning these journeys, usually it's a difficult enough challenge to find dates free on everyone's calendar. You don't usually have the luxury of worrying about what other events are happening during that time in the region you are traveling to. But time and time again, it is apparent the Lord has ordered our steps and brought us to the exact place and the exact time he chose before the foundation of the world. It is truly humbling to experience it.

New Orleans was one of these divine setups; the Lord brought us to New Orleans on the same weekend as the Heritage Jazz Festival. In addition to this, warships from the US, UK, and Canada were gathering on the Mississippi as part of a special event the Navy was hosting. What a picture of what was happening in the Spirit—the warships were certainly convening in that city! The estimates were of an excess of five hundred thousand extra people in town because of everything that was going on. We couldn't help but feel that all those people were on a collision course with destiny, as were we.

Keith and Cindi Stone once again graciously hosted the rest of the team on this leg of the journey. They moved to New Orleans in the aftermath of Hurricane Katrina to help a community that had been absolutely ravaged and needed help rebuilding, both physically and spiritually. Part of their ministry to that community involved setting up and running healing rooms. We wanted to come into agreement with their prophetic declaration that New Orleans is made to be a city of prophetic worship.

A small church just east of New Orleans opened its doors to us and hosted our first few meetings. It was a small gathering of believers in the natural, but James had helped engrain in us the truth that there are no small gatherings in the Spirit. When we worship we intentionally link our worship with the angels, elders, and cloud of witnesses worshipping around the throne of God. When we pray, we intentionally link our intercession with every other righteous intercessory prayer raised on behalf of that region or that group of people. When we link our worship and prayer with these much larger eternal realities, it is hard to ever again think of worship or prayer meetings as "small," regardless of the attendance. We may be just a drop, but we are riding on a tsunami of eternal worship and prayer. After all, meetings that shape history usually just involve a few people, not large crowds. Even Jesus, who only elected to walk with twelve disciples, had an even smaller inner circle of Peter, James, and John when he chose.

Our team was joined by Eddie and Deanna, a local pastor and his daughter who played bass guitar and drums with us. Coming from a musical family myself, it was great to meet and get to play with this local family of fantastic musicians.

It is the year of the whirlwind. Everything is being repositioned. We are aligning sound portals in New Orleans. We release a whirlwind of light that causes bloodlines to awaken to their eternal destiny.

Our intent that first night was to release sound that unlocks sight. Isaiah 9:2 says "The people that walked in darkness have seen a great light; those who dwelt in the land of the shadow of death, upon them a light has shined." As the light shines on us, we can begin to see what Father intends for us and for our region. We wanted to release a sound that would cause people to begin to vibrate with Father's heart for the region, and this is exactly what happened in the meeting as we began to play.

The voice of the blood is speaking. New Orleans is rising in the sound of Judah. Royalty is being restored through the glory of the blue note. The waters of the anthem are rising. Baptism angels are being released. Deep is calling out to deep. The red hot love of the Father is painting every heart in town.

Visions

Several people began to share visions they had seen as we worshipped. The first vision was shared by a sister named Darnicia, whose name means "hidden." This seemed appropriate, since our meetings there were hidden, in a sense: In light of everything else going on all over town with the Jazz Festival, we felt like we were in a "secret place" type of gathering. Darnicia described seeing a large dragon raised up over the New Orleans region, but that a wave of water was cresting over the city blocking the dragon. She went on to share about how alcoholism has been running rampant, especially in the youth, and that she discerned this was at least part of what the dragon represented. Substance abuse is in many cases an attempt to cope with trauma, and it becomes a snare of the enemy to keep people in bondage. With this in mind, we raised up a wave of worship and declared mercy and freedom over every bloodline and family tree that had been caught up in addiction of any kind.

A brother named Tim shared a vision, and honestly, at first this one really puzzled us. He said he saw a wave rising up out of New Orleans, and that on top of the wave was a penny that lay heads up. The part about the wave wasn't difficult to understand; in fact, James had been speaking about a wave or tsunami of glory rising up in New Orleans that would fill the region with the glory of God and shift everything in a moment—the way Katrina did-but it would awaken rather than destroy. So we prayed into that and declared things for a while, but the part about the penny was still a bit puzzling. Of course, the heads side of a penny bears the image of Abraham Lincoln, the president that led our country through one of our darkest hours. He arguably did more to undo the trauma caused by slavery than anyone else in our history. Jamie shared that the Lord had been speaking to him about Abraham Lincoln as we traveled to New Orleans, but what connection Abe Lincoln had to the New Orleans region, he didn't know . . . until he did some digging.

Lincoln is said to have traveled by flatboat down the river to New Orleans in the summer of 1831. Since his parents, his church, and even his state were all of the abolitionist viewpoint, he was aware of slavery in some sense; but he had not seen the horrors of it until he came to New Orleans.

"In New Orleans, for the first time, Lincoln beheld the true horrors of human slavery," wrote Mr. Lincoln's legal colleague, William H. Herndon. Lincoln's fellow traveler on the boat that day, John Hanks, recounted: "The whole thing was so revolting that Lincoln moved away from the scene with a deep feeling of 'unconquerable hate.' Bidding his companions follow him, he said, 'By God, boys, let's get away from this. If ever I get a chance to hit that thing [meaning slavery], I'll hit it hard."[3]

And hit it hard he did. It would certainly seem that the very man who would ultimately issue the Emancipation Proclamation, changing the legal status of millions of slaves to "free," made up his mind about slavery in New Orleans. The penny on top of the wave seemed to speak of a people that would love what God loves and hate what God hates the way Abraham Lincoln did. But the Lord had much more in store for us regarding this simple vision of a penny. (More on that in the chapter about Memphis.)

On the evening of our second night at the church in Chalmette, the atmosphere shifted and it began to pour rain. The weather was so intense that the Jazz Fest events were all cancelled, but we thanked the Lord because we were still able to pray and worship. We reflected on the fact that a sudden atmospheric shift had cancelled the sound that was being released throughout the city, but that we were still able to release our sound. We pondered what sounds might have been released, and what altars might have been built that night but weren't, because of the storm.

---

[3] William H. Herndon and Jesse W. Weik, *Herndon's Life of Abraham Lincoln* (Indiana: Obscure Press, 2009), 63-64.

The lightning strikes and the thunder rolls. There's a shifting in the atmosphere. There's a holy sound in the fairgrounds, It's a second line turnaround. Every lost soul is coming home. The Father is waiting. Just a closer walk with thee. There's only one sound heard tonight, and there's only one king over New Orleans, King Jesus!

Congo Square

Our assignment for the next day was to release our sound in Congo Square, which is described by some as the "soul of New Orleans." It has been maintained as an open meeting area since New Orleans was founded almost 300 years ago, in 1718. Prior to the 1800s, the square was a spot where slaves could gather informally to socialize, sing, dance, drum, etc. In 1817 a law was passed that gave African slaves the ability to gather on Sundays for dancing and singing, and this was to take place in Congo Square as well. For many years, African slaves gathered here to release their sound and their dance, sometimes numbering in the hundreds. African cultural expressions here eventually developed into Mardi Gras, second line, and New Orleans jazz traditions. For this reason the square, now located in what is known as Louis Armstrong Park, is famous for its history of African-American music. In many ways there couldn't have been a better spot for us to worship and release light into the sound and song of every bloodline connected to that land.

In more recent history, Congo Square is the birthplace of the New Orleans Jazz Heritage Festival, an annual celebration of New Orleans culture, and more specifically, indigenous music. Drawing a crowd of only 350 with acts like Duke Ellington and Fats Domino, the first festival in 1970 was not an overnight success. It grew very quickly year after year, and soon started to draw crowds in the hundreds of thousands. Something very interesting happened that first year though. Famous gospel singer Mahalia Jackson decided to show up and sing, despite not being booked to perform. Mahalia was well-known not just for her singing, but also as a civil rights activist. Mahalia was the granddaughter of a slave, so she was well acquainted with the suffering and trauma that cause many to sing the blues. But Mahalia didn't sing the blues, in fact, she flat out refused to sing anything but gospel or sacred music. "Blues are the songs of despair," said Miss Jackson in an interview with the New York Times.

> *"Gospel songs are the songs of hope. When you sing a gospel song, you have the feeling there is a cure for what's wrong, but when you are through with the blues, you've got nothing to rest on."*[4]

Wow. What light and revelation to be walking in! Mahalia experienced firsthand the trauma and pain caused by slavery and prejudice, but she knew where her hope was. Maybe it was for this reason Mahalia was chosen to sing at Dr. Martin Luther King's rally at the Lincoln Memorial in 1963, where the "I have a dream" speech was delivered.

In any event, despite being in poor health and not being booked to perform, Mahalia Jackson showed up to the first New Orleans Jazz Heritage Festival in 1970. She proceeded to perform an impromptu rendition of "Just a Closer Walk with Thee" while being backed up by a brass band, and the Jazz Fest was born. And it was on this day—exactly forty-five years

---

[4] Alden Whitman, "Mahalia Jackson, Gospel Singer, and a Civil Rights Symbol, Dies," *New York Times.* January 28, 1972, accessed 26 April, 2016, http://www.nytimes.com/learning/general/onthisday/bday/1026.html.

later—that the Lord brought us to that exact spot in Congo Square to release our sound, but also to agree with the sound and the light that had been released by Mahalia so many years ago. How we even were able to secure a permit for Congo Square in the middle of the festival falls into the long list of miraculous circumstances the Lord orchestrated.

Congo Square

We were once again set up under a large, live oak tree that must have been old enough to have witnessed some of the early roots of the Jazz Fest, and possibly before that. The square itself is a large open area paved with cobblestones, so our sound carried well throughout the area. A number of onlookers stopped to see what we were doing as we worshipped there. While most of us were stationed in one place, connected to the sound system by our cables, our saxophone player, Byron, was able to really test out his wireless system as he walked all over the square releasing the sound of worship. A number of people joined us and filled the square with dancing and colored flags of worship. As we worshiped, we held every bloodline that had released its sound from this location in our hearts, and we agreed with the song and the prayer of Mahalia Jackson.

> *We magnify the King of Glory. His love sets every captive free. We were made to walk with thee. Kingdom light is shining in the darkness. Turn the beat around, turn the beat around, through the blood of the Son. This is holy ground. Mercy is flooding the city. Angels, do what you came to do. We release shalom over New Orleans, nothing missing nothing lacking, nothing broken.*

As was starting to become a bit of a pattern, the atmosphere shifted quickly as we were playing, and we were barely able to pack up our gear before a huge downpour began. We only got to play a short time in Congo Square, but we felt we did what we had come to do.

With our time in New Orleans at an end, we set our sights on traveling through the Mississippi Delta along Route 61, otherwise known as the Blues Highway.

CHAPTER 6

The Delta

O ur first stop along the Blues Highway was in Vicksburg, Mississippi. Vicksburg is well-known among Civil War history enthusiasts, as it was the location of one of the more strategic and remarkable campaigns of the Civil War. General Grant attacked the Confederate Army's strategic river fortress here with very little success. In fact, he suffered so many casualties that he decided to stop attacking and instead lay siege to the city. It took forty-seven days, but eventually the confederate forces surrendered. This is considered to be a turning point in the war, as the Union forces took control of the Mississippi River and would hold it for the duration of the war, sealing the fate of the Confederacy. The strength with which Vicksburg repelled the initial attacks was amazing. We discerned in the Spirit that Vicksburg is a place of hardness, a place of strength, and a city of warriors, and that is why it was such a difficult city to take.

The music history of Vicksburg and its influence on the blues is something still being discovered, but being well-positioned halfway between New Orleans and Memphis, it was a place where bluesmen would stop to play their music on their travels. The numerous juke joints in town were a breeding ground for the blues sound, and blues music continues to be a strong part of the culture today, as it seems to be in almost every major town along the Blues Highway.

The door the Lord opened for us in Vicksburg was to worship at River City Rescue Mission, a ministry that helps men rebuild their lives and re-enter society. The men here thought they were coming to hear a concert, but obviously we weren't there to perform for them. In fact, the Lord had something amazing in store for them.

James oftentimes will ask people what their names mean. We know from Scripture that God cares a great deal about names and that our names are tied to our identity and our destiny in him. Many times we tell people what their name means, and we honor them for who they really are and were named to be. When we do this, something dormant in them comes alive. This is what happened in Vicksburg. As we began to ask the guys what their names were and what they meant, we heard names like Charles, Keith, and William, which are names that mean strong, warrior, hard, and protector. This just confirmed to us that Vicksburg was and is a city of warriors. We began to sing over the men, honoring them and releasing them into their destinies.

Oftentimes we mistake drug dealers, crime bosses, witches, psychics, etc. as enemies of the kingdom of God, but Paul makes it clear that our battle is not with flesh and blood. These are just precious men and women created with divine purpose—gifted by the Lord in a certain area, but who have been hoodwinked into using their gifts to advance darkness rather than release light. Many drug dealers are apostles serving the wrong kingdom. Witches and psychics are just prophets that have been tricked by the enemy into using their gifts for the wrong kingdom. The way James puts it, they just have their ladder on the wrong wall. There is a real enemy who seeks to steal, kill, and destroy. The Devil operates in darkness. Our assignment as believers is to release so much light that he can't operate anymore.

We release the light of the Lord over every bloodline and every family tree in Vicksburg! We call you out of darkness and into glorious light.

Part of releasing light over individuals is honoring who the Lord made them to be. As we honor them, we unlock the full glory of everything they represent in the kingdom. As we sang over the men in Vicksburg that night, just about every single one of the seventy-five or so men wanted us to tell them what their names meant and sing over them. Something special was unlocked in many of their hearts that night, and I believe their bloodlines were eternally impacted for the kingdom of God as we ministered to them. One of the men's names meant "smooth soaring eagle." What fun we had singing over him! As we sang over Terrance, I started to play the groove from Sade's song "Smooth Operator," and we changed the words to "smooth soaring eagle, free to fly." We sang over him and began to prophesy about warrior eagles rising up out of Vicksburg.

The next morning we ministered at a church called Jubilee Revival Center. What a name! A lot of the men from the night before were in attendance. James taught a bit about the release of eternal sound and that Vicksburg has a sound to release to the nation. When we release prayers and songs birthed of the Spirit, those sounds enter the eternal realm. Many of us have had mothers or grandmothers who have prayed for us, for example, and those prayers are as alive today as the moment they were uttered, even if the person who prayed the prayers is no longer with us. Chances are that if you are serving the Lord, it is because someone in your bloodline prayed for you and blessed you to be able to do so. The songs and prayers you release over your bloodline, and even over your city, are powerful. That morning we agreed with every Grandma's prayer that blessed her children and her children's children with enough light to fear and serve the Lord.

> *The lion is roaring in Vicksburg. There is a mighty army of warriors rising up. Judah is rising. We are walking in Grandma's prayers. It's my time to walk it out. We open every gate within us. I'm a Jubilee eagle and I'm free to fly. I'm a smooth-soaring eagle.*

Dockery

That afternoon we drove north along the Blues Highway to our next stop—Dockery Plantation. Dockery was a cotton plantation established in Cleveland, Mississippi, in 1895 by Will Dockery. Within a few years it had grown to a massive scale, housing several thousand sharecroppers and itinerant workers. The plantation had its own commissary, post office, school, doctors, churches, and even its own currency. Dockery Plantation is regarded by many to be the birthplace of the blues. B.B. King was quoted as saying, "You might say it all started right here."[5] This is not due to it being the first place blues music was written or performed, necessarily, but more so because of the number of famous blues performers trained and sent out from it. Will Dockery is said to have taken little interest in the workers' music, but he was known to be very fair in his treatment of them and took a very gracious approach to this form of entertainment. This was in contrast to many other plantations and towns that were intentional about running the blues musicians off because of the trouble they generally started.

The family of Charlie Patton moved to the plantation around 1900. Patton is recognized by most historians to be one of the earliest and well-known pioneers of the blues sound. So much blues music has been traced to Patton and his contemporaries (such as Tommy Johnson, "Son" House, Robert Johnson, and "Howling Wolf") that Dockery is considered to be one of the more pivotal centers for the development and spread of the blues. Utilizing the local railroad called the Peavine, and the other rails it connected to, bluesmen were eventually able to travel back and forth to places like Memphis, Chicago, and even Detroit. From 1910 – 1930, Dockery Plantation was preeminent as a center for the definition and propagation of blues music throughout the Delta.

We were blessed to meet and chat with the executive director of the Dockery Farms Foundation, Bill Lester. Bill showed us the steps of the old Commissary building. The building unfortunately burnt down in the '70s, but the steps are still mostly intact, other than being grown over with weeds.

---

[5] B.B. King, "Quotes."
http://www.brainyquote.com/quotes/authors/b/b_b_king.html.

Steps of the Commissary

On Saturday afternoons, Bill told us, the workers got paid and came to the Commissary to pick up what they needed, rather than walk five miles to the nearest town with stores. Patton and company used this opportunity to perform their music in front of a captive audience. Bill recalled,

> "They would play there at the [Dockery] Commissary for thirty minutes and get everybody all riled up, and then they'd walk across the one-lane bridge that's gone now. There was a one-lane metal bridge—to the first house on the right, which the bluesmen and everybody on the place called the "frolicking house." You had to be fifteen years old to be able to go into the frolicking house, so you can imagine the performances were probably pretty wild. They'd move all the furniture outdoors and place coal-oil lanterns in front of mirrors they brought, so that when it got dark, the house would

illuminate and you could see it from all over the place."[6]

Patton and the other bluesmen would charge twenty-five cents to come listen to them play all night in the frolicking house. In this way, they would make more in a single night than the average worker made in a month. Some of these early bluesmen were also gifted entrepreneurs and led lifestyles that put them on a significant pedestal. This helped with the propagation of the blues sound in the region.

Bill told us several stories about the history of the plantation, but one of them was of special interest to us. Right in the center of where most of the main buildings stood (only some of them are still standing), there is a very large concrete water trough that was used to water mules, but also for baptisms by the local churches. The nearby river wasn't suitable for baptisms because it was so full of snakes and alligators, and too many people were getting bitten, so they dunked them in this watering hole instead. We were struck by the many thousands of bloodlines and family trees baptized in this "dipping pool." How many eternal destinies had been birthed and changed on this ground? Bill told us that people still come back to see the place where their parents or grandparents were baptized.

As we worshipped that night in a large barn-like structure on the farm we were joined by Michael, a drummer, and Ian who played bass. We were also joined by Betty Love (who really helped make the way for us in the Delta region), a team of local intercessors, and even some random tourists. We prophesied

---

[6] Amy Evans, "Bill Lester," August 9. 2012,
http://www.southernfoodways.org/assets/Bill_Lester_Interview_Dockery_Farms.pdf.

over the ground and every bloodline that had been affected by the sound coming out of the Delta. We released joy over every soul whose family tree became a God-fearing family tree as a result of that dipping pool. We released Jubilee to the sons and daughters of the Delta.

Dockery was a place of sending out, thanks to the Peavine; however, it was something catastrophic that caused many to leave the region and never return. The Great Mississippi Flood of 1927 is still considered to be the most destructive river flood in the United States' history. Thousands of square miles were covered with water up to thirty feet deep. Hundreds of thousands were displaced. Many would never return home, instead joining the Great Migration of southern African Americans into more northern cities. There are those in the South today who believe that many of those who never returned home are prodigals.

Many blues songs and lyrics were written about the Great Flood of 1927, like those in Blind Lemon Jefferson's song "Rising High Water Blues" and Charlie Patton's "High Water Everywhere."

Interestingly enough, the rivers were swollen and in flood stage while we were there as well. We declared it was a holy flood—one of mercy and awakening light affecting every soul in the Delta. And we bless every prodigal son and daughter of the Delta with Father's love, and we call you back home. That is the sound of Jubilee—returning to your inheritance, the land the Father has ordained for you.

A Messianic Jewish brother Jonathan, who had joined us for worship that evening, felt we should direct this call of the prodigal sons returning toward God's people, Israel. So he led us in a song he had written, and we were blessed to join him in praying for the apple of God's eye.

We prophesy to the ground the Delta turnaround. We plant it deep, five layers down. Angels are ministering to the bloodlines. Joy has come. Step into the dipping pool. The waters are rising; it's a mercy flood. What you said you would do is done in our daughters and sons, the sons and daughters of the Delta. Even those who have run away. Jubilee to the sons and daughters of the Delta. Sweet winds are blowing from the Delta. Sweet shalom. Nothing missing, nothing broken. The glory of the blue note is being released from the Delta to Israel, from Dockery to Jerusalem.

We finished our night of worship by honoring a couple that was also instrumental in making a way for us in the region. They are faithful intercessors in that region, and chose to spend their forty-fifth wedding anniversary with us that night. Father, we bless the Youngs, wherever they may be right now.

It's hard to say how privileged we all felt over being given the opportunity to release our sound from this amazing place. What an honor!

Indianola

Our next stop on the Blues Highway was Indianola, Mississippi, the place where modern-day blues icon B.B. King grew up. It was here that B.B. made a living shining shoes and started to play the blues. Church Street was the main drag there for the African-American community. At the corner of Church and Second Street, there are even handprints and the outline of his shoes in the cement—right where he used to play for passersby, as well as a representation of his famous guitar, Lucille. B.B. said of his favorite spot to play blues, "It was just like a good fishing place—it seemed like a nice spot to be. You'd find me on the corner on Saturdays and sometimes after I got off work. I never passed the hat, but the people knew that I'd appreciate a dime if I played a tune they requested."[7]

It was a cloudy grey morning as we set up our gear right on Church Street in an abandoned parking lot, a block or so down from B.B.'s spot. We were hoping we wouldn't get rained out, since we had no cover to play under, but what happened next really blew us away. We had been playing B.B.'s popular groove "The Thrill Is Gone" in basically every city we had visited, but we thought we had better not miss the opportunity to play it in his hometown. When we began to play that pattern, the entire atmosphere literally shifted. The sky that had been gloomy and overcast was clear and sunny within minutes; the wind suddenly changed direction; and people began to come out of their houses and businesses to see what was going on and listen to the sound. It really was unlike anything else we had experienced. We know the spiritual atmosphere of a place can be affected by sound, but this was as if the natural atmosphere recognized the sound and was responding. It seemed almost too sudden and dramatic to be a coincidence. James said it was like every molecule recognized and responded to the sound.

As we were standing there playing, we had no idea that, simultaneously, B.B. King was having major health issues, and that by the time we got home from our trip he had been moved into home hospice care.

We honor B.B. King for all that he carried and released as a true artist and innovator. Like all of us, B.B. could only release his sound and walk in the light he had. While he enjoyed a very successful musical career with many accolades, he was a man whose "thrill was gone" in many ways. B.B. first began to sing

---

[7] B. B. King, "Quotes."
http://www.brainyquote.com/quotes/authors/b/b_b_king.html

the blues as a young boy because he resonated with the sound. Raised in a segregated society, he inherited the pain and trauma carried in his family tree, and the blues gave a voice and a measure of comfort to that. "The blues was bleeding the same blood as me," B.B. would say. Our mission on this journey, though, was to bless every bloodline and family tree with light—to awaken and come out of the "blue" sound they had known and enter into the fullness of the color blue and all it represents. While the blues may give you comfort for a time, they will never take you to your destiny.

A few weeks after being in Indianola, James was out on the west coast with a few members of the Blue Journey team, though it was on an assignment not specifically related to the Blue Journey. At one point in the evening, the team seemed to all at once suddenly know they needed to release that "Thrill" pattern, and they were obedient to this prompting of the Lord. Later on that same night, word came that B.B. had gone home.

It was rather surreal for all of us that just a few short weeks after we had been in B.B.'s hometown declaring a shift in the atmosphere and a new sound being released that B.B. would be laid to rest. I don't pretend to fully understand it, but the fact that the man many call the "last great bluesman" died during this trip, and very shortly after we visited his hometown, seemed very significant and represented a major spiritual shift.

The darkness is fleeing and the sun is coming out in Indianola. We agree with every grandma's prayer for the children of Indianola. We bless the children and the children's children; we bless your future. Hope and a future. The wind has shifted. The wind is blowing on your dreams. The Father has a dream just for you.

Clarksdale

Our last stop in the Delta was at the Delta Blues Museum in Clarksdale, Mississippi, whose mission statement says it exists for the purposes of "exploring the history and heritage of the unique American musical art form of the blues." The museum is home to blues-related artifacts, memorabilia, and works of art portraying the blues traditions. Many well-known artists have raised significant amounts of money to make the Blues Museum what it is. Unfortunately, the museum was closed while we were there, but we were stationed in an outdoor amphitheater right next to the museum. It is located (appropriately) on Blues Alley and faces down a main strip through town, so our sound could travel a long distance. We were thankful for a beautiful clear Mississippi sky that night as we set up, although for once we did at least have cover if it had started to rain.

It was our final night in the Delta region and in the great state of Mississippi, and it seemed like a fitting way to conclude our time there. We held the entire region in our hearts that night as we released our sound. From Vicksburg to Cleveland to Clarksdale, we declared the Jubilee rivers were flowing, releasing the glory of the blue note to every bloodline and family tree, and unlocking dreams and destiny. We prophesied over all the minstrels and psalmists in the region, that they would be awakened to their eternal destinies and original intent, and the dreams of the Father would be awakened in them and in the entire Delta region.

We were joined by some faithful intercessors that had been traveling the region with us, a few tourists, and a couple of what seemed like drunk vagrants. It's an interesting dynamic when you are minding your own business and worshipping and praying for a region and a couple of clearly inebriated individuals start interrupting and panhandling. On one hand there is the temptation to be annoyed at the interruption, but that would be a mistake. One of the mistakes the Pharisees (in Jesus's time) made was to be so absorbed in their religious activities (in praying and declaring the Word) that they missed the Word made flesh. They were so busy praying for the Messiah to come that when the very Messiah they were praying for was riding by the temple on a donkey, they viewed it as an interruption and told the kids shouting "hosanna!" to keep it down.

This is where the rubber meets the road. Those men represented bloodlines and family trees in that region that needed awakening light. They were exactly who we were there for. They and their generations might be the next ones to release sounds from the Delta that will shake our very nation. We prayed for those men that night, and I'm not sure exactly what inspired James to pray this, but he prayed, "Father, body slam those guys in your love." This lead us into a whole new musical movement where we sang about the Lord's "body slamming love." Only James. We found out afterwards that one of the guys asked for a Bible, so some seeds were planted.

Later that night, after we were packed up and in our cars, an SUV pulled up next to James's van. Turns out it was the mayor of Clarksdale, and he invited us to come back again to his town. The mayor is the co-owner (along with actor Morgan Freeman) of a well-known blues club near the museum called Ground Zero, which we got to visit while we were in town. His offer to have us come back and release our sound there again was a very nice gesture.

Holy rhythm, holy melodies. Our hearts beating as one is the sound of Clarksdale. The glory of the blue note is released in Clarksdale. The windows are open; it's time to dream again. Dream the Father's dreams.

Healing rivers are flowing, from Clarksdale to Cleveland to Vicksburg the rivers are flowing.

Jubilee rivers are flowing down, releasing the glory of the blue note to every bloodline and every family tree, unlocking dreams and unlocking destiny.

It's the time of Jubilee in Mississippi; it's the time of the Father's dream. It's time for the Delta dream.

There's a new sound in the Delta. Every psalmist in the Delta, it's time to sing. Every minstrel in the Delta, it's time to pick up that slide and prophesy.

Robert Johnson's Crossroads

The following morning we were to make our way to Memphis, but we felt we needed to make one last stop. There is a story that has become a legend about one of the more prolific bluesmen of the Delta, Robert Johnson. Johnson was enamored with Charlie Patton and some of the others on Dockery Plantation, and he had an intense desire to become a famous bluesman. The legend states that a voice instructed him to take his guitar to a nearby crossroads at midnight. There he would meet a man (the Devil) who would make him a master of his instrument. As the story goes, Johnson gave his guitar to the Devil, who tuned it, played a few songs on it, and handed it back to him. In essence, the legend states that Robert Johnson made a deal with the Devil and sold his soul in exchange for mastery of the blues guitar.

There are several versions of the legend floating around, and no fewer than five sites that claim the be "the" crossroads where Johnson sold his soul. Other accounts place Johnson in a graveyard instead. Many dismiss the legend altogether, claiming it began many decades after Johnson died.

We parked our cars at one of the locations thought to be (if the legend is true) the site where it happened. What was important to us wasn't whether or not the legend was true, or whether we had found the correct location. What we chose to focus on instead is that all minstrels and psalmists will at some point find themselves at a crossroads, faced with the question of who they will serve with the gifts they have been given. Our prayer for every one of those minstrels and psalmists is that they would be awakened and have the wisdom to make right choices, and choose light instead of darkness; that they would lay their gifts at the feet of the Father of lights—from whom all good and perfect gifts come—and become an instrument in his hands.

CHAPTER 7

Memphis

A s we drove the rest of the way back up the Blues Highway toward Memphis, there wasn't much to see other than flat miles of endless yet beautiful farmland. It was a striking, clear, sunny day, and as I watched some egrets keep pace with our car, I reflected on all those who would have traveled this same route while releasing their sounds into the atmosphere. The earliest blues practitioners might have only traveled by train, but later artists such as John Lee Hooker and B.B. King would have certainly traveled frequently along this route. Elvis Presley would have traveled here as well. It's been said his rock-and-roll music was as rooted in the Delta as a cypress tree in the lowland muck. The Delta was and is a place where new sounds are birthed, and this highway is how the sound was spread to nearby, major music hub cities, and eventually the nation and the world.

We arrived in Memphis with enough time to see some of the sites before we had to set up our gear. Beale Street is the major tourist attraction for blues music aficionados. In 1903, W.C. Handy was hired by the mayor of Memphis to write several campaign songs, leading Handy to make Memphis his new home. Handy wrote one song which would eventually be called "Memphis Blues," and another called "Beale Street Blues." The "Blues on Beale Street" was born. Over the next few decades, artists that regularly performed here included Louis Armstrong, Muddy Waters, Albert King, Memphis Minnie, and B.B. King. Beale Street later fell on hard times, but it has since been redeveloped and preserved for its historical significance, and was declared "Home of the Blues" by an Act of Congress in 1977. Today, Beale is home to major tourist attractions like B.B. King Blues Club; the Hard Rock Café; W.C. Handy's historic home; and many other clubs, bars, restaurants, and gift shops.

As we walked down Beale Street, you could hear blues music streaming out of almost every window and door. Outside one of the restaurants, a live band was performing blues music on the sidewalk. A middle-aged African-American man was there wailing on his electric guitar with his band behind him, and he was a real showman, playing his guitar with his teeth and then even with his tongue! He was gracious enough to let both Keith and I take a turn borrowing his guitar and jamming with his band for a bit. It was a truly unforgettable experience to be playing blues music with some of the locals on Beale Street.

Lorraine Motel

We also wanted to visit the Lorraine Motel in Memphis, the place where Reverend Dr. Martin Luther King Jr. was assassinated. Martin Luther King carried a sound for his generation—a sound of racial reconciliation and of the healing of bloodlines and family trees. King understood that the answer to these problems was not hatred but love, and that we must turn to God, the source of all love. "I refuse to accept the view that mankind is so tragically bound to the starless midnight of racism and war that the bright daybreak of peace and brotherhood can never become a reality. I believe that unarmed truth and unconditional love will have the final word," said King. He was also quoted as saying, "Darkness cannot drive out darkness; only light can do that. Hate cannot drive out hate; only love can do that."[8]

In the aftermath of the Civil War, the assassination of Abraham Lincoln had, in many ways, left the South as orphans. Lincoln was a wise and compassionate leader who would have fathered our nation into a great level of healing of those wounds, but the enemy had other plans. Likewise, I believe Martin Luther King was a voice that would have brought great healing to our nation. Even with all he accomplished, countless additional bloodlines and family trees might have found healing from ancient traumas, and racial reconciliation might have been moved forward exponentially, had King been able to carry his message for several more decades.

It was an emotional experience for some of us as we walked around the Lorraine Motel, reading the various placards regarding what had happened there, especially because we had just been hearing news that the previous night there had been rioting and burning in Baltimore over another race-related incident. Being from Philadelphia, this felt very close to home.

---

[8] Martin Luther King, Jr., "Quotes."
http://www.brainyquote.com/quotes/authors/m/martin_luther_king_jr.ht
ml

Jamie and I were particularly struck by one stone engraved with Genesis 37. With our backs toward the building where the assassin fired the shot from, we read: "They said to one another. 'Behold, here cometh the dreamer . . . let us slay him . . . and we shall see what will become of his dreams.'"

We felt there was something profoundly significant about the fact that Martin Luther King's sound was silenced here in Memphis. We knew part of our assignment while in that city was to honor and agree with the message and the sound that King released, and to come against any opposing sound that would seek to drown it out or silence it.

And then we received an uncanny confirmation. Remember the vision about the wave coming up from New Orleans with a heads up penny on it? Well, it was shortly after this that Keith Stone spotted a penny on the ground. It was heads up, and the date on it was 1968. He picked it up and handed it to Jamie. There were a couple of amazing things about this. First, the vision was of a wave from New Orleans with a heads up penny on top of it, and Keith Stone is from New Orleans and he was the one to pick up this heads-up penny. The next thing was that it was from 1968. Most currency this old is taken out of circulation, so it was odd to find something that old. More importantly, 1968 is the year Martin Luther King was assassinated, and we found it right after visiting the Lorraine Motel. Lastly, upon researching it further, Jamie discovered it was most likely minted in Philadelphia—where we are from. Here we were, just a few days after someone we didn't know had seen this vision, and it was being fulfilled right before our eyes. This little penny connected Philadelphia, New Orleans, Memphis, Abraham Lincoln, Martin Luther King, and the year of his assassination all into one random piece of copper laying on the ground – heads up. This was either a very unlikely coincidence or it was a "kiss from heaven," as Keith would call it. We felt we were receiving a significant confirmation that we were exactly where the Lord intended us to be.

Handy Park

The place where we worshipped that night was an outside amphitheater located in W.C. Handy Park, right on Beale Street. A large statue of Handy looms at the entrance to the amphitheater, and it stirred up memories of many of the things we dealt with in Florence. So many sounds had been released from this street and even this park, but probably not very many like the sound we intended to release. Even as we set up, we could hear multiple other groups playing and competing for the airwaves, but we just began to thank the Lord for the release of the heavenly anthem that drowns out all other music but its own.

Handy Park on Beale Street

There was definite warfare there. We sensed spiritual darkness unlike anything we had yet encountered on our journey. It may have had something to do with the overall climate in that city, but we identified several other factors. There was a national atheist convention around the time we were there, and Marilyn Manson was performing his "Hell Not Hallelujah" tour at around the same time as well, so the city was likely filled with many people lost in darkness, or even celebrating it. Also, the park we were in was named for W.C. Handy, and we already knew about his issues from having been in Florence.

As we worshipped we sang over Memphis, "the City of Kings." Memphis is sometimes called "the City of Three Kings" for Elvis "the King" Presley, B.B. King, and Martin Luther King. We declared there is only one king in Memphis—Jesus! —and that all those found in him are rising and taking their places as priests and kings in the earth. Memphis is indeed a city of kings.

At one point in the evening, Jamie began to prophesy and sing about a scarlet thread running through Memphis, and that the scarlet thread and the blue note were together bringing life to the land. The scarlet thread in Scripture is referenced several times, probably the most notable of which was when Rahab the harlot helped the spies Israel had sent into Jericho. She and her entire city were destined for destruction, but the spies told her that because she had aided them, she should tie a cord of scarlet thread outside her window so she and her house would be spared when the city fell. Scarlet is symbolic throughout Scripture for the atoning work of Christ and his shed blood. This story in particular reminds us of the blood being put on the doorposts of the house at the time of Passover, when Israel was being delivered from Egypt, but all of this speaks very directly of the cross and the Lamb of God who would be slain for all. In fact, sometimes Bible scholars use the scarlet thread to mean the interweaving of the story of Christ's blood redemption; you will find this scarlet thread woven into every book of the Bible.

The meaning I took from what Jamie was releasing was that the scarlet thread (or the redemptive blood of the Lamb) was being applied to the sound of the land. The blood was renewing the sound of the blues, and the new blue sound was one that would bring life to the land. The blood redeems, cleanses, and brings authority to the sound. This was something that came up again later in our journey.

We worshipped for a while that night before feeling like we were having any real breakthrough. Quite a few people stopped and gathered to hear our sound, since it was a very public place with a lot of foot traffic, but unlike many of the other places we had played, we felt our message was very counterculture here. At one point in the evening, when James was blowing his shofar, we noticed smoke was pouring out of our speakers. Needless to say, that brought our time to a hasty conclusion! I'm not one to spiritualize every equipment malfunction, but given the warfare we were experiencing, it seemed like more than a coincidence that our speakers caught fire right as we were breaking through. I think most of us felt we had unfinished business in Memphis that night. Perhaps it was the Lord's strategy that we weren't there for a longer time, but we set in our hearts to at some point return to Memphis.

Hope and healing are rising in Memphis. Every psalmist and minstrel prophesy.

Not black, not white, but the glory of the blue note.

The scarlet thread and the blue note bringing life to the land.

There is a pure fire going into the heavens and there is breakthrough for Memphis and Beale Street.

The waters are stirring. God is troubling the waters. Salvation spring up from the ground. Healing break forth. Freedom break out.

CHAPTER 8

St. Louis

S t. Louis was a very different leg of the journey from what we had been doing up to that point. Instead of being out on the land in many different locations, we merged this leg of the journey with an annual weeklong gathering that James organizes called Tribe Quantum Worship Congress. We did release worship over the region, but it was just as much a time for us to be refueled and to receive vision for the rest of our journey. In fact, we received vision not just for the rest of the Blue Journey, but also for an assignment the Lord had for us once the Blue Journey was over. I have learned from James to pay careful attention to what happens in gatherings during worship. Sound unlocks sight. When the ekklesia (governing body) convenes, we all release the light that we carry, and in a corporate environment, this magnifies what the Lord is doing in and through each one of us. With such a release of light, we can see things we weren't able to see before. We might see a new dimension of the Lord, or we might receive an anointing, a mantle, or an assignment. Pay attention to what you see in the midst of worship, and to what all those around you are seeing. One of the things that sets apart the type of meetings we do is that usually there will be an open mic for people to share revelation, or we will intentionally stop and ask people what they are seeing or hearing in the midst of worship. Most church gatherings make no room for this because it's messy and difficult. Generally, it is left to the pastor or worship leader alone to hear from the Lord, and the rest of us are just there to receive or, worse, be entertained. But, the church is made strong by the gifts that every joint supplies. The woman on the third row might have the next verse the Father wants sung that morning. One of the children might have the word of the Lord for that moment. The guy that straightens the rows of chairs may have a burden to lead the congregation in powerful intercession that the Lord wants released. Part of where I believe the church needs to go is to establish this culture of honoring the sound and release of every member, and not just the ones who are getting a salary.

The Season We Are In

Chuck Pierce is a leader who has established this very thing, and is one who sees in the midst of sound. He is a very accurate prophetic voice that many of us have come to trust, and he was one of the main speakers at the gathering in St. Louis. The previous year, at the 2014 Tribe Quantum Gathering (before the Blue Journey began), Chuck prophesied something very powerful. Here are some excerpts:

> Here is what God spoke to me tonight when we came in here and started worshipping: He showed me that St. Louis would become the dividing line of America. Now

when I say St. Louis, in the Bible a city like this was called a Decapolis. It would have ten key cities around it, and it wouldn't be just St. Louis. There would be ten surrounding cities in the region that made up what God was doing, and so this would become the dividing line.

There is a harvest mentality the Lord is attempting to bring back to this nation that I don't think we have seen in many generations, which is so important for us to grab a hold of. You have to understand harvest; you have to understand cycles. So it's very important right now that we are remembering that God has a harvest. The problem that comes right now is that the enemy has gotten embedded in the harvest.

Now hear me carefully: I want to be clear on this. This becomes the area, this Decapolis in America, becomes the dividing line where the sound of heaven can enter in and start separating wheat and tares for the future. And the harvest begins tonight!

This is such a time when we want to see God's plumb line for the season. When the plumb line drops, everything begins to realign because God is remolding. He's redecorating or he's re-mantling what needs to be re-mantled, and he wants it is in his order in a new way.

The Lord is going to start setting a new plumb line in front of you that he will use to realign the apostolic-prophetic measure that is presently in the earth. And so let's look at what the plumb line does once it drops from heaven. It repositions you. There is this divine repositioning occurring with God's people that we want to understand. And sound is so important in it. It causes you to start coming into completion, in line with what has been destined and postponed; he drops the plumb line because he is ready to build it and finish the building he has started in you.

When I saw the plumb line come down, faith exploded. There is a realignment of power going on between heaven and earth right now that the enemy cannot stop, and it's being motivated by sound.

In this season Judah will go first. That means there is going to be such a shift in God's order because Judah now is taking the role in the earth that God has intended for this generation. There is a Judah people rising up. Now when Judah goes first, that means God has a new order for victory. One order has come, but now all of a sudden we say Judah is going first. A new order is coming.

Now Judah was the tribe that operated in government, in war, and you have a new sound. It means to actually extend your hand and sling a rock and release the sound that can take out any disqualifying voice trying to impede the atmosphere. I'm here to say again: A Judah tribe is arising.

How you know you are moving in a Judah anointing is your praise is louder than the enemy's voice trying to test you. Your praise is much louder. This sound of Judah is loosing restoration through the land. It's coming down in very strategic places in this nation. Not every generation allows the Judah tribe to arise. This generation is not only allowing the Judah tribe to come forth, but three generations are aligning in this Judah sound, and that's what is causing the earth to start shaking in a new way.

God's says he is realigning the sound of heaven in this season, at this place, in this portal, at this time. And he is going to cause a dividing line to come down and start dividing in this nation the wheat and the tares. He will do it in states. He will do it in counties. He will do it in cities. He is going to cause his Judah people to arise.

The Lion of the tribe of Judah has triumphed!

To try and summarize what he released that night (and there was much more to it), St. Louis and the surrounding areas were becoming a dividing line. The wheat and the tares have grown up together, but they must now be separated because the Lord is causing a great harvest to be reaped. The plumb line of the Lord is being dropped, realigning things in the region, and it is being carried by the sound of a multigenerational company of Judah people. In this season of dividing, as we release our sound, the Lord is causing us to have victory over our enemies, and a great harvest will be reaped all across our nation.

Tribe Quantum Worship Team

The Dividing Line, And The Judah Sound

Chuck was very transparent in the fact that he said he didn't fully understand what the word meant. In fact, I think none of us knew what "becoming the dividing line" meant at the time. But fifty-one days later, an eighteen-year-old black man named Michael Brown was fatally shot and killed by a white police officer named Darren Wilson in nearby Ferguson. The shooting sparked tension between the community and the police department, and eventually protests and civil unrest ensued. During the day there were peaceful protests, but at night riots and looting broke out. The city burned as anger and rage were the sounds that dominated the airwaves. Various groups came from all over the nation, and even other countries, to stir the pot and release their sound in Ferguson. Over the course of the next year, we saw this same scenario being played out in city after city: Chicago, Cleveland, New York, and Baltimore, to name a few. What had started in Ferguson, St. Louis seemed to be spreading around the nation. In city after city the sound of rage was lifted up. In fact, we were reading about Baltimore burning on the morning we visited the Lorraine Motel. Martin Luther King knew rage was not the answer. Someone pointed out that we have moved into an "age of rage." It is a Psalm 2 time when the kings of the earth are shaking their fists at God and stirring up hatred and division, but the answer to the age of rage is raging love! The Judah company must arise in our cities, bringing the plumb line sound and trumping the sound of rage with the sound of raging love. As we watched the news, we wondered which city would be next and where the Judah company was.

Then in June of 2015, almost exactly one year to the day Chuck Pierce had given this word, Dylann Roof (a young white man) walked into a prayer meeting and killed nine African Americans in one of our nation's oldest black churches in Charleston, South Carolina. This young man had obviously come into agreement with the sound of rage, even stating that his very intent was to start a race war. War that has divided our nation has broken out from Charleston before: the first shots of the Civil War were fired there, and obviously the enemy intended for another war to break out there. But something happened in Charleston that didn't happen in Ferguson or anywhere else. The children of the victims of this senseless act of violence made the unbelievably difficult decision to publicly forgive the perpetrator.[9]

> *"I forgive you and my family forgives you, but we would like you to take this opportunity to repent. Repent, confess, give your life to the one who matters the most, Christ, so he can change it, and change your ways, no matter what happened to you, and you'll be okay through that. And better off than how you are right now."*

— Anthony Thompson (husband of Myra Thompson)

> *"I forgive you. You took something very precious away from me. I will never talk to her ever again. I will never be able to hold her again, but I forgive you. And have mercy on your soul. You hurt me, you hurt a lot of people, but God forgive you, and I forgive you."*

---

[9] Leyla Santiago, "Families of Charleston Victims Forgive Shooting Suspect in Court," WRAL, June 19, 2015, accessed April 26, 2016, http://www.wral.com/families-of-charleston-victims-forgive-shooting-suspect-in-court/14725682.

— Nadine Collier (daughter of Ethel Lance)

One by one, the families of the victims addressed Dylan and chose forgiveness over bitterness, love over hatred. Alana Simmons comments were particularly poignant.

"Although my grandfather and the other victims died at the hands of hate, this is proof, everyone's plea for your soul is proof, that they lived and loved and their legacies will live in love. So hate won't win."

— Alana Simmons (granddaughter of Rev Simmons)

This was the Judah sound. This is the sound of raging love that trumps the sound of rage, anger, and division. It is the same sound Jesus released when he hung on the cross and said, "Father forgive them, for they know not what they do." And when this sound was released in Charleston, the entire atmosphere over that city shifted. The various groups inciting violence and rage in other cities didn't know what to do with the sound. The media didn't know what to do with it. The anger that burned in the streets of many of the other cities found no foothold there, and what seemed like a hopeless situation that was spiraling out of control in our country was quelled in some measure. It was as if someone had put out a lighted fuse with a cup of cold water.

There is an old hymn from 1852 called "Crown Him with Many Crowns" that we have been singing a lot the last few years. The third line of it says "Hark! How the heavenly anthem drowns all music but its own!" When we as the sons of God in the earth—his called-out ones—begin to release the sound that comes from his throne, the heavenly anthem, it drowns out every other sound and every other song. The sound of heaven trumps other sounds the way a bright light trumps the darkness. It's not even a struggle; darkness simply can't exist where there is light. And the heavenly anthem in Charleston had done just that.

Of course we weren't the only ones praying in or for Charleston, but we couldn't help feeling like this was a very direct answer to our prayers from four months prior. Our intent and release was that every family tree and bloodline in Charleston would be blessed with awakening light so that a sound could be released that would shift our nation. And that is exactly what happened. Could it be that if those families had not had light enough to be able to forgive that young man, a race war would indeed have broken out? Thankfully we will never know.

A Word over Us

It was in the context of all of this that James hosted the Tribe Quantum Gathering again in 2015, and Chuck prophesied the next part of our journey to us.

> I saw something. I don't even know how to describe it, but I'm going to say it the way I saw it. The Lord said you are going on a journey in a different way this year and the year ahead. The Lord said it will be called "The developing wedge for this nation." And I saw you going through certain cities that formed a wedge, and what now is being stirred up here will be able to open up the future; this wedge will create the opening for the future of this nation.

> And I saw you going to St. Louis. And I saw you going to Memphis. And then I saw you going into these interesting

cities: Chicago, Toledo, Cleveland, and Cincinnati. I saw you going into Detroit and then back to Indianapolis. And the Lord said this will create a wedge and a weapon that this nation must have, for without it being created, that will also be the wedge that destroys this nation.

So when you go in, you are actually going in before the enemy develops his stronghold in this nation for the future. For I say to my people tonight, I must have a nation that knows it is now in the clash of conflict, and my people must take the reins of what is happening now.

This is the beginning of removing from the enemy's strategic board that which would destroy this land in the future.

Like I said earlier, you never know when you're going to receive your next assignment, and we had just received ours (we would start calling it the Wedge Journey) only halfway through the one we were already on. It certainly seemed like an extension of the Blue Journey.

The Lord is in this hour uncovering and exposing ancient wounds that have been carried through bloodlines for generations, and it is time for the body of Christ to rise up and deal with it. Many wounded ones may have released the sound of the blues in our nation, but there is a new blue sound being released by those who have been redeemed, know who they are, and know the power in the sound they carry. The word "wedge" can refer to a separating or to a bringing together. The enemy would seek to divide us, but what he intends for evil, God is planning to use for good.

Charleston's mayor at the time, Joe Riley, summarized it perfectly, "This hateful person came to this community with some crazy idea he would be able to divide it, and all he did was make us more united and love each other more."[10]

There is always a powerful release of worship and intercession when the Tribe Quantum family comes together. Despite not being out on the land like we were in most of the other cities, we had some incredible times of releasing worship over the city and the region. Here are three of the themes or musical movements that came forth.

The dance of the two camps, heaven and men, at the crossroads. He is stirring up the water, stirring up the fire, stirring up the wind.

It's the place where the new sound begins, at the crossroads. The anthem of the cross is burning at the crossroads, setting every heart on fire.

Every family tree is a burning bush at the crossroads.

We declare the wedge of Father's love breaking off rejection and trauma. We call you to a higher sound: it's the song Father's singing over you; there's no greater frequency around.

Calling in all the prodigals: you have a tall destiny—you are the apple of my eye. No longer orphans but kings, you're clothed in royal blue. There's a place at my table just for you. I put my ring on your finger, my robe on your back.

---

[10] Leyla Santiago, "Families of Charleston Victims Forgive Shooting Suspect in Court," WRAL, June 19, 2015, accessed April 26, 2016, http://www.wral.com/families-of-charleston-victims-forgive-shooting-suspect-in-court/14725682.

The power of covenant love is piercing your darkness, drowns every other sound. Plumb line sons are rising up. The sons are rising in the thrill of living again.

There's a tsunami of glory breaking on the land; the water is rising.

There's purpose in the sound tonight, speaking into the darkness and releasing the light. It's a whole new blue, St. Louis blue.

We magnify the new blue sound; we make it big; it's big enough to touch the nation. It's eternal blue; it's the sound of blue justice.

We release blue justice in the streets of Ferguson. Holy blue.

CHAPTER 9

Chicago

Some say that while the blues may have been birthed mainly in the Mississippi Delta region, it was in Chicago that they became a more significant and lasting part of American musical culture.

In Chicago, the blues were amplified and electrified. Electric guitars and harmonicas were played through a PA system, replacing some of the acoustic instruments and becoming staples of the blues sound there. The blues birthed in Chicago would become a major influence on modern rock music at home and abroad. Famous blues artists like Willie Dixon, Bo Diddley, Son House, Muddy Waters, Howling Wolf, and others (some of whom had made their way up from the Delta around the time of the Great Flood or as part of the Great Migration) would perform at blues clubs located primarily in the predominantly black neighborhoods of Chicago's south side. Labels such as Chess Records did a tremendous amount to feature and promote blues music, and it was even described as

"America's greatest blues label." But it was the likes of Columbia Records, RCA Records, Victor Records, and Paramount Records that promoted blues music into having international influence. The blues being birthed in Chicago at that time eventually made it to Europe and the UK, having a profound influence on many of the British rock bands at that time, such as the Rolling Stones.

Our host in Chicago was a friend of James who we know as "the Bishop." The Bishop is one of the most interesting men I have ever met. His motto for hospitality is "lavish and unique," and it certainly was that. We stayed in Aurora, IL, at an old commercial building he had purchased and fixed up which he affectionately labeled "the hut." Aurora is nicknamed the "City of Light" because it was the first city in the nation to use electric lights to publicly light the entire city. I thought it was very fitting that we would stay in the City of Light, as we were there to release light into Chicago and into every bloodline and family tree. Chicago is lighting up!

That evening, the Bishop hired a personal chef to come cook us an incredible meal while we sat around a large table and heard about what was going on in the region. We also strategized about our release of sound in the Windy City. Now that's lavish and unique.

In most cities we were eager to release our sound from the same places the blues players from years ago did, but in Chicago, very few of the venues still existed because many of those areas have since become gentrified. While the blues music history was fascinating to all of us, our primary assignment for the city was to release awakening light that invades every bloodline and family tree. We chose to go to some of the most spiritually dark places in the city to release our sound. Chicago has been leading our nation as the city with the highest number of murders committed each year, so we knew the spirit of murder was something running rampant in Chicago. That would become the focal point of most of our time there.

Statesville Prison

We first went to a place where families, both local and from many other states and countries, lived. It was also a place where many had come into agreement with the spirit of murder: Statesville Prison. Statesville is a large prison housing several thousand inmates, and also ranks among the worst to be in, by some metrics. The Bishop serves as a chaplain in Statesville, and he had made arrangements for us to worship with some of the inmates in one of the prison's auditoriums. A percentage of the inmate population have become believers, and they have been organizing 24/7 worship, prayer, and fasting in the prison for several years now. They are serious about contending for the lives of the inmates, particularly those who may have been unjustly imprisoned.

Bringing our whole team and all of our equipment into a maximum security facility was a difficult task. The security protocols alone were a lot to overcome, but it was compounded by the fact that one of the other workers there was vehemently opposed to us coming in, and they were going to be one of the ones going over our gear and determining what could be brought in. There didn't seem to be any logical rationale for this hostility. It certainly seemed like a spiritual struggle. Whatever spirit that person was in agreement with sure didn't like what we were coming in there to do, but praise the Lord, we had favor and all of our gear made it in.

The room we were in could have easily held a few hundred guys, but for security reasons they limited it to seventy-five. I've been involved in prison ministry before, but at very different types of facilities. I'm fairly sure this was the first time I have led worship with multiple snipers having guns trained on the worshippers. Generally they wouldn't have even been allowed to all stand and worship, but they allowed us a little leeway with that, thankfully.

Statesville is a maximum security facility for those with many years to serve. I'm always stunned to meet someone who has been in a cell since before I was born. Just about everyone in there was serving between twenty years to life sentences, as the vast majority had been convicted for some degree of murder. Of the seventy-five guys that came to worship with us, it is likely most were murderers.

I think the inmates were expecting a concert, probably because they wouldn't have had the language for what we were actually there to do, with the exception of some of the believers. As we started to worship, we could tell they were very engaged with us. We started to make some decrees and have the guys make them with us. We declared and sang that their bloodlines were being made holy, the joy of the Lord was their strength, and that they could change the world from inside their cells, just as some of the early apostles did.

The Bishop took some time to talk to the guys about their identity and being free to be who God made them to be. We made a lot of declarations over them to break off every false identity the enemy had tried to put on them or keep them trapped in.

At one point we started singing over the city of Chicago and binding the spirit of murder. Remember, these are guys who had at one time come into agreement with that spirit, having committed murder themselves, and were now being freed from it. They now had authority over the very thing that had once dominated their hearts, and the grace to conquer it in their land. What a powerful time it was as seventy-five murderers declared in one voice, "We bind the spirit of murder over Chicago."

> *Holy. Holy is in my bloodline. Holy is moving in me, shaking my family tree. Changing the world from my cell. The joy of the Lord is my strength. We release joy to every heart, every cell. We bind the spirit of murder from here to Chicago through the blood of the Son.*

There are some amazing things that happen in these prison communities. I was particularly impressed by one man I met who had taught himself how to play the piano by practicing on a cardboard cutout made to look like a keyboard. He helped form a choir, and its members have written over sixty original songs! It is amazing what we take for granted sometimes.

I believe tremendous light was released over those guys, and that many seeds were planted that day. It was an eye-opening experience for some and a huge encouragement to others. Light was penetrating even the darkest of hearts. As we wrapped up our time there, each and every one of the guys wanted to shake our hands and thank us for being there. Inmates are certainly among the most grateful people I have met.

Calumet Park

Our venue for worship and prayer the next day was Calumet Park, right on Lake Michigan. Calumet is a strategic location, being right on the border of Illinois and Indiana, and on a clear day you can also see Michigan. It is also the location of an international port and Coast Guard Station Calumet Harbor.

It was only late morning, but it was already blazing hot and a heat advisory was in effect. This didn't stop large crowds from gathering by the lake for cookouts and all kind of recreation. We found a shady area to set up our equipment where we could release our sound over all the people there and over the water. God was good to us, and a strong breeze started to blow almost as soon as we started to set up. It turned out to be a beautiful sunny day.

Calumet Park

A man named Rich prayed for us and welcomed us into the land. He was telling us about an answer to prayer they'd had—a nearby old building named Dominion had been polluting the environment, but it was being decommissioned and removed. We started to thank the Lord and declare that power structures that have been polluting the area are being torn down, both in the natural and in the Spirit.

We were also joined that day by some singers from a local church. We had an amazing time worshipping there and making decrees over Chicago, over the land and waters, and over everyone who could hear our sound.

> *There is wonder-working power in the blood. Signs, wonders, and miracles are breaking out. Release your joy. Jubilee! From the south side the west side to the north, every prayer that has been prayed for Chicago is breaking forth. Everywhere that darkness is, we release God's light. Everywhere that death has reigned, we release God's life.*
>
> *The waters are stirring. Ancient gates are opening. A spiritual tsunami is rising up; it's the prayers of the saints. The water, the Spirit, and the blood agree. Chicago is free! The winds of change have come.*

The Dragonfly Invasion

Just as we finished worshipping there, a very strange phenomenon occurred: Thousands of dragonflies began to swarm the area. Many people pulled out their phones and cameras to take pictures of these clouds of dragonflies. We didn't realize it at the time, but we were witnessing the beginning of what some started calling the Great Chicago Dragonfly Invasion. Within the following few days, thousands upon thousands of dragonflies rose out of the waters of Lake Michigan and descended on the city of Chicago in a way that had some people comparing it to a biblical plague. The good news is that dragonflies are not harmful or really irritating to humans as they don't bite or sting. In fact, they perform a valuable service—one of their favorite things to eat is mosquitos, and this many dragonflies certainly would decimate the mosquito population. These dragonflies can live in the water for a long period of time, and no one seems to be exactly sure what could have caused the sudden onslaught. It was certainly unusual according to local biologists. In hindsight, I find it extremely interesting that we were there declaring blessings over the water at the exact time and location that scientists would eventually pinpoint as the very start of the invasion. So who knows? Someday we will see all our prayers accomplished in the earth. For now we thanked the Father that every bloodsucker in Chicago was being consumed in Jesus's name. After we finished at the park, we ducked into a local restaurant for some of Chicago's famous deep dish pizza, and there we met one of the most colorful waitresses I've ever met who we all called "Mama."

Murder Castle

The next day our assignment was to deal with something we believed was a root for the spirit of murder in Chicago. H.H. Holmes is considered to be one of the first and most notorious documented serial killers in modern times. In the late 1800s, Holmes opened a hotel he had designed and built specifically for the purpose of murdering people. His hotel later became known as the "murder castle." His reign of terror lasted for a number of years until he was finally caught in Boston, and later imprisoned and executed in Philadelphia. While he confessed to only twenty-seven murders, his body count is often estimated to have been as high as two hundred. Some even speculate Holmes may have traveled to London at one point and been responsible for the murders there attributed to Jack the Ripper. In any case, the man was filled with evil intent.

The land that Holmes's hotel used to sit on is in one of the worst neighborhoods in Chicago—Englewood—and it is currently a post office. The Lord gave James the strategy to drive a wedge into the ground, a literal one, somewhere near the site as a prophetic act, and then worship and release our sound. We showed up at the site not really knowing what exactly we were going to do or where we were going to do it, but we were believing God to work out the details, like he always seems to do. We eventually found the spot where we felt we should drive the wedge in the ground, but for obvious reasons, we were trying to be discreet. About a dozen or so of us were there huddled around as James led us in breaking off the spirit of murder from this place, and we prayed for a covering of the innocent bloodshed that had given the enemy legal access to operate here—that it would be covered by the blood of Jesus. We agreed with the prayer of every mother who had lost her child to the violent streets and wept and prayed for justice. We released light into the atmosphere that exposed anyone who was in agreement with the spirit of murder.

As we were praying and preparing to drive the wedge, a man and his wife none of us recognized came and stood close to our little huddle. Again, we were trying to be discreet, so James asked them, "Do you know why we are here?"

"Oh, we know why you are here!" they replied. "We are pastors in the area, and the Lord has been telling us to come to this spot and deal with these things for over two years now, but we never felt released to come on our own. The Lord told us, 'Wait until I send my reinforcements,' and we believe you all are the reinforcements."

Wow, what a divine appointment! Talk about being at the right place at the right time. We all prayed together and took communion. As we finished releasing what the Lord had shown us in this location, the Bishop had the honor of driving the wedge deep into the ground—as the representative of that region and someone who had authority. It was a difficult job as the ground was extremely hard there, both physically and spiritually.

Pastor Louis and his wife also told us they had sensed a major shift in the Spirit the previous afternoon, and asked us if we had been doing anything in the area. Of course, we had been worshipping at the lake and getting swarmed by dragonflies! The Lord was definitely up to something.

James conveyed to our new friends that we were looking for a place to set up and worship that night, and that we hadn't found one yet. Well, the Lord had already taken care of us, Pastor Louis's church was just a few blocks away, and they were happy to have us come and release our sound there.

Englewood

On the way to their church on Wolcott Street in Englewood, I felt the Lord very clearly speak to me about releasing brotherly love. This is not all that uncommon. Being from Philadelphia—the City of Brotherly Love, Jamie and I often feel it is our assignment to release brotherly love in all the places we travel to. It's something we carry not just as Philadelphians, but also as brothers. But this time was different. I felt there was something urgent about this release on the Lord's heart, and when we got to the church I discovered why. Right there on the opposite corner from the church were two things that were incredibly significant to me. The first was a five-foot-tall stone bust of Abraham Lincoln. Lincoln had already marked our journey significantly from New Orleans and Memphis, and this was just another confirmation. The same spirit of murder we had been wrestling with is what ended Lincoln's life, as well as that of Martin Luther King and many, many others. How many people meant to live out the purposes of God have been cut short by this thing? After I did a little research, I learned that the statue had been sitting there for almost ninety years. It had seen the neighborhood change time and time again, been painted over and over—including by some gangs to mark their territory—and now was in a state of complete disrepair, with many of the features barely recognizable. There are many statues in Illinois, the land of Lincoln, but this one seemed to speak volumes about the condition of this neglected neighborhood.

The second thing we saw, as soon as we arrived, were two men yelling at each other so angrily that I really thought we might have to call the cops. The rage in their voices was unnerving, demonic almost. They were standing mere feet from the Lincoln statue on the same corner. I knew immediately why the Lord wanted us to release brotherly love. The sound dominating the airwaves before we arrived was rage and hatred, but did that ever change.

As soon as we got set up, we began to release the raging love of the Father over Englewood and all of Chicago. Without the Father's love, there is no brotherly love. As we worshipped, people were popping their heads out of their windows up and down the side streets to see what was going on, and some began to come congregate with us on the corner. We were particularly blessed that some young kids came and showed an interest in what we were doing, and we let them play our instruments. Our keyboardist had a child on each knee playing, our drummer handed the sticks over to another young man, and a girl that had been eyeing my guitar for a while mustered the courage to come up and give it a few strums. We sang over and blessed the next generation of Englewood.

> *Holy is moving in Englewood. We release strength to all of Englewood. We release the glory and the movement of the blue note to Chicago. Father's love is burning in Englewood, and brotherly love is here. Anything is possible.*

Santo Fuego

The following morning was Sunday, and we worshipped with a Hispanic church in another part of town. It was a morning filled with holy fire—santo fuego. It was already a hot summer morning in the city. We had to lug all our gear up several flights of stairs to their meeting place, and the air conditioning was not working. We were all soaked with sweat before the meeting ever started.

James shared a little bit about what the Lord had been doing on our journey, and it was a real encouragement to them. Obviously the murder and overall crime rate in Chicago is of major concern to the churches there, and a focus of their prayers. James shared that many of these criminals are gifted pastors, apostles, and evangelists that have simply been duped into working for the wrong kingdom. Like Saul before he became Paul, they just need enough light released into their lives to see the right way. We got to minister to a number of beautiful saints that morning, and even a few who were giving their lives to Christ for the first time. The pastor and his team were a blessing to us as well. He prophesied over our team that there were angel musicians joining us everywhere we went, one thousand strong, and they were moving with us and following our lead. What an encouragement!

Pastor Louis, whose church we had worshipped at the night before, came in toward the end of the meeting. He told us his congregation had experienced a totally different atmosphere in their church that morning; there was a freedom in their worship that was totally new. What an answer to prayer!

We finished our time in Chicago with a blowout time of worship and prayer with a group of about 200 intercessors that come together once a month to pray and worship over their region. We shared with them about the Blue Journey, and they were greatly encouraged and joined with us in an intense time of intercession. Honestly, after all the dark and intense places we had been over the past few days, it was a welcome change to be in this totally free atmosphere of worship with these radical believers. We were so blessed to have a Native brother there named Eddy, who also happened to be a blues guitarist. I was so honored that Eddy got up and released his sound with our team on my guitar. I've had Native brothers and sisters play my guitar several times in the past, and for some reason it always feels like such an honor—like some part of my sound is being released through them, and a piece of who they are is being added to my instrument and my sound.

Toward the end of the meeting, James led us all in releasing the roar of the Lion of Judah over all of Chicago, and I have never heard a shout so loud in all my life. There was truly a shout in the camp of the people of God that night.

Arise and shine, Chicago, your light has come. The thankful army is rising up. We release the power of thankfulness in Chicago. No king but Jesus. He's our God. We crown you with many crowns. The heavenly anthem drowns out all other sounds.

CHAPTER 10

Detroit

Detroit was a very different experience, for Jamie and I especially, as it was the only leg of our trip we brought any of our kids on. Jamie has three kids and I have four. Gabriel (my oldest) and Maggie (Jamie's oldest) are very close, as they were born only three weeks apart. At the time of this trip they were eight years old. It was their first time on an extended ministry trip like this, and their first time on a plane, so their excitement levels were through the roof.

Raising up the next generation of worshippers and intercessors is something very important to us, and something I feel the body of Christ does not spend enough time thinking about. Oftentimes we can be so preoccupied thinking about how to pay the bills this month or, at best, what the next two to three years may hold, that we are almost never intentional enough to think about how we can impact the next few generations fifty to one hundred years from now.

God reveals himself as the God of Abraham, Isaac, and Jacob, so we know that family and thinking generationally are important to him. In fact, throughout Scripture we see the dreams, destinies, and promises of one generation fulfilled in a subsequent one, even through some of the great heroes of the faith like those mentioned in Hebrews 11. In our culture, we tend to get impatient when it takes more than a few weeks or months to see a harvest in our lives, but it could be that the greatest fruit of our lives will only be realized by sowing intentionally and faithfully into generations that may not even be born yet.

One of the passages James likes to use to illustrate this point is in Judges 15. Samson slew 1,000 Philistines (enemies of God's people) with the jawbone of a donkey. Perhaps more significant is the fact that as a result of the battle and Samson's obedience, a spring of water opened that generations were able to drink from. It was still watering God's people over a hundred years later, when the book of Judges is thought to have been written. Part of our intent as we traveled through these cities was to dig wells that generations after us would benefit from.

Another mistake we sometimes make is not expecting the Lord to move through our young ones. God made Samuel a prophetic voice to Eli at a very young age. The Lord called and used Jeremiah at a young age, despite his lack of confidence.

I once heard someone say there is no junior-sized Holy Spirit. If our children love the Lord and are filled with his Spirit, they should be able to hear from him the same way we can. Some would even say children can hear his voice more easily than us, because they don't carry the baggage of cynicism and past disappointments. Natural maturity is not necessarily a credible indicator of spiritual maturity. In our gatherings we try very hard not to put a ceiling on what we can expect from our young ones, and instead we allow them the freedom to move, make mistakes, and experience God in whatever ways they are ready to.

We had been in some pretty intense, dark, even dangerous places in Chicago, and I knew Detroit was going to give us a similar experience. While Chicago has the most overall murders in our nation, Detroit and Flint (both on our itinerary) exceed Chicago's numbers and are the two cities with the highest murder rate per capita. To be quite honest, I was a bit nervous about having the kids along with us on a trip like this. At the time we planned it, we were mostly just looking for an affordable trip we could take with our kids. But as the time of the trip grew closer, I began to get more and more anxious about having them there, and about our abilities to keep them out of trouble (with everything else we were going to have to focus on). I began to ask myself why we had picked this trip and was questioning the wisdom of it, but the Lord had a purpose for them being there, and I was about to find that out.

A few weeks before our trip, I found a news story about a very disturbing event in Detroit. In what was called "the largest public satanic ceremony in history," a nine-foot, one-and-a-half-ton statue of a goat-headed Baphomet was unveiled. Baphomet is an ancient symbol of idolatry that has become closely associated with Satanism. There were close to 700 people reported to have attended the unveiling ceremony, all of whom were required to sign a "Release of Liability, Film Notice, and Transfer of Soul Agreement." Yes, you read that right. The attendees were required to pledge their soul to Satan, despite the organizing group's official and paradoxical stance that Satan doesn't really exist. Wow, are they deceived! This was disturbing enough, but when I finally saw a picture of it, what caught my eye was that on either side of the Baphomet creature stood two young kids: a young girl on the left and a young boy on the right. They were very similar in appearance and age to our kids, and were both looking up to the Baphomet. I immediately knew what God's plan was and why our two kids were coming with us to Detroit. You see, the Devil has a plan for our generations just like God does. John 10:10 says "The thief comes only to steal and kill and destroy; I [Jesus] came that they may have life, and have it abundantly." The Devil's plan for our bloodlines is either to end them altogether or, at the very least, keep us forever lost in darkness and lies. God's plan is to fill us with his light and truth. I knew after seeing the statue that we were traveling there as a multi-generational company to counteract what the Devil and some very lost souls had been perpetrating in that region. Instantly, the anxiety over having the kids with us in some dangerous areas was gone, because I knew it was a setup from the Lord and that they had an assignment there as well.

Monroe

It was a gorgeous, warm, breezy day as we traveled to our first destination in the region. We had some extra time, so we took the opportunity to drive down to the edge of Lake Erie and put our feet in. Monroe is a small city located south of Detroit on Lake Erie. Named after President James Monroe, it has played a significant part in Michigan's history, stretching all the way back to the period of time just after the War of 1812, when the Michigan territory was being organized. Because of its history, some of the local intercessors feel that this little city, now dwarfed by some of its larger neighbors, is an important gateway into the state of Michigan. We are so thankful for

Anita Christopher and all the intercessors who made a way for us and traveled with us through the region.

We worshipped that night under a pavilion in the heart of town, across from the city hall. A fair number of intercessors came and joined us from all over Michigan, and most ended up traveling with us to each of our destinations in that state.

We started off with just the sound of drums to break open mercy and release awakening light to every family tree. We blessed Michigan from that gateway as we watched the sun slip down behind the buildings. Many of the folks who joined us saw visions in the sound we were releasing. There was a sweetness and a beauty in the sound that night that was unusual—a sound of peace, purity, and healing. At one point Isaac led us in a musical movement while we played. We declared for hope deferred to be broken off and for fresh hope to fill Michigan. We played and people danced in the presence of the Lord, while the soft orange glow of the streetlamps flooded the area. It was a beautiful night and set my expectations high for the rest of our time in the Detroit area.

We bless the gate of Michigan. Peace to these streets, every heart, and every home. We release shalom. Every gate in Michigan is blessed tonight through the mercy of the blood. We call every bloodline and family tree out of darkness and into light. Michigan is the state of the restored voice. The voice of every family tree is being restored.

We release angels of mercy. There's mercy at every gate. The justice of mercy from the courtroom of heaven. Through the Monroe gate you're kissing the state. Bringing back the voice of pure Michigan. It's a voice of declaration.

Paradise Valley

Paradise Valley is a neighborhood in Detroit with a significant music history. "As Detroit's manufacturing base boomed during two world wars (1917-18 and 1941-45), large numbers of African Americans moved here to work in the factories. Detroit's African-American population increased from 5,000 in 1910 to 300,000 by 1950. Throughout this period, segregationist policies restricted where blacks could live, own businesses, and spend their free time. During the 1930s, a commercial center emerged in the area known as Paradise Valley. Some nightclubs, called 'black and tans,' were frequented by blacks and whites alike. African Americans owned and operated all of the businesses in the valley." — From a Michigan historical site placard

Paradise Valley, along with neighboring "Black Bottom" (actually named for the richness of the soil, not for the black folks that lived there, as some might presume) served as Detroit's entertainment and business district. Detroit is known today primarily for Motown, but long before Motown was birthed, nightclubs along the famous Hastings Street, and throughout this area, would have been abuzz with their own flavor of jazz and blues music. Early acts like Bessie Smith and later ones like John Lee Hooker delivered the industrial sounds of Detroit mixed with the classic Delta blues, and they birthed something unique to the region.

Unfortunately, none of the original landmarks from this time are still standing. The rapid population growth these neighborhoods experienced in the 1930s and '40s resulted in overcrowding and slum-like conditions. The city built some housing projects to help alleviate the overcrowding, but the idea backfired. As folks moved out of Black Bottom, it became abandoned and blighted. Instead of pouring money into a neighborhood in desperate need of repair, city officials opted to demolish and redevelop the entire area. Highways and larger modern buildings now occupy the space.

We met at a parking garage along a busy highway early one morning, just to worship on the ground that used to house the sound released all those years ago. Even though the entire area has been redeveloped, the ground still remembers the voice of its Creator. The area is still very much a sound portal. The bluesmen who released their sound here were in many cases looking for work and a better life. They were searching for what would bring freedom and healing to the trauma and pain in their souls. We began calling forth the jewels in every bloodline still in the land. We agreed with everyone who prayed that their grandkids would have a better life than them.

We call forth the jewels in Detroit. Redemption is here. Chains are broken. Detroit is blossoming forth, especially the African-American community. We praise the Creator of paradise. The king of the harvest is dancing through Paradise Valley. There is a magnified light in Detroit moving into the fullness of the blue note and God's original intent. There's a new blue sound from Motown. It's the sound of the lion shaking the ground. It's shaking every family tree. We release the light, the life, and the love of the Father.

Dearborn

We then worshipped at a church in the western part of the city, not far from nearby Dearborn. Dearborn and nearby areas have experienced an explosion in their Muslim population in recent years, and it is of major concern to the churches there. We declared from that place that the sound of true worship to the living God would dominate the airwaves, and not the sound of the Muslim call to prayer. The heavenly anthem is drowning all music but its own. We also entered into the "Boom, boom, boom" sound (from John Lee Hooker) for the first time. We Released it this way:

> *Out with the old and in with the new. Every dark gate must fall! Boom, boom, boom*
>
> *We release the order of the King. Boom*
>
> *We release the justice of the King. Boom*
>
> *The awakening train is here. Boom, boom, boom*

Victory, victory, victory. The sound is breaking the hardness of the people of Detroit. Bitterness and hope deferred are being broken off. Michigan is meeting mercy.

Pontiac

That night we worshipped in Pontiac, Michigan. When you hear the word Pontiac, you might think of the Pontiac cars produced by General Motors, but they were named after the city that produced them. The city, in turn, was named after an Ottawa war chief in the eighteenth century named Chief Pontiac. Chief Pontiac's life was marked by the bloody wars he fought against British military occupation, so great bloodshed and broken covenants have marked this region. In the end, Chief Pontiac is said to have cursed the white men and their generations for defiling the land through broken covenants.

This history and the issues that have come down through the generations play a significant role in the sound and the song of the people in that land. The saints here are believing for a complete healing and restoration of the land, and that the city of Pontiac will turn to the Lord.

Pastor Lee welcomed us into his city and church. We set up in the parking lot, where the church had laid out about 100 folding chairs. Pastor Lee said God had told them he was sending some reinforcements. That wasn't the first time we had heard that. We had an awesome time of worship that night, declaring the word of the Lord over Pontiac and over every bloodline and family tree, regardless of what condition they might find themselves in.

The words of men are being broken by the blood of the Son. Every bloodline is blessed, beginning with the Native people. Every reservation is moving in the sound of freedom.

We release healing. This is the night of Pontiac's healing. There is a new sound in Pontiac. It's the sound of blessing and not curses. Everything changes when holy is in the air.

While we were worshipping, James had all the women come to the front. All the men surrounded them and symbolically covered the women by lifting their hands up around them. This is something James will often do in meetings. The Lord showed him this strategy a few years ago. One of the tactics the enemy uses to bring an end to our bloodline is through the deception of abortion. The Lord told James that if the men had covered the women properly, there would be no abortion issue in our land. Far too often, women have been left to make decisions and deal with situations they never should have had to face alone. Too many men have shirked their responsibilities and told women their pregnancies were their problem to deal with. This left our culture susceptible to a major deception of the enemy. The widespread abortion problem we see today is really innocent bloodshed, and it brings defilement on our land. James had all the men pray a prayer of repentance and ask forgiveness from the women there, as a prophetic act.

As we were doing this prophetic act, a woman named Ako began to weep uncontrollably. She was eventually able to share with us that in that atmosphere, she was able to finally forgive generations of men in her family that had treated her, her mother, and her grandmother as property and hadn't covered them properly. As she continued to weep and receive a major healing from the Lord, we sang over her.

> *We bless you, Ako. You are a shining star because of whose you are. Your bloodline is a shining star. In every home where women have been property, we release mercy. We release awakening light. The awakening is here. Nothing can stop it!*

We prayed and released over Ako, but more was happening. When the Lord prompts us in these ways, we need to realize it is bigger than just our meeting. It's always bigger than who is in the room. Our meeting is just the tip of what the Lord is doing in a city, region, or people group. James gives the analogy of receiving a vaccination: The needle enters one tiny spot, but what's delivered through that needle affects the entire body. If the Lord is releasing healing, deliverance, or repentance on a gathering of believers, we should receive what he has for us, but then we should also turn and release it into the region and into the entire body. Ako received something special that night, but we believe many other bloodlines did as well while we released that out into the region.

It was a powerful night of worship in Pontiac. We probably would have continued a little longer, but we were getting absolutely swarmed by mosquitos and felt we needed to call it a night. I guess we needed some of those Chicago dragonflies to come join us in Michigan.

Motown

Like many of these cities influential in the release of the sound of blues music, there were many other styles and genres that grew out of, or alongside, that sound. Muscle Shoals is celebrated for its contributions to rock and roll, New Orleans for its contributions to jazz, and Detroit for Motown.

Motown is a combination of two words: motor and town, which had become a nickname for Detroit due to its car manufacturing, and was the name of a record label started by Berry Gordy in 1960. The Motown Sound, as it became known, was an instant and unparalleled success. With artists such as Marvin Gaye, Stevie Wonder, The Jackson 5, Smokey Robinson, Diana Ross, and The Supremes, Motown Records produced over 100 top ten hits in the 1960s, and close to 80 percent of the Billboard Hot 100 record charts for the same decade.

Unlike the blues venues of the '30s and '40s, Studio A and the rest of the houses and buildings where Motown was birthed in the '50s and '60s are very well preserved. A museum and guided tour are available as well.

Just like The Swampers were key to the success of Muscle Shoals Sound Studio, Gordy had put together a very talented and tight-knit team of musicians that recorded on many of the albums. They were known collectively as the Funk Brothers. A documentary from 2002 publicized the fact that the Funk Brothers played on more number one albums than the Beatles, Elvis, the Rolling Stones, and the Beach Boys combined.

Motown Records also played a critical role in the racial integration of music as it reached a crossover audience of both black and white markets. This almost certainly had something to do with Gordy's significant attention to artist development, which taught these young, inexperienced artists how to handle themselves with great dignity and play against some of the negative stereotypes of that time.

Outside Motown Museum

As we went through the museum, the thing that struck me was how righteous the roots of Motown were. The story behind the Gordy family is an impressive one I won't take the time to lay out here, but it is worth hearing. Also, the intent of almost all of the artists was to release songs of peace, hope, and love, and in many cases whole families released their sound as one voice. Obviously this message and this music resonated strongly in our nation. We prayed there and blessed the sound of Motown.

> *Every bloodline connected to the Motown sound is being visited with mercy. Holy is the sound of Motown.*

Chene Park

That afternoon we went down to the Detroit River, which is also the US/Canadian border. We gathered at a place called Chene Park. We learned that Aretha Franklin and the Isley Brothers would be performing there that night, but we were on the strip there because the Baphomet Statue had been unveiled in a warehouse there.

We felt the Lord directing us to a place between the warehouse and the river. It was such a beautiful day. The sun was shining and the scenery down by the river was just beautiful. It was hard to believe that such intense darkness could reside in such a peaceful looking setting. We were traveling light, so we began to worship, sing, and release over that land with just a single acoustic guitar.

A number of people were seeing prophetically in the sound, and we released a lot. My son Gabriel had a vision of an oak tree growing up that was connecting heaven and earth, and so we prayed through and released Isaiah 61:3. With Jamie leading us, we broke off every form of idolatry, whether it was idolizing statues or idolizing singers and performers. We repented for any part we had played in idolatry, of any form.

> *He's giving beauty for ashes, oil of joy for mourning, and garments of praise for the spirit of heaviness. The trees of Detroit are righteous; they are the planting of the Lord.*
>
> *The earth is the Lord's and the fullness thereof; the water and the blood and the Spirit agree; heaven and earth agree with this freedom song.*
>
> *Detroit is free. Detroit is free of idolatry.*

We were by a small hill, and someone felt Gabriel and Maggie should release their sound from the top of this high point. They released the sound of their worship with shofar and mattah in hand, over every young person—like the ones looking up to the Baphomet in the statue. We joined with them in breaking the influence of the enemy over the youth. It was a proud papa moment for sure.

Wish Egan Park

Our next stop was to set up near a community youth center in Wish Egan Park. James had asked some of the local law enforcement officers where some the darkest areas of the city were, and this was one of them. We wanted to be intentional about going into the darkest areas to release the light. We set up our full sound system outside the youth center on the corner of the property under some trees. It was a steamy, hot afternoon in urban Detroit, but we were thankful for the shade.

Apostle Diane, who is a powerful intercessor and mother in the faith in the region, welcomed us and opened with prayer. A few dozen folks from the community joined in with us as we began to worship and release light over the neighborhood and the city.

Releasing joy and the strength of the Lord over every bloodline. Praying for every person in the city who administers justice, that they would know the just one and would administer his justice. If you don't know him, you are setting yourself up for corruption.

We bless the city of Detroit. What happens here reverberates back to every city on the Blue Journey so far. The 8 Mile is no longer a dividing line but a place of new beginnings.

Mercy is on the throne of Detroit. The sons are coming to this land. Rising out of Babylon, the sons are set free, the hidden ones and the prisoners. I AM is the song of their hearts/song of their mouths.

We are seeding the land, restoring the roots, releasing the righteous fruit.

There was a powerful flow of revelation as we worshipped there. Many people were seeing in the Spirit and releasing it into the natural. At one point a little boy named Emmanuel came to the mic and started singing, "There is power in the name of Jesus." We were so moved when his grandmother shared that one of her other grandchildren had been killed in the streets of this neighborhood. We thanked God they had not become bitter, but that they were a family tree that was releasing light in its community.

Burning up the heavens, burning up the darkness. The horses are out of the stalls and running free. Where there is hatred, now there is brotherly love. Detroit is free. We release Jubilee.

Fire in Detroit, boom, boom, boom!

Fire in the pulpits, boom, boom, boom!

Fire on Aretha, boom, boom, boom!

Flint

Our final stop in the land was with our good friend Pastor Ed and the saints at Gateway Hope Center in Flint, Michigan. Ed leads a radical group of worshippers and intercessors, so we felt very at home there. We were hoping to play outside, but the weather wasn't looking good so we decided to just worship in their building. We released blasts from Flint to Detroit to Chicago. Flint is a hard, hard place, but we felt the reason the enemy is so active there is because he is afraid of the fountain of life rumbling under the ground. We declared that the gates were open and that pure living water was flowing through Flint to Detroit and the whole region. It was a powerful time of worship with our friends and a fitting way to conclude our time in that region.

> *The sons of glory are kicking out the snakes and creeps. He has given us dominion to drive out the enemy, secure the borders, and release the glory. The new wine is being poured out.*
>
> *We're turning the lights on. Darkness has no place in wet sunshine.*
>
> *We release the waters and the warriors of Flint. Blind and bitter no more.*

CHAPTER 11

Austin

U nfortunately, the time we were scheduled to be in Austin ended up not being a good weekend for most of the team, so instead of having the usual team of six to eight of us, there were only three of us: James, Isaac, and myself. In many of the cities we had been down a person or two and had been blessed to have local musicians join with us and fill in the gaps, but in Austin we were going to be more dependent on that than ever. Thankfully, we were absolutely thrilled with the amazing musicians and intercessors the Lord connected us with when we went. Rocky Ivey from Open Gate Ministries was so gracious in paving the way for us, and we were so thankful for him. Not only were we not lacking, but Rocky was able to connect us with some of the finest musicians we had played with on our journey.

When most blues music lovers think of Austin, Texas, they immediately think of Stevie Ray Vaughn. He was one of Austin's favorite sons, and certainly brought a lot of national attention, but Austin was a hotbed for the blues long before he arrived on the scene. During the '40s, '50s, and '60s, Austin had a vibrant blues scene. Clubs like Charley's Playhouse and the Victory Grill (which has claimed the nickname "Austin's First Home of the Blues) were abuzz with the sounds of the blues, sometimes until the early morning hours, and even as far back as the 1920s. Blind Lemon Jefferson, who was also from eastern Texas, was one of the fist blues artists to be recorded, earning him the nickname "the Father of Texas Blues." After Jefferson's commercial success, blues singers from all over the South flocked to east Texas—Austin, Dallas, etc.—in hopes of being recorded. "Lightning" Hopkins was another bluesman who helped put east Texas on the map musically in the late '20s.

Called Together

Race relations played a big part in the development of the music in Austin. In 1928, Austin, which was divided east from west, created a Negro district in the east side. The division was completed by building a road, then called East Avenue, today called I35. But despite the institutional racism, blacks in Austin developed a thriving community, including music venues that were an integral part of the "Chitlin Circuit," a string of venues throughout the region where blacks could safely perform and listen to music. The Chitlin Circuit derived its name from chitterlings or pig intestines—a cheap local dish that would be served at or near many of the music venues.

East side music venues and restaurants thrived, initially because there was nowhere else for the black folks to go, but eventually the blues music caught the attention of the white community, particularly the university students. So great was the interest in blues music among the college-age white community that some of the blacks grew to resent it, as entire bars and clubs would be reserved and filled with white audiences, leaving no room for the locals. While blacks were not nearly as welcome on the west side of town as whites were on the east side, the love for the music helped forerun the eventual desegregation of Austin in the late '60s and '70s.

Today, Austin is still very much a sound portal, touting the nickname "Live Music Capital of the World," and with good reason. Austin has more live music venues per capita than any other US city. It is also home to a show called Austin City Limits, which has been airing live music from its namesake for over thirty years, making it the longest-running music program in television history. The show also helped inspire the annual Austin City Limits Festival that draws close to half a million music lovers each year to Zilker Park, Austin.

It seems the Lord has been calling many worship leaders and worship musicians to move to Austin in recent years. Many of them have come for different reasons, but somehow they've come. I believe this is another outworking of the Jubilee season we are in. The Lord is repositioning many in Austin to fulfill the destiny he has placed on them and on the city. Some have even been starting to call it the "Live Worship Capital of the World." It will be interesting to see in the years ahead what the Lord begins to establish with all those he has called together in this city.

Oak Hill

On our first night in Austin we were hosted by Rocky at his ministry, which is located in a strip mall and comes off as more of a live music/art venue or cafe than a traditional church building. It is a fitting expression of what it means to be a community of worshippers in Austin, and it speaks of how highly they value the arts. Folks that might not walk into a traditional church building would feel comfortable here, and they come in to receive ministry. We were joined that night by Jeremy and his son, Devin, on guitar and bass, and a drummer named Roman. There were many, many worship events going on around town that weekend, so we were grateful they took the time from their busy schedules to come flow with us.

We felt it was important in that atmosphere to enter the land in honor by honoring the sound of some of these musicians that carry the sound of their region, and we wanted to have them lead us. It was a powerful time of worship that night, with many of those gathered seeing in the Spirit and releasing it for the whole room to own together.

One had a vision of a master builder laying a foundation, but he was dancing and spinning as he built it. Every sound he released and every dance move he made laid another stone into the foundation. Sounds turned into brushstrokes and brushstrokes turned into engravings.

Another sister had a vision of a river flowing toward Austin, but as it grew close she realized it wasn't a river of water but one of warriors on horses. As the river came to her, she was swept up in it and joined the army of warriors. As the river advanced toward the city, the warriors starting banging their swords on their shields. Finally, the river crashed into the city, creating a huge cloud of glory that rumbled through all of Austin.

James likes to always ask people what their names mean, because *who* is sharing is just as important as the words he or she is saying. In that night's small crowd, there were three women that shared, all named Michelle. Michelle means "who is like God," so we declared that phrase was rumbling through all of Austin.

> *We bless the sound of the live music capital of the world. Awaken, Austin! Arise and shine. The winds are blowing on the embers. Austin is ablaze. Every gate in Austin is being set aflame. Strange fires are being snuffed out. The muddy waters are being made clear.*

Another woman shared a vision she had of a statue of Stevie Ray Vaughn that was crying because that which he'd longed for was being released this night. It is said that Stevie Ray Vaughn, toward the end of his life, had apparently gotten cleaned up and saved, and he had longed to raise up sons to carry what he carried. Jeremy prayed and thanked God that we were releasing a first fruits offering of the authentic sound of the sons of Austin.

Open Gate Ministries

There was another young son of Austin there that night named John David, who we wanted to release his sound. We prayed and released honor over him that night, and declared he was the injection point for every other minstrel and psalmist in his generation—that they would hear a clear sound from heaven and release all that they are and what God made them to be in their sound. As we were praying for John David, someone spoke about three generations worshipping together, which is something very near and dear to my heart. We realized there were a few young ones in the room, so we had them come up and stand for their generation while we prayed and released one last time. We were absolutely stunned to find out that the first and middle names of the two young boys were Johnny Cash and Miles Davis! This idea of the sons of Austin releasing their authentic sound would become an anthem we would carry with us through our entire time in the land.

The next day Rocky took us downtown to see some of the places where blues music had been played over the years. Some of the neighborhoods where guys like Stevie Ray Vaughn lived and gigged are still there, but large portions of the city are gentrifying. It was a bit surreal to see little bungalows that might have been rented for $25/month now towered over by expensive high rises. In a nearby park, we stopped off for a photo op with a large statue of Stevie Ray Vaughn.

Rocky took us past many of the music venues still standing, and other spots where they've been torn down or moved on to other locations. We had lunch at a place called Threadgills. Now open in two locations, Threadgills started out in 1933 as a filling station turned music bar, and it quickly became a popular spot for traveling musicians to spend time at. Kenneth Threadgill welcomed all kinds of acts into his venue through the years, and was known to walk out from behind the bar, grab a mic, and sing along with the performers on stage. Threadgills had a "no hate" policy, and welcomed both black and white artists and audiences. Singers like Janice Joplin cut their teeth singing here. The more southern of the two Threadgills locations now pays homage to the Armadillo Headquarters that was once nearby, and whose owner now owns Threadgills. The "dillo," as it is sometimes called, was another popular performance venue through the '70s.

Real Street

A few hours later we arrived at what would be our venue to release our sound for the next two nights. It is an inconspicuous building that used to house the Austin House of Prayer and is now an art gallery. It is located on Real Street.

This was one of these places that really had me guessing for a while. I couldn't figure out why the Lord had us in this location. It just seemed like a rather strange place for us to end up, but I believed God had a purpose in it, and that all would soon be revealed.

We were joined by two amazing musicians and great guys, Jerry on drums, Dave on bass, and of course Rocky on guitar and vocals. As we began that night, Rocky began to sing the Lord's prayer in an awesome way, unlike anything I had heard before. I can only describe it as an indigenous type sound. We came up under him and started to make many declarations over Austin.

Every kindred tribe and tongue in Austin is saying yes to you, Lord. Austin city says yes. The sound of Austin is coming up to the next level. Austin is getting its voice back.

> *Rusty gates are opening. Gates the occult has established are being brought into righteous alignment. There's thunder in the skies and lightning in the air. Lift up your heads, oh gates, and let the King of Glory in.*

During one of our sessions on Real Street, I began to sing something I had woken up with that morning. The phrase rumbling around in my spirit was, "The scarlet thread, the blue note, and the violet crown." I really wasn't sure what it meant, but I knew it was something I needed to release, so during one of our sessions I did, and in the moment the Lord gave me the next piece.

> *The scarlet thread, the blue note, and the violet crown,*
>
> *Sons of Austin, release your authentic sound.*

I did a little research and found out another one of Austin's nicknames—albeit unknown to many of the locals—is "the City of the Violet Crown." The violet crown actually refers to an atmospheric phenomenon that causes the sky and hills west of Austin to sometimes show a lush purple color at sunset. Most likely it is the same atmospheric phenomenon known as the Belt of Venus, which would certainly not be unique to Austin, but might be more spectacular or more frequent here than in other places due to Austin's prime conditions. A local man named David described having witnessed it:

> "I have lived in Austin most of fifty years and have always heard about the "Violet Crown." Just as the sun went down yesterday, I was standing outside and the sky went purple. I live on Koenig near Woodrow. I probably looked like an idiot

staring up at the sky, but it was worth it. You could have knocked me over with one finger. I always thought it was a legend or folklore or whatever. It was incredibly beautiful, real, and I saw it. I would say lavender is the closest color to what I saw. I was so bowled over I forgot to take a picture. I ran inside for a camera a few minutes later, but it was gone. It was only visible for two or three minutes. Amazing."[11]

Athens, Greece, has also been called the City of the Violet Crown by some of its poets. There are references to it going back as far as 400 B.C. In the late nineteenth century, Austin became home to the University of Texas. Residents were so proud of the school that they started calling Austin "the Athens of the South," linking their city with Athens. Athens is a city known for its institutions of higher learning, including one of the oldest known universities in human history, the Platonic Academy, which was founded by Plato. It is probable that this link is responsible for Austin acquiring the nickname "City of the Violet Crown." It is also likely that the first time it was used to reference Austin, it was in jest at Austin residents' somewhat sensational claims regarding their universities. But it also may be that the Belt of Venus is more predominantly seen in Austin, due its abundance of cloudless yet dust-filled sunsets. Today, a number of Austin businesses and organizations bear the Violet Crown moniker, but most residents probably don't even realize why.

I was still trying to put together what the scarlet thread and the blue note had to do with the violet crown. Part of what it

---

[11] Susan Burneson, "Just What Is a Violet Crown?" *Voices of the Violet Crown.* Accessed 26 April 2016. http://www.violetcrownvoices.com/just-what-is-a-violet-crown

meant to me was that the blood of Christ was redeeming the sound of the land, reclaiming the glory of the color blue, and obviously red and blue together make purple, but I still wasn't getting it.

I went back to some of the notes I had been keeping about our journey, and I realized the last time we had been prompted to sing about the scarlet thread and blue note was on Beale Street in Memphis. I explained all of this to Rocky and he was able to fill in a missing piece: When the house of prayer was in that building on Real Street, one of their slogans was "From Beale Street to Real Street!" He explained that it spoke to them of recognizing and embracing their roots, but of being free to release a sound that was authentic to who they were, and not to be a copy of someone else. This is exactly what we had been releasing all along., and it was the last piece of the puzzle. When we release our authentic sound (our blue note) through the power of the blood, there is a crown of glory over us and over our land. I believe this is why the Lord brought us to Real Street—to receive this revelation and to decree the scarlet thread, the blue note, and the violet crown over all of Austin from this well.

The men and women who pioneered the blues sound on Beale Street and elsewhere did not do so by trying to copy someone else's sound. Stevie Ray Vaughn was as good an example of this as B.B. King or Charlie Patton. They released an authentic sound of who they were in the light they had, and that sound swept our nation. We, in the body of Christ, must realize that we will not have the impact for the kingdom of God we want if we only try to copy someone else's gift. God has given each of us a unique sound to release, and that means there is something of the heart of God that goes unexpressed in the earth if we are not true to who we are made to be.

The city of Austin actually has an unofficial slogan to "Keep Austin Weird." It's a call to support small businesses over big corporations, and indie- and community- based projects over cookie-cutter commercialism. But I believe it is also a prophetic call to the sons and daughters of Austin to stay true to what the Lord has placed in them, and to resist the temptation to become a clone of something else for the sake of some perceived level of what we would call success.

The scarlet thread, the blue note, and the violet crown: This phrase brought a lot of things full circle for me, not just in what we were releasing over Austin, but over the course of the whole journey. When we allow the power of Christ's blood to cleanse and redeem us, we become free. The ultimate freedom is to be exactly who God made us to be without any competing influences – to release our authentic sound, our blue note. When we release the glory of who he made us to be, we and our land (our sphere of influence) are crowned with glory.

> *The scarlet thread, the blue note, and the violet crown.*
>
> *Sons of Austin, release your authentic sound. You are free, bonds are broken, your atmosphere is changing right down to the ground. Original intent and authentic sound are springing up out of the ground. From Beale Street to REAL Street releasing the authentic sound.*
>
> *The victory is the Lord's; the victory grill is the Lord's. Yahweh, maker of fire, copyright owner of the whole earth.*

During our last session at Real Street, we didn't have a drummer. But you know what they say, necessity is the mother of invention! I once again needed to use the app on my iPad to create drum loops, so that was our drummer for the evening.

This had happened once or twice previously on our journey, but this time it really became a focal point in the sound. We released powerful decrees over Austin to a groove I can only really describe as EDM (Electronic Dance Music) infused with blues. It was a powerful time, but it was also a new sound for us, and it birthed in us a desire to experiment with this electro blues sound more and see where it would go. God is so good. Even when we think we are lacking something, he uses it as an opportunity to birth something new and unique in us. As the electro blues sound was pumping, our thoughts were drawn back to the Victory Grill, where so many artists released their sounds. James began making powerful declarations and giving a whole new meaning to the Victory Grill.

Victory has always been Father's plan for this capital land. Victory is here, it's burning hot on the grill. There's a whole new meaning for victory grill. Fire on the alter, flames in the air. The incense of holy worship. The victory is the Lord's, the victory grill is the Lord's. Yahweh—maker of fire—copyright owner of the whole earth. The angels are dancing in Austin tonight. The victory is the Lord's.

At the end of the meeting, a dear sister who had been worshipping with us the whole time shared that she had been in a car accident recently and had been in a lot of pain, so much so she was unable to dance in worship. For the two nights she was with us, though, her body was working perfectly and she was able to dance. Hallelujah!

Out of the Box

We were back at Rocky's for our final night in Austin. Their community was in a season of transition and they were about to relocate their ministry, as the Lord would lead. In fact, our meeting there that night was the last meeting they were going to hold in that building. They weren't sure exactly where the Lord was leading them, but they were stepping out in obedience anyway, much like Abraham was called to do. James felt it was a prophetic picture for the region: that they are being called to get out of the familiar, out of the box, and allow the Lord to lead them into fresh territory and fresh revelation.

We were joined again that night by Jerry on drums and Austin on bass and keys. We really were blessed to have such amazing musicians to flow with us. We started out by just releasing Revelation 4 and the picture of the throne of God. God had been speaking to us through colors, and I was reminded of the rainbow around the throne, since God is the source of everything, even all the colors of the rainbow. We joined with the living creatures and elders in singing "Holy, holy, holy."

While we were worshipping, a young man named Johnathan had a vision of a lion roaring over Austin, and the lion was roaring, "Mine!" You could begin to feel the zeal of the Lord over the city of Austin as he shared this vision. I believe the Lord is zealous for the city of Austin, and he wants it to be a city that knows how to release the sound of pure worship, the authentic sound only it can release. The original intent of the Father is being fulfilled. Austin is a worship capital.

The mountains melt like wax. The fire is falling all over Austin. All flesh is burning with the fire of God. The land is mine. The water is mine. Austin is mine says the Lord!

CHAPTER 12

Kansas City

K ansas City wasn't actually on our initial itinerary for the Blue Journey. This wasn't due to a lack of interest, but rather due to the fact that it was simply not possible to visit every town or city that had birthed the blues. While we had visited some of the larger well-known places where the blues had evolved, the reality is we barely scratched the surface. Blues music was born on thousands of front porches and juke joints. Its earliest practitioners were from all across the deep South, and they rarely stayed in one place for very long.

But the Lord knew we needed to complete our journey in Kansas City and, thankfully, two faithful women of God in Kansas City knew it too. Debra and Lauren had been tracking along with the rest of our journey and contacted James about the team coming to Kansas City for the final leg.

Even before blues music was popular in Kansas City, ragtime was the main sound of the region here and in nearby

St. Louis. Ragtime was birthed by the intermingling of minstrel or vaudeville shows with the Africa-originated influence of syncopation. Its name comes from "ragged time," which also references its syncopated or unusual timing. The most noted ragtime composer in the late 1800s, and beyond the turn of the century, was Scott Joplin. Joplin, who was dubbed "King of Ragtime Writers," achieved fame with songs like "The Maple Leaf Rag," and "The Entertainer." Joplin's death in 1917 is considered by many to mark the end of the ragtime era and the beginning of the blues and jazz eras. His sound was formative for many artists in the region, and indeed throughout the nation, crossing over into styles beyond blues or jazz, and even big band and swing.

In the '20s and '30s, Kansas City became well-known for its distinctive jazz music, but if Kansas City jazz had a secret ingredient, it would have been that it was firmly rooted in the blues. Charlie Parker, Count Basie, Jay McShan, and others perfected their blues-based jazz sound here. "Big Joe" Turner was the quintessential blues shouter of that time. He was known as "the Boss of the Blues," and was also later considered a founding father of the rock-and-roll sound. Like so many of these musical pioneers, Big Joe discovered his love for music through his involvement with a local church, and by the time he was a teenager in the 1920s, he had quit school and was working as a singing bartender throughout clubs in Kansas City. He teamed up with boogie-woogie pianist Pete Johnson, and together the pair became quite well-known throughout the region, eventually playing with Benny Goodman and others in New York City's Carnegie Hall, and introducing a much wider audience to their brand of blues and jazz.

The duo of Turner and Johnson reminded me of our approach to music on the Blue Journey. We didn't generally have a set list or a plan of almost any kind when we worshipped and released sound. We would pick a key to all start in and see what happened from there. The whole goal was to enter into the sound the Lord showed us to release over the land.

Jay McShan, one of the most noted jazz and swing bandleaders responsible for the Kansas City sound, said this of Big Joe Turner and Pete Johnson:

> *"These guys did one tune and it would last for an hour, and you would wonder where all the notes and words were coming from."[12]*

When we got to Kansas City, the eyes of the nation were on it: The American League Championship Series of Baseball was being played between the Kansas City Royals and the Toronto Blue Jays. Kansas City is known as "the City of Fountains," because it has more operating fountains than any other city in our nation. In fact, it is said to be the city with the most fountains in the world, second only to Rome. Because both of the teams in the world series used blue as their colors, the city had dyed the water in many of its fountains blue. Here we were to release the glory of the blue note in Kansas City, and when we got there all the fountains had been turned blue. Woah! The Lord was already speaking.

Kaw Point Riverfront Park

Our first place to worship in the land was Kaw Point Riverfront Park. The park is right in the heart of the city, and

---

[12] Terry Waldo, "Kansas City Blues." Accessed 26 April 2016. http://library.umkc.edu/spec-col/parisoftheplains/webexhibit/musical/mus-01.htm

it gets its name from the fact that it is situated exactly where the Kansas and Missouri rivers intersect. Rivers are always very significant and strategic places. Before there were highways, rivers were the highways. All travel, commerce, and life in general revolved around rivers. The confluence of these rivers was the reason for the geographical location of Kansas City. The area had been explored by Lewis and Clark back in 1804, and a silhouette statue of them stands at the intersection of the rivers on the southwest side.

Kaw Park

The park was beautiful, and we found a spot right on the water where we could set up and worship. The only downside was that we couldn't get our cars anywhere near that location, and so ended up having to lug all of our gear about 150 yards into the park, but it was worth it. From that vantage point, there was a great view across the water of the downtown area, and we really felt like we were singing over the city.

As we worshipped I was reminded of the lyrics Sydney Brown wrote in 1904 to one of Scott Joplin's most famous songs, "Maple Leaf Rag." I thought they were particularly poignant:

Oh go 'way man I can hypnotize dis nation,

I can shake de earth's foundation wid de Maple Leaf Rag[13]

Exactly. Sounds can do that. There was a lot of profound truth in that statement, whether Brown or Joplin realized it or not. It reminded me very much of the lyrics to that old hymn "Crown Him with Many Crowns" that we had been releasing along this journey. The heavenly anthem drowns all music but its own.

There's a lot of musical history in Kansas City, but the city also released a recent sound that has swept our nation. Under the direction of Mike Bickle, the International House of Prayer has been holding 24/7 worship in its prayer room since the late 1990s. This sound and model have resulted in the formation of literally hundreds of similar ministries devoted to worshipping God 24/7. The sound they are releasing has started an entire movement. Kansas City is clearly a place the Lord has ordained to release sounds that shift our nation, and that is part of what we released as we sang over the city from across the river.

The atmosphere is changed. DNA is rearranged at the sound of holy, holy everywhere the river runs. Eternal purpose and original intent.

There is a river whose streams make glad the city. The earth moves at the roar of the lion. Every molecule responds. It

---

[13] Ray Argyle, *Scott Joplin and the Age of Ragtime* (North Carolina: McFarland, 2009), 34.

hypnotized the nations, shakes the earth's foundation, the earth moves.

The heavenly anthem is shaking the nation. The glory of the blue note is shaking the nation—blue glory where the rivers meet. A people of justice. Royal blue. Heavenly blue. Blue flame is burning in bloodlines and family trees.

Jubilee is here. Jubilee awakening and salvation spring up from the ground. The ancient tribes are coming alive. The ancient dances are being danced. Come alive! The eyes of the Lord are looking over the land from Kansas City tonight. You're the God who sees and brings Jubilee to every tribe and tongue.

As the sun set behind us, the city in front of us lit up and the city lights reflected on the relatively calm river waters. We kept worshipping there, even though it was getting dark. Eventually the sun was all the way down and we couldn't see anymore because there were no lights near us. When I looked down I couldn't even see the neck of my guitar well enough to play anymore. Needless to say, we had a fun time trying to wrap everything up, find black wires lying in the grass in the dark, and lug it all the way back to the car in the pitch black. Thank God for cell phone flashlight apps.

Gem Theater

The next day we trekked to a place near downtown Kansas City called 18th and Vine. This is a part of town known for its musical heritage, and is to this day a hotspot for musicians and music lovers, particularly in the jazz genre. In the early twentieth century, clubs were found throughout the city, but the 18th and Vine area was fertile ground and had the majority of them. Blues and jazz seemed to mix and mingle effortlessly in the clubs there, and a distinctive style of music was birthed by the likes of Jay McShan, Charlie Parker, and Count Basie during the '30s and '40s.

One of the buildings in this section is the Mutual Musicians Foundation. The MMF has been hosting late night (1 a.m. – 6 a.m.) jam sessions for local musicians since 1930. Called a living museum, the MMF is a living, breathing testament to the rich musical heritage of Kansas City. Another hotspot in the area is known as the Blue Room—a very well-known jazz club that people come to visit from all over the nation.

In the center of this area is the Gem Theatre. Built over 100 years ago in 1912, the Gem was originally a silent movie theater, and it quickly became a fixture in the community. The Gem stopped being used in the 1960s and fell into disrepair, but in the 1980s it became the centerpiece of the city's renovation and revitalization efforts, and today it is a beautiful venue that hosts community events and productions, including the annual 18th and Vine Jazz Festival. It was this theater we had rented for the day, and where we would have our next release.

Our time at the Gem was different to anything else we had done on our journey. For one thing, we were in a state-of-the-art theatre, a far cry from setting up our gear out in the grass or in a parking lot somewhere, as we had done many times so far. Also, since we were at the end of the journey, we wanted to use the opportunity to recount the story of all the places we had been and talk about what the Lord had been doing and showing us in each leg of the trip.

Gem Theater

James is a prophetic artist, and he used images he'd created to share the vision with groups we met with all the way through our journey. Behind us on the stage at the Gem was a huge backdrop we were able to project these images onto. We began to tell the story of the Blue Journey, starting all the way back at Charleston, South Carolina. With the huge, beautiful images behind us, James talked about each leg while we entered into some of the sounds we released in each region. A small crowd joined us in the theater and worshipped with us, blessing each of the cities we had been to. It was an incredible time of reliving and thanking God for all he had accomplished so far. We finished our story that afternoon and took a break for dinner. Our gracious hosts were kind enough to treat us to some of Kansas City's famous barbecue at one of the local hotspots.

Crown and Throne

We returned that night for our second session in the Gem, with our intent being to turn and bless Kansas City. Over dinner we had been talking about the significance of the blue fountains, the Royals, etc., but when we got back to the Gem that night, a brother there shared another piece with us. Kansas City sports teams have always reflected the call of God to be a city of kings and priests unto the Lord. The baseball team is called the Royals. The football team there is called the Chiefs. The basketball team that was in town (but has now moved) was called the Kings, and even the old negro league team was called the Monarchs.

Another piece we were carrying with us was a prophetic word from a friend of ours named Rick Ridings. Rick prophesied a few years back that 2000-2010 was focused on the harp and bowl. If you aren't familiar with harp and bowl, it is based on the imagery from Revelation 5:8: Each of the elders around the throne has a harp, which represents worship, and a bowl, which represents intercession. Harp and bowl is basically the mingling of worship and prayer in meetings. Depending on where you worship, that might seem a rather simple concept, but in most churches—even twenty years ago—it was revolutionary. The International House of Prayer in Kansas City has been possibly the greatest driving force behind spreading the idea of harp and bowl-style worship. This time, Rick prophesied that in the second decade, 2010-2020, the Lord would add the understanding of the crown and throne. Each of those elders with a harp and bowl also has a crown and a throne. Whereas the harps and bowls speak primarily of priestly ministry, the crown and the throne speak of kingly authority.

There is a marrying together of the priestly and the kingly in our worship that the Lord is orchestrating. The term we use to describe what the Lord is moving us into is governmental worship. I believe Kansas City is destined to once again be instrumental in helping the body of Christ transition into the next revelation God has for us.

> *Kansas City is a city of royals and chiefs. Kansas City is a city of kings and priests moving in the fullness of the scarlet thread, blue note, and violet crown. Righteous red and royal blue.*
>
> *Sons of Kansas City, release your royal sound. We release governmental worship from Kansas City to the world, on earth as it is in heaven.*
>
> *The fountains are blue. The royals are after the crown. We honor harp and bowl ministry. We release the crown and throne authority from heaven to the sons of Kansas City, from the sons of Kansas City to the world.*

We ended that night with calling forth the thankful army in Kansas City and thanking God for each city along our journey.

One of the security guards at the Gem came up to me after we were done playing and said that from the moment he had arrived in the theater and we started to play, he could feel the presence of God in a way he was not used to. He said he began to cry as he felt the Lord draw near, and he immediately called his wife to have her come join him so she could experience it too. What a testimony.

As it turned out, this guard and the woman running the theater were connected with the Jazz Museum across the way, and they offered to bring us over for a private, after-hours tour of the museum. The museum is fascinating, and we also got to hear about some of the programs going on the city, particularly among the youth. These programs are helping to raise up the next generation of musicians and insure Kansas City remains a place of excellence and empowerment in the arts. After we had toured the museum a while, we were invited into the attached jazz club—The Blue Room—and got to hear some of the local jazz talent. We felt really honored and appreciated by all the staff, both at the Gem and the museum.

The Way KC

Our final stop in Kansas City was at a local church called The Way KC. They had recently moved into a new building, and people had been there night and day painting, cleaning, and getting things ready for that Sunday. We were joined by some of their musicians: Alice on violin, Cedric on trumpet, and Caleb—their worship leader. The worship that morning was intense, and the Lord was really moving. Many people in the congregation saw visions and shared them as we worshipped. One man saw a vision of a sword cutting the head off a snake, but as it continued to swing, it was cutting the strings off puppets. God was releasing a new level of freedom for his people, freeing them from every place the enemy had his hooks in and was pulling the strings. Another vision was of fire falling all over Kansas City, and the people of God were containers of his glory and fire. We prayed and released blessings over everyone there who felt that they were not a container of his glory, and prayed they would be filled with the revelation of who they are in him.

Another man named Brian saw angels all over our team as we worshipped. We prayed and released light over Brian, who had just come out of alcoholism. We stood in honor and blessed this mighty man of God; he is a gift from the Lord. Some people even started spontaneously sowing into him financially. He never knew his name meant high and noble. I think Brian started to see himself very differently after finding out what his name meant and being honored in that way.

When we were getting close to the end of the meeting, James asked Pastor Derek to give us some direction for our final musical movement. Derek shared that everything we had released so far had been right on with what the Lord was showing them. He said the Lord had called them to that region to kick the doors open in Kansas City, so that became the theme of the final sounds we released on the Blue Journey.

> *We kick the door open. The way is open. The way is open from Kansas City. Lift up your heads, you gates; be lifted up, ancient doors. The King of Glory is here. From this gate to every gate, the doors are open.*

We wouldn't find out until a few weeks later that the Royals won the World Series in a dramatic fashion. Some prophetic voices started to point out that there was a message of hope for our country in the fact that Kansas City won the pennant. The Royals had suffered a heartbreaking loss the year prior, and had been counted out many times in the 2015 playoffs, as they were behind bigtime, both during individual games and in their overall series. It was a dramatic come-from-behind victory that allowed the Royals to take the crown for the first time in thirty years. Just like the Royals, America has suffered heartbreaking losses as far as our values are concerned. And even as a sense of hopelessness has been setting in among the body of Christ, the Lord seemed to be speaking to many through the World Series that even though the situation has seemed hopeless, and even though it seems like we are down by a few runs in the bottom of the ninth, it is never too late for him to show his power. He can, and will, and is moving in our nation. I keep coming back to the verse the Lord gave me at the very beginning of our journey. Hope deferred makes the heart sick, but longing fulfilled is a tree of life. I would never presume to say our worship and prayer meetings had anything to do with the outcome of the World Series, but a few intercessors told us they thought it did, and even went to the trouble of buying us some championship souvenir T-shirts. All I know is that we were where God showed us to be, doing what he showed us to do, and nothing is impossible for him when he has a willing servant to work through.

Afterword

After a journey like this it is good to look back and reflect on what was accomplished. I believe it is healthy and appropriate to measure the effectiveness of our prayers in whatever ways we can. Some of the responses from the people and atmospheres we released our sound in gave a clear indication that the Lord was at work. But the truth is we don't know exactly what all of the fruit of our journey was, nor do we really need to. God is good to give us a peek behind the curtain every now and then, but someday we will clearly see everything our prayers, worship, and simple acts of obedience accomplished in the earth.

One bit of fruit that is undeniable is that the journey changed those of us who were on it. I believe this is the primary function of all worship and prayer in the first place. Yes, the goal is to establish God's kingdom on earth, but the first place it is established is in our own hearts. Psalm 115 and many other Scriptures make it clear that we become like that which we worship–whether that is God or something else. I believe that as we journeyed through these lands and released our hearts to the Lord, he was simultaneously releasing his heart to us and granting us perspective on some things we had not seen clearly until this trip. He was also preparing us for our next assignment: The Wedge of Worship, as we would begin to call it. Chuck Pierce prophesied that journey over us in St. Louis. Even as I am writing this story, we have begun that journey, and we have already realized we would not have been prepared to walk this assignment out if we had not been prepared by our previous assignment.

Just as when the first blues musicians released their sound in the earth, our journey probably seemed unremarkable to many, but it may have created ripples that will affect things we will never witness firsthand. At the very least, our sound won't go unchronicled like theirs did. And perhaps, as Ray Hughes said in his foreword, someone somewhere will reflect on this journey and say "Once upon a time." Perhaps, even as we were walking in the footsteps of those blues musicians from so many decades ago and releasing our sound in the light we have, someone else will follow in our footsteps and release their sound with a far greater light in the land. The greatest fruit might be if the pinnacles of our journey become the platform from which another generation could stand, see, and release a greater revelation of the Father, awakening and blessing every bloodline and family tree into its divine purpose and original intent.

About the Author

Jonathan Fitt is a singer, songwriter, multi-instrumentalist, worship leader, speaker, and author that has been serving the body of Christ in the areas of music and worship since 1997. He has been featured on a number of full-length studio and live worship albums, and he has written or co-written many worship songs.

Jonathan is a cofounder of Philadelphia Tabernacle of David, a ministry focused on raising up worship and prayer throughout the region, and he currently serves as its assistant director. Jonathan's main passion is to see artists equipped and released into the fullness of their destinies.

Jonathan currently resides in Rushland, Pennsylvania, with his wife, Ashley, and their four children.

Contact Jonathan

Web: www.jonathanfitt.com

E-mail: jfitt@me.com

Travel

MILAN

AND THE ITALIAN LAKES

ROWLAND MEAD

NEW
HOLLAND

NEW
HOLLAND

★★★ Highly recommended
★★ Recommended
★ See if you can

Third edition published in 2012
by New Holland Publishers (UK) Ltd
London • Cape Town • Sydney • Auckland
10 9 8 7 6 5 4 3 2 1
website: www.newhollandpublishers.com

Garfield House, 86 Edgware Road
London W2 2EA, United Kingdom

80 McKenzie Street
Cape Town 8001, South Africa

Unit 1, 66 Gibbes Street, Chatswood
NSW 2067, Australia

218 Lake Road, Northcote
Auckland, New Zealand

Distributed in the USA by
The Globe Pequot Press, Connecticut

Keep us Current
Information in travel guides is apt to change, which is
why we regularly update our guides. We'd be grateful
to receive feedback if you've noted something we
should include in our updates. If you have new information, please share it with us by writing to the
Publishing Manager, Globetrotter, at the office nearest
to you (addresses on this page). The most significant
contribution to each new edition will receive a free
copy of the updated guide.

This guidebook has been written by independent authors
and updaters. The information therein represents their
impartial opinion, and neither they nor the publishers
accept payment in return for including in the book or
writing more favourable reviews of any of the establish-
ments. Whilst every effort has been made to ensure that
this guidebook is as accurate and up to date as possible,
please be aware that the facts quoted are subject to
change, particularly the price of food, transport and
accommodation. The Publisher accepts no responsibility
or liability for any loss, injury or inconvenience incurred
by readers or travellers using this guide.

Publishing Manager: Thea Grobbelaar
DTP Cartographic Manager: Genené Hart
Editors: Thea Grobbelaar, Nicky Steenkamp,
Melany Porter
Cartographers: Genené Hart, Carryck Wise,
Nicole Bannister
Design and DTP: Nicole Bannister, Lellyn Creamer
Picture Researchers: Shavonne Govender,
Colleen Abrahams
Consultant: Tracey Gambarotta

Reproduction by Hirt & Carter (Pty) Ltd, Cape Town
Printed and bound by Times Offset (M) Sdn. Bhd.,
Malaysia.

Cover: *The view from the lakeside walk above Lake
Maggiore.*
Title Page: *Milan Cathedral.*

CONTENTS

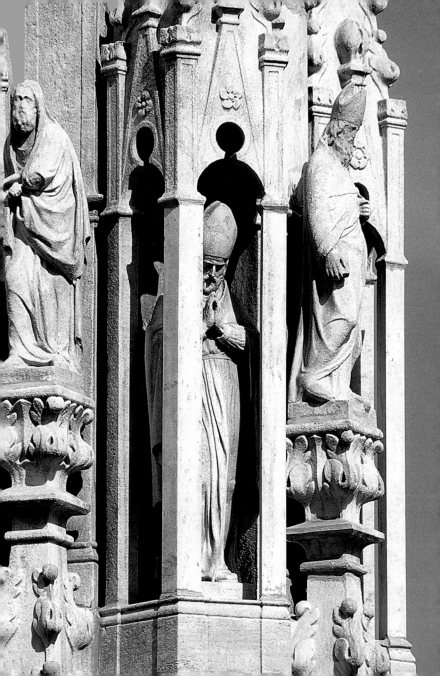

1. Introducing Milan and the Italian Lakes

Many people consider that wealthy Milan should really be the capital of Italy. Admittedly, it does not have the ancient remains of Rome, the waterborne charms of Venice or the elegance of Florence, but Milan is the industrial and commercial powerhouse of the country. It differs from the somnolent south of Italy – no long afternoon siestas for the Milanese, who like to think of themselves as being more northern European in attitude. They pride themselves on their timekeeping, their industry and their ability to make things function properly. Greater Milan's population of around four million accounts for barely 4% of the Italian people and yet they contribute nearly a quarter of the country's tax returns. No doubt they will put on an efficient show when EXPO (with a theme of 'Feeding the Planet, Energy for Life') comes to the city in 2015.

This application and creativity can probably be explained by Milan's geographical position. Located on the fertile Lombardy Plain drained by the River Po, Milan's backdrop is the snowcapped Alps. Throughout its history, invaders from the north, from the Lombards to the Habsburgs, have poured through the Alpine passes bent on conquest, but often staying to settle and thereby adding their skills to the population's accomplishments.

Although Milan can boast few of the ancient monuments that grace Rome, there is enough of historical interest to satisfy a tourist for many days. Few could fail to be impressed by the imposing Gothic Duomo, or

TOP ATTRACTIONS

*** The Duomo: Milan's cathedral, the finest Gothic cathedral in Italy.
*** The Arena at Verona: the Roman amphitheatre that seats 25,000 people for summer operas.
*** Borromean Islands: three beautiful islands on Lake Maggiore.
** Villa Carlotta: on Lake Como – the most opulent of all the lakeside villas.
** La Scala: Milan's world-famous opera house.
** Leonardo's *Last Supper*: fresco at the church of Santa Maria delle Grazie.

Opposite: *Statues on the façade of Milan's cathedral.*

Above: *Torbole on Lake Garda, which can easily be reached from Milan.*

cathedral, which took over 500 years to complete and which is resplendent with 135 carved pinnacles. No visitor would want to leave Milan without seeing Leonardo's *Last Supper* in the refectory of Santa Maria delle Grazie or enjoying an opera at La Scala. There is much more. There are galleries and museums by the score. Who could resist shopping in the Via Monte Napoleone? Here the Milanese passion for style and fashion comes to the fore and the visitor can browse in the boutiques at the creations of Gucci, Versace and Armani. Football fans, too, are catered for and they can watch a match at the San Siro Stadium (*see* page 47).

Furthermore, it is easy to leave the city of Milan behind and within an hour be in the **Italian Lakes** region. Lakes such as Como, Maggiore and Garda are long and narrow in shape and owe their origins to the Ice Age, when glaciers moved down from the Alps eroding deep valleys that later filled with meltwater. Throughout history the lakes have been the haunt of the wealthy, from the Roman Pliny to the pop stars of today. The shores are graced by elegant villas and tree-lined promenades backed by terraces of citrus fruit and olives, with the snowcapped Alps forming a stunning backdrop. The Milanese flock here for their relaxation, mixing with tourists from many parts of the world, many of whom come back time and again.

THE LAND
Mountains and Rivers

The scenery around Milan and the northern Italian Lakes owes much of its present-day appearance to the

Ice Age, which took place in the Quaternary geological period. The Alps, a mountain range that has its origins in the action of volcanoes and the movement of the earth's plates, was one of the first parts of Europe to be affected when the Ice Age started around a million years ago. Glaciers flowed slowly down from the Alps along pre-existing river-worn valleys towards the plains to the south. The glaciers scoured out the valleys to a considerable depth, often below sea level, while at the snouts of the glaciers, streams washed out fine rock material known as moraine. Between 10,000 and 20,000 years ago the climate became milder and the glaciers retreated. Streams filled the scoured out valleys forming the **ribbon lakes** so typical of northern Italy. The southern outlets of the lakes were often dammed by the moraine, deepening the lakes even further. The deepest point of Lake Como, for example, is 410m (1345ft), with the lake's bed 300m (984ft) below sea level. Other types of moraine along the lake shores provide favoured spots for settlement or agriculture. Today the snow and ice have retreated back to the highest parts of the Alps, remaining throughout the summer to form a magnificent photogenic backdrop for the lakes area. The hilly area around the southern parts of the lakes is often termed the **Pre-Alps**.

Further south, the glacial material has been reworked by the **River Po** and its tributaries, such as the Sésia, the Ticino, the Adda and the Adige, to form a fertile plain. In the past the rivers flooded regularly, leaving a layer of silt that further added to the plain's fertility. Today, the Po Valley is the richest agricultural region in Italy, growing rice, grapes, maize and a variety of fruit and vegetables. The Po, which is Italy's longest river, has also been important for navigation, and large ships can still reach as far inland as Pavia, just 38km (24 miles) to the south of Milan. The river was a safe transport route to bring stone for the construction of churches and palaces, transport soldiers in times of war, and carry goods from all over the world into the heart of northern Italy.

ITALY'S LAKES

It is estimated that there are around 1500 lakes in Italy. They have been formed in a variety of ways. The most common are the **alpine glacial lakes**, which are small, usually round and occupy cirques where glaciers were originally formed. **Crater lakes** are found in the craters of extinct volcanoes, mainly in the south of Italy. **Coastal lakes** are in the form of lagoons and can be seen along the Adriatic coast. The largest and most scenically spectacular lakes are the **ribbon lakes**, such as Lake Como in northern Italy, which occupy the over-deepened valleys carved out by glaciers in the Ice Age.

With a length of 405km (251 miles), the River Po is Italy's longest river. It rises in the Cottian Alps and enters the Adriatic Sea, 56km (35 miles) south of Venice. It is navigable as far as Pavia, 38 km (24 miles) south of Venice. Its main tributaries are the Ticino, the Adda and the Adige. The River Po plain is the richest agricultural area in Italy. It is also Italy's most polluted river – 136,000 tonnes of nitrates, 250 tonnes of arsenic and 60 tonnes of mercury are pumped into the river daily.

To the south of the Po Valley are the **Apennine Hills**, which form the spine of Italy. On a clear day it is possible to stand on the Apennines and see the snowcapped wall of the Alps rising above the haze of the Po Valley.

Climate

The Po Valley and the Italian lakes have unusual weather in that the area lies at the junction of the Mediterranean and Alpine climatic types and has the best (and worst!) features of both. The city of **Milan** has cold, raw winters, with a January average of 2°C (36°F). Snow is experienced regularly and fog can last for days on end, both in the city and on the surrounding plains. The summer months of July, August and September can be unbearably hot and sticky, with July averaging 26°C (78°F). August can be particularly humid and everyone who can do so leaves Milan for more agreeable climatic venues. Rain falls throughout the year, falling in late summer in thunderstorms.

The **Italian lakes** have a more moderate climate. The Alps shield the lakes from the more extreme weather in winter, when temperatures range from 4°C (39°F) to 6°C (43°F), allowing a wide range of plants to survive. Snow is usually confined to the higher ridges between the lakes. Summers are hot, with July temperatures averaging 24°C (75°F) at Lake Como and 25°C (77°F) at Lake Garda. Rain falls throughout the year, but mainly as spectacular thunderstorms in late summer. These can reverberate around the Alps for days. The heat of the summer is tempered by refreshing breezes blowing down the lakes. These winds can reverse their direction according to the time of day, providing good conditions for sailors and windsurfers.

Climatically, the best time to visit the lakes is either in spring, when the flowers, blossom and birdsong are at their best,

COMPARATIVE CLIMATE CHART	MILAN				MAGGIORE				GARDA			
	WIN	SPR	SUM	AUT	WIN	SPR	SUM	AUT	WIN	SPR	SUM	AUT
	JAN	APR	JULY	OCT	JAN	APR	JULY	OCT	JAN	APR	JULY	OCT
AVERAGE TEMP. °C	1	10	22	12	5.2	12.9	23.9	10.1	4	13.2	24.5	14.7
AVERAGE TEMP. °F	35	51	72	54	41	54	74	50	39	55	76	58
RAINFALL mm	62	82	47	75	90	61	20	22	31	62	72	89
RAINFALL in	3	3	2	3	4	3	1	1	1	3	3	4

or autumn, especially late September, when the temperatures are balmy and the autumn colours are spectacular.

Wildlife

It has to be said that northern Italy is not one of Europe's prime wildlife sites. This is largely owing to the hunting and shooting that has been traditional in the country for centuries.

Don't expect to see much wildlife in **Milan**, apart from the thousands of pigeons that inhabit its squares and a few bedraggled specimens of wildfowl on the lakes in the city's parks. The situation is little better on the **Lombardy Plain**, where during the hunting season from August to March, and particularly on Sundays, the fields reverberate with the thunder of guns as hunters with their feathered Alpine hats blast at everything that moves, whether the creature is protected or not.

Around the **lakes**, the situation improves. Water birds such as mute swans, mallards and coots can be seen everywhere along the lake shores. There are encouraging numbers of great crested grebes and, where there is more shelter and vegetation, little grebes often breed. There is also the chance of seeing a kingfisher on boughs hanging over the water. Fish abound, particularly trout, charr and pikeperch (which northern Europeans will know as zander). There is an active fishing industry, especially on Lake Maggiore, and these fish all appear on restaurant menus. The forested slopes of the lakes are home to many species of woodpecker, including the large black woodpecker, plus, in the summer, many species of warbler, redstarts and flycatchers.

At the northern end of the lakes, on the approach to the **Alps**, the amount of wildlife increases. The coniferous forests are the habitat of a variety of mammals including red squirrels, wild boar, and introduced deer. Badgers and wildcats are also around but as they are nocturnal they are unlikely to be seen. Predators include stoats and foxes.

Above: *Mute swans are found on all of the northern Italian lakes.*

THE MARMOT

Anyone visiting the Alps to the north of the Italian lakes in summer stands a good chance of seeing a marmot (*Marmota montis* – literally mountain mouse). It lives in the Alps above 1800m (6000ft) and spends much of the daylight hours feeding on vegetation. It lives in burrows and hibernates during the winter. It is most vulnerable to predators in spring when it emerges from hibernation and its senses are not fully alert. Its warning call is an eerie, high-pitched shriek.

Above: *Carpets of wild flowers can be seen in spring in the Alpine meadows to the north of the lakes.*

Above the tree line, chamois and ibex can be seen in good numbers. In many areas marmots, a mouse-like creature the size of a cat, are so widespread that lynx have been introduced to control their numbers. Their main predator, however, is the huge golden eagle, which also takes mountain hares. Other raptors include the short-toed eagle (which can hover like a kestrel), the honey buzzard and the long-eared owl. The rocky peaks are the natural habitat of the alpine chough, which is immediately recognizable by its electric call.

Italy has some 15 species of snake, some of which are venomous. A few of these can be found in northern Italy, but the chance of a visitor encountering one is slight. Lizards, however, are common and include the green lizard, the wall lizard, the gecko and the huge ocellated lizard. Butterflies are prolific in the summer, when the visitor can expect to see the small Apollo, clouded yellow, grayling, ringlet and a host of small blues.

However, it is the **flora** that draws many visitors to northern Italy, particularly in spring and early summer. The mild winter climate of the lakes (Garda has only frozen over once and that was in 1701) means that a wide range of exotic flowers, shrubs and trees can be grown in the gardens and hotel grounds along the waterside. The gardens on Isola Madre and Isola Bella on the Borromean Islands of Lake Maggiore are a wonderful example. Try not to miss the azaleas and rhododendrons at Villa Carlotta on Lake Como during April and May.

Many visitors are attracted to the Alps where wild flowers such as the gentian, edelweiss and saxifrage appear in spring after the snows have melted. Lower down the slopes, orchids like the lady's slipper are now fully protected. Other plants such as arnica are collected for their medicinal properties.

THE GOLDEN EAGLE

Visitors to the northern parts of the Italian lakes might be lucky enough to get a glimpse of the golden eagle (*Aquia chrysaetos*). With a wingspan of 2m (6ft), it can be seen soaring over the alpine meadows and forests in search of prey such as mountain hares, ptarmigan and marmots.

Wildlife Protection in Northern Italy

Italy is often the despair of its neighbours in northern Europe when it comes to environmental matters. In theory and on paper, there is a whole series of conservation bodies ranging from National Parks (*Parchi Nazionali*) down to small Nature Oases (*Oasi Naturali*). In practice, conservation and protection are slipshod and the responsibility of a confusing variety of bodies. Officially some three per cent of the country is protected – compare this with 21 per cent for the United Kingdom and 28 per cent for third-world Costa Rica. The main problems are bureaucracy and the vested interests of bodies such as the hunting lobby, which prevent the organizations from carrying out their environmental responsibilities. The liming and netting of birds is still common, while hunting and poaching of protected species continues to take place. The nearest protected areas to the Italian lakes are the **Adamello-Brenta** to the northwest of Lake Garda and the **Val Grande** and the **Alta Valsesia** reserves, which lie between Lake Maggiore and the peaks of Monte Rosa.

HISTORY IN BRIEF

The history of the Lombardy Plain and the city of Milan in particular has been a gruesome catalogue of invasions, sieges, plagues, wars and, in recent years, bombings. It is a characteristic of the area that it has always pulled itself together, recovered and returned to prosperity.

Below: *There is little in the way of wildlife in the city, but there are plenty of pigeons for tourists to feed.*

Early Days

The retreating ice sheets left behind a fertile landscape which was quickly occupied as early as Bronze-Age times by Ligurians from the west and Etruscans from the south. Milan itself was probably founded around 600BC by the Insubres, who were a Celtic tribe from Gaul. In

STONE AGE DISCOVERY

Evidence that man occupied northern Italy in Neolithic times was given credence in 1991, when a corpse was discovered preserved in the ice of an Alpine glacier to the north of Trentino. Dating methods have revealed that this cadaver, christened Oetzi the Iceman, is 5300 years old. He was dressed in clothes made from the skins of deer, goat and bear, while his weapons included a long bow, arrows and a copper axe. Sophisticated tests suggest that Oetzi had a diet of vegetable matter and mountain goat. Sadly, he appears to have died a violent death. There is also evidence of Neolithic villages around the shores of some of the northern Italian lakes.

222BC, the Romans arrived in the area, and Milan became the major settlement of Cisalpine Gaul, quickly becoming the Empire's second largest city after Rome. In the 3rd century the Roman Empire was divided into two by Diocletian, and Rome became the capital of the Western Empire. In 313, Constantine issued the Edict of Milan, which officially recognized Christianity as a religion. Thereafter the city became an important religious centre, helped by the appointment of the respected Sant'Ambrogio (Ambrose) as Bishop of Milan.

The fall of the Roman Empire marked a period of decline for Milan, which could not defend itself against barbarians such as the Huns and the Goths who both pillaged the city. The next group to invade were the Lombards, who set up their court at Pavia and gave their name to the province that covers most of the area described in this book. The *longobardi* (*see* panel, page 14) were not entirely vandals, however, and they set up law courts and eventually converted to Christianity. They were defeated by the Franks led by Charlemagne in AD774, and Milan regained its position as the main town of the area.

The Middle Ages

The economy revived under the Franks and, helped by a series of influential bishops, Milan, in 1045, declared itself a *comune* or city-state. The next three centuries were characterized by conflict between Milan and other city-states such as Pavia, Cremona and Como. A new city wall

Below: *The old part of Bergamo has a wealth of city walls, gates, towers and historic churches.*

was built, but this was demolished in 1162 by Frederick Barbarossa on behalf of Como. The walls were speedily reconstructed and the Lombard League was set up under the leadership of Milan to afford additional protection. These inter-city struggles were typified by support for either the pro-pope *Guelfs* or the *Ghibellines* who represented the emperor.

The Dynastic Families

The 13th century saw the first of the dynastic families come to power. This was the Torriani family, who were part of the pro-pope faction. They were not to last long, however, as they were soundly defeated in 1277 by the **Viscontis** representing the Ghibelline element. By this time Milan had a population of around 200,000 – making it probably the largest city in Europe. The greatest of the Viscontis was Gian Galeazzo (1351–1402) who bought the title of Duke of Milan and at the height of his power controlled most of northern Italy. He also commissioned the building of the Duomo, the Castello and many palaces. Unfortunately, Gian Galeazzo died from the plague in 1402 and within 40 years the dynasty had died out.

Above: *The tower of this church near Lake Como is typical of many in the area, which have a top-heavy appearance.*

Milan immediately declared itself the Ambrosian Republic, but within three years the city had come under the control of the first of the **Sforza** family. Francesco Sforza, who claimed the dukedom because he had married an illegitimate daughter of the Viscontis, adopted a different approach from the preceding dynasty, preferring to acquire peace for the city rather than expansion. The castle was rebuilt and renamed the Castello Sforzesco, and work was started on the Ospedale Maggiore. The golden age of the Sforzas came with Francesco's son Ludovico el Moro, who was a great patron of the arts. He brought to his court such talents as Leonardo da Vinci (1452–1519) and the architect Donato Bramante (1444–1514) who restored many of Milan's churches.

Ludovico's downfall came when, in 1494, he encouraged Charles VIII of France to invade Naples. Alarmed by their success, he led a coalition of forces to drive the French out of Italy. After some initial success, he was forced out of power in 1499 by Louis XII, who marched into Milan and claimed the city for himself. The population, who were weary of paying taxes to support the Sforza regime, welcomed Louis with open arms, while Ludovico was obliged to spend the rest of his life in exile.

MASTER BUILDERS OF COMO

The magnificent churches and cathedrals of northern Italy owe much to the *Maestri Comocini* – the master builders from the Como area. They were travelling groups of architects and stonemasons who used the marble and granite of their home area to wonderful effect. They worked from the 7th to the 17th century and were probably at their peak during the 12th century. Their work can be seen, not only in northern Italy, but as far afield as Poland and Russia.

Above: *Finding a postbox to send cards and letters home is not difficult in the cities of northern Italy.*

SINISTER LOMBARDS

One of the first tribes to take advantage of the fall of the Roman Empire were the Lombards who flooded into northern Italy in 568. It has often been suggested that this Germanic group got its name from their long beards, but in fact it was from their long *bardi*, or poleaxes, that terrified their enemies. They had a reputation for barbarism supported by the story of their king, named Alboin, who forced his wife Rosmunda to drink from her father's skull. In revenge for this indignity she stabbed him to death. The Lombards conquered much of Italy and in fact came nearer to unifying the country than any group for the next 14 centuries. The Lombards' name also lingers on, with a street in London, a region of Italy, a river plain, and even a political party.

Foreign Domination

For the next three centuries Milan and the Plain of Lombardy were to languish under foreign powers. Virtually the only good to come out of this period was the spell in office of the Archbishop of Milan, San Carlo Borromeo (1538–84). He was a patron of the arts, built numerous churches and social institutions for the poor, and got rid of the corruption that was rife in the area. The plague of 1630 brought Milan's population down to around 60,000 and this was a low point in the city's social and economic standing.

The French were soon removed by the Spanish, who had control over Milan until the War of the Spanish Succession (1701–13), after which the Austrians took over. Enlightened despots such as Maria Theresa (1740–80) and her son Joseph II did much to introduce economic reforms during this period. The Austrians, in turn, were forced out by the French, and when Napoleon's army entered Milan, the troops were welcomed as liberators. Napoleon proclaimed the Cisalpine Republic and in 1800 he crowned himself King of Italy in Milan Cathedral. Napoleon modernized the city, reforming the administration, setting up schools on the *lycée* model, and starting many public building projects. The population, however, were heavily taxed and many of Milan's art treasures were removed to France. The Milanese were therefore not too unhappy when the Napoleonic Empire collapsed and the Austrian forces returned in 1814. Austrian control was officially recognized at the Congress of Vienna in 1815, and the Habsburgs were to remain in charge of the city for the next 50 years.

Unification

Movements for uniting the country immediately began to appear. The most influential figures were Guiseppi Mazzini (1805–72), an important political agitator; Guiseppi Garibaldi (1807–82), a charismatic military figure; and Count Camillo Cavour (1810–61), who owned

HISTORICAL CALENDAR

600BC The Etrucscans settle in Lombardy Plain.
222BC Roman Conquest. Mediolanum (Milan) becomes the capital of the Western Roman Empire.
AD313 Constantine the Great issues the Edict of Milan allowing tolerance of the Christian faith.
374 Ambrose (Sant'Ambrogio) becomes Bishop of Milan.
476 Fall of the Western Roman Empire.
568 Lombards invade northern Italy, making Pavia their capital.
773 Charlemagne conquers the Lombards, incorporating their land into the Frankish Empire.
1045 Milan becomes an autonomous *comune*.
1162 Milan is taken by Frederick Barbarossa.

1176 The Lombard League defeats Barbarossa at Legnano.
1277 The Visconti dynasty begin their rule over Milan.
1477 Francesco Sforza is made Duke of Milan. Later Ludovico el Moro patronizes Leonardo da Vinci as well as other artists and architects.
1499 Milan occupied by the French under Louis XII.
1525 Milan becomes part of the Habsburg empire.
1540–1706 Spanish rule.
1701–13 War of the Spanish Succession. At its conclusion the Duchy of Milan comes under Austrian rule.
1796–1814 Napoleon conquers Lombardy and makes Milan the capital of his Cisalpine Republic.
1815 Milan once again becomes Austrian.
1815–59 The rise of the *Risorgimento* independence

movement. Milan becomes the industrial and financial capital of a free Italy.
1919 After World War I Mussolini founds the Fascist movement in Milan.
1939–45 Milan suffers serious bombing during Allied raids. Mussolini is shot while fleeing to Switzerland in 1945.
1950s Milan leads Italy's postwar economic revival.
1960s and 70s Student unrest and terrorism.
1992 *Tangentopoli* corruption scandals focus on Milan.
1995 Maurizio Gucci is murdered in Milan.
1997 Gianni Versace is murdered in Florida.
2001 Self-made media mogul from Milan, Silvio Berlusconi, begins first term as Italian prime minister.
2002 Euro is introduced.

the newspaper *Il Risorgimento*, which gave its name to the unification movement. The first action came in March 1848 when the Milanese staged a revolt known as *Cinque Giornate* – the five days that the revolt lasted. The insurrection was brutally crushed by the Austrians, but the unification movement was gathering pace. Supported by Louis Napoleon, the Austrians were defeated at Magenta in 1859 and the northern part of Italy was united under Piedmont. Victor Emmanuel II of Piedmont marched into Milan through the triumphal arch that was built by Napoleon and which is now known as the Arch of Peace.

Unification was only half complete, but Garibaldi's forces soon overthrew the Bourbons in the south of the country and King Victor Emmanuel II was proclaimed King of Italy in February 1861. Complete unity was achieved with the addition of Venice in 1866 and Rome in 1871.

When Napoleon marched into Milan, the city welcomed him with open arms. Eighteen years later, with the collapse of the Napoleonic Empire, the Milanese had had enough and were glad to see the back of him. On the credit side, he had established Milan as the capital of the Cisalpine Republic, inaugurated extensive public works, reformed the education and legal systems on French lines, founded Milan's Fine Arts Academy and the Brera Museum and Gallery. On the other hand, his administration imposed high taxes on the populace and plundered art treasures from churches and private collections. Perhaps Napoleon's most lasting memorial is that he put into many people's minds the potential for a single unified Italian state.

Below: *Even the most discerning shopper will find plenty of interest in central Milan.*

For the remainder of the 19th century Milan concentrated on building up its economic base. The industrial revolution generated a variety of industries, including chemicals and textiles, while in the city centre the stock exchange and banks flourished and the opera house established its reputation. Milan was now the business and commercial capital of the newly united country.

World War I and the Growth of Fascism

After being neutral at the start of the war, Italy entered the conflict on the Allied side in 1915, expecting some rewards in the form of land at the conclusion. The war turned out to be a disaster for Italy. Its army was ill equipped and at one battle alone – Caporetto in 1917 – half a million Italians died. It was estimated that of the 5.5 million Italians who were mobilized some 40 per cent were killed or wounded.

It was not surprising that after the war there was considerable social and economic unrest in Italy and the **Fascist** movement came to the fore. Both the Fascist movement and its leader, Benito Mussolini, had close links with Milan. Mussolini became dictator of Italy in 1922 and his plans for buying weapons of war made him popular with the middle-class industrialists of Milan.

World War II

Mussolini took Italy into the war, making a pact with Hitler. The Allies invaded Italy in 1943 and later that year the Italian government signed an armistice with the Allies. The Germans now took control of the north of the country and established a puppet government at the resort of Salò on Lake Garda. It was during 1943 that Milan, with its heavy industry, became a target for Allied bombers, which inflicted heavy damage on the city. Meanwhile the Italians had formed a determined Resistance movement that continually harassed the Germans. It was these partisans who finally caught

Mussolini as he was trying to escape to Switzerland. He was shot along with his mistress, Claretta Petacci, and his body was later strung up from the roof of a petrol station in Milan's Piazza Loreto, where some partisans had been shot a few weeks earlier.

The Postwar Years

In 1946 King Victor Emmanuel III abdicated and Italy voted in a referendum to abolish the monarchy. The postwar period was typified by political instability. Most governments were coalitions and they fell and were replaced with regularity – there were nearly 60 governments between the end of World War II and the close of the century. Milan, however, led the postwar 'economic miracle'. Helped by generous Marshall Aid, the city re-established its heavy industry. Later came new high-tech industries, while the banks and the stock market thrived. Less savoury were the student protests of the 1960s and the terrorist activity of the 1970s.

Above: *This Roman amphitheatre is the venue for outdoor opera performances during July and August.*

Even more sensational were the bribery and corruption scandals of the early 1990s, when Judge Antonio de Pietro lifted the lid on the racketeering and bribery that was rife in politics and business. Milan became known as **Tangentopoli** or 'Bribe City'. Milan also produced **Silvio Berlusconi**, a self-made man and media mogul who became the country's prime minister in 2001. His various terms of office have, however, been plagued with allegations of fraud, corruption and sexual misconduct.

Art and Architecture

The earliest architecture to survive dates from **Roman** times. Examples are few, however, and confined to a handful of villas on the southern shores of Lake Garda, the forum at Brescia, and the magnificent amphitheatre at Verona. In Milan, there are some remains of the curving walls of the circus, which must have been one of the largest constructions in the Roman Empire, while a few private houses in the same area have some fragmented mosaics. By far the most interesting Roman architecture in

> ### CAVOUR (1810–61)
>
> Count Camillo Benso di Cavour was the brains behind the unification of Italy. He was born in Turin, but for many years he worked for the Kings of Sardinia. It was to his great personal satisfaction that when Italy became united it was Victor Emmanuel II of Sardinia who became its first king. An able politician, Cavour believed that progress lay not in revolution but in social and economic progress. Sadly, he died a year after Italy achieved unification.

Above: Como's cathedral
is a curious mixture of
Gothic and Renaissance
architecture.

DONATO BRAMANTE – MASTER ARCHITECT

Donato Bramante (1444–1514) has always been recognized as the greatest Renaissance architect in Italy. Born in Urbino, he was brought to Milan by Ludovico el Moro. He worked on a number of churches in the city, including San Satiro, the tribune of Santa Maria delle Grazie and the cloisters of Sant'Ambrogio, and drew up a new plan for the cathedral at Pavia. While in Milan, Bramante also painted and wrote poetry, and it is believed that he had close relations with Leonardo da Vinci. Bramante left, in 1499, for Rome, where he continued his glittering career working, among other projects, on the rebuilding of St Peter's.

the city lies outside the Church of San Lorenzo, where a row of 16 Corinthian columns dating from the 2nd or 3rd century AD have been erected, having been brought there from some unidentified temple.

The **Romanesque** period was one of the most vital phases in Italian art and architecture, Lombardy standing out for its numerous churches of quality. The Lombard Romanesque had a style of its own, reflecting the architecture of southern Germany, with essential simplicity alongside round arches, and decoration confined to the apse or main portal. The work was carried out by travelling bands of master builders such as the *Maestri Comacini* from Como. Classic examples from this period include Sant'Ambrogio in Milan, San Fedele in Como, and the Basilica of Santa Maria Maggiore in Bergamo.

So successful was the Lombard form of Romanesque that the **Gothic**, so popular in France, was resisted in northern Italy. The glorious exception is the Duomo in Milan, which is probably the most strongly Gothic religious building in Italy. The Lombard builders never totally adapted the Gothic style, rejecting the striving for height and the resulting flying buttresses, but maintaining the thick walls and horizontal lines. At this time, a small number of artists and sculptors were beginning to throw off the shackles of Byzantine art, particularly in sculpture and in early frescoes.

The **Renaissance** marked a rebirth of art and science as the Greek and Roman ideals were 'rediscovered'. The movement originated in Florence and quickly spread to other parts of Italy, including Lombardy, where the wealth of the region was poured into the sponsorship of talent by merchants and bankers. Ludovico il Moro brought Leonardo da Vinci into his court, and his many talents were to inspire a whole range of followers, such as the painter Bernardino Luini (d. 1532) and the sculptor

Cristoforo Solari (1439–1525). There are some superb examples of Renaissance architecture in Milan, first appearing in the middle of the 15th century, when Francesco Sforza brought in Filarete to design the Ospedale Maggiore (based on an example in Florence). Later Ludovico il Moro hired the incomparable Donato Bramante (1444–1514), who contributed the apse of San Satiro, the cloisters of Sant'Ambrogio and the wonderful tribune of Santa Maria delle Grazie. Elsewhere in the region, Brescia became a major centre for Renaissance painting. Mantua, with the wealthy Gonzaga family spending freely, sponsored much Renaissance work. The court painter here was Andrea Mantegna (d. 1506), who established a considerable reputation for his frescoes. The Palazzo Tè, just outside the city, also dates from this period.

The **Baroque** period covered the 17th and 18th centuries. In Milan, these were austere times, with the plague decimating the population and San Carlo Borromeo keeping a firm hand on the tiller. The best painting in these times came from Bergamo, Brescia and Mantua. The mid-18th century saw the emergence of two fine northern Italian painters, Alessandro Magnasco (1667–1749), who worked in Milan, and Giuseppe Bazzani (1690–1769) from Mantua. Architecturally, the period saw the construction in Milan of the Palazzo Reale and La Scala.

Italy made little contribution to art and architecture during the 19th century. One exception in Milan was the Galleria Vittorio Emanuele II, designed by Giuseppe Mengoni and something of an engineering triumph, making a it worthy neighbour of the Duomo. Some fine villas appeared around the shores of the Italian lakes during this period, many with superb gardens. Of the Italian artists of the time, the best known is Amedeo Modigliani (1884–1920), although he spent much of his working life in Paris.

During the early years of the 20th century, the Italian version of Art Nouveau, *Lo*

ART IN MILAN

Visitors interested in art will find much to occupy their time in Milan. All the city's churches have frescoes to delight the eye, with the star exhibit being Leonardo di Vinci's *Last Supper* at the Church of Santa Maria delle Grazie (*see* page 36). There are a large number of art galleries, and few would want to miss the Pinacoteca di Brera, which holds one of Italy's most important collections and features work from the country's best-known artists. Enthusiasts of modern art should head for the Galleria d'Arte Moderna in Via Palestro.

Below: *The Italian lakes are lined with houses and villas displaying a variety of architecture. Many have their own boathouses.*

THE GROWTH
OF TOURISM

Tourism in the Italian Lakes region began to take off in the late 19th century, when a host of writers, artists and musicians were drawn to the area by the stunning scenery, attractive waterfront villages, subtropical vegetation and the amenable climate. Composers such as Verdi and writers who included Ibsen, D.H. Lawrence and Goethe, all gained inspiration from the area, which in turn drew in royalty, politicians and those simply seeking health cures. Today, the Lakes remain a popular location for the discriminating tourist, while Milan has recently become a stylish venue for a weekend break, particularly for those seeking retail therapy.

Stilo Liberty, found its form in many of the hotels around the lakes. Mussolini's major contribution to architecture was the massive Stazione Centrale in Milan, which defies any stylistic definition. The post-World War II period saw Milan's first skyscrapers, with the 1960 Pirelli Building remaining the pick of the bunch. In the early years of the century the art scene was enlivened by the Futurists, who glorified the new mechanistic age and attempted to drag Italian art into modern times. In latter years Milan's artistic endeavours seem to be in designing motor cars or making fashion statements rather than in fine art.

GOVERNMENT AND ECONOMY

Since 1946 Italy has been a democratic republic. Government takes place in Rome where the president is largely a figurehead. The decision-making is carried out by the lower house known as the Chamber of Deputies. The upper house consists of senators from the 21 different regions of Italy. The regions also have a measure of self-government. Each region is divided into provinces. The lowest level of government is the local council or *comune*.

Voting

Every Italian is expected to vote as his civic duty, although there is no penalty for failing to do so. In fact, Italy has a higher turnout at election than any other European country – often over 90 per cent. The proportional representation system and the large number of political parties in existence led to a vast number of coalition governments in the post-war period. The bargaining that went on fed the corruption that was endemic in Italian politics, so that in 1993 a new system was introduced whereby 75 per cent of the upper and lower houses were elected by the first-past-the-post system, with the remaining 25 per cent elected by proportional representation.

Below: *The Italian flag has green, white and red vertical sections and is flown at all official functions.*

Political Parties

The strongest political party in the post-war years was the centre-right Christian Democrats, who usually shared power in a coalition with three or four other parties, thereby keeping out the communists. The bribery and corruption scandals in recent years, and the north's frustration with the backward south of the country, has spawned new parties known as *leghe* or leagues, such as the Lega Nord, which are northern-based coalitions in favour of a federal Italy. Anti-Mafia parties have also sprung up in the south. The two main parties, the Christian Democrats and Socialists, have been almost annihilated in recent elections, and new parties have been formed, like Sylvio Berlusconi's centre-right Forza Italia and the centre-left party of Romano Prodi. The centre-left were in power in the late 1990s but were defeated by Forza Italia in 2001. The Milan-based media mogul, Sylvio Berlusconi, formed Italy's longest lasting post-war government, but his period of power was marred by charges of corruption and money laundering. He forced through backdated legislation to put the premier above the law of the land in order to get himself out of trouble, but this was later overturned in court as being unconstitutional. The voters finally had enough and returned Romano Prodí to power in 2006. Berlusconi was later re-elected but his period of office continued to be marred by allegations of misconduct.

The Economy

A grasp of the contrasts between the north and south of Italy is essential in understanding the Italian economy. The south of the peninsula is on the fringe of Europe, with all the disadvantages of industrial location and transportation. It is hot and dry and lacking in energy, raw materials and resources. In addition it is dominated by the Mafia whose influence extends into all parts of daily life, preventing initiative, enterprise and investment. In complete contrast, the north, based on the industrial triangle of Milan, Turin

Above: *A funicular railway takes tourists to the hill above Como.*

GAETANO DONIZETTI (1797–1848)

Donizetti was born in Bergamo to a poor shop-keeping family. His musical talent was soon recognized, however, and he gained a scholarship to study at Bologna. His first opera was performed when he was 25 and for many years he was acknowledged as the leading Italian opera composer. Donizetti composed more than 60 operas, including *Lucia di Lammermoor, La Figlia del Reggimento, La Favorita* and *Don Pasquale.* His fall from grace began in 1843 when the syphilis he had caught in his youth began to cause uncontrollable fits of temper and eventually madness. He returned to Bergamo where he died in 1848. His tomb, with a fine memorial, is in the church of Santa Maria Maggiore, while his former home in Via Arena is a rather sad little museum.

Above: *Senior citizens are respected and well provided for in northern Italy.*

and the port of Genoa, is the powerhouse of the modern country. The climate is more favourable for agriculture, and there are power sources in the form of natural gas and hydroelectricity. Milan, itself with a population of around two million, is the country's economic capital. With its thriving industry, fashion houses, stock exchange and artistic heritage, it is a major European city. The Milanese and their fellow northerners feel that they are subsidizing the south, and there is frequent talk of federalism or even partition, but after a hard-won unification campaign, this is unlikely to happen.

THE PEOPLE
Language
Much of the Italian language is derived from Latin, so that visitors with a knowledge of French or Spanish will find the basics easy to pick up, particularly as each syllable is pronounced as it is seen and no letter is silent. There are vast numbers of regional dialects in Italy, and it was not until Dante wrote in the Tuscan dialect that this became the educated Italian to use. Some Italians even speak a different language, with German used in the Alto Adige region and French spoken in the Valle d'Aosta. The media, however, and particularly television, are gradually eliminating Italy's linguistic diversity.

Few Italians are good linguists, but the ability to speak good English confers some status. Visitors should find that in the tourist industry there will be someone in most of the hotels and restaurants who speaks English. Nevertheless, the ability to speak a few words of Italian will be greeted with smiles and pleasure.

Religion
The Roman Catholic church has been a dominant factor in Italian life for centuries and it still subtly permeates

---

SENIOR CITIZENS IN NORTHERN ITALY

Elderly visitors will find that the Italian lakes are an ideal destination. The pace of life is slow and hotels and attractions are well prepared for the senior citizen. Pensioners will find that many concessions are available, such as lower entrance fees to museums and monuments. Be prepared, however, to produce proof of age.

society today, although it no longer has the political power or social influence that it had in the past. Today, although 97 per cent of Italians are baptized and church marriages are the norm, fewer than 10 per cent regularly attend Mass. The strict rules of the past have been relaxed – both contraception and abortion are readily available, and the barriers to divorce have largely been removed. Despite this trend, the support for saints' days is undiminished, perhaps because all Italians enjoy a good party. Most saints' days involve a religious procession, when the statue of the saint is paraded through the streets. These are particularly atmospheric at Easter.

One of the pleasures of holidaying in northern Italy, however, is in visiting its cathedrals and churches. Few will be unimpressed by Milan's **Duomo**, the third largest cathedral in the world, and the city's clutch of ancient churches, many containing priceless works of art. The towns of the Italian lake region are also well endowed with historic churches, such as those at Como and Bergamo. (Visitors should remember that beachwear and shorts are not considered appropriate dress in churches.)

The Family

The family has always been a major influence in Italian life, probably due to the country's agricultural past and the need for cooperation in order to survive, plus the teachings of the Catholic church. Today, children, particularly males, tend to live at home until their thirties. Most students attend their local university and continue to reside at home, maintaining the traditional link between mother and son. In Italy the matriarchal structure is alive and well!

The north of Italy has seen a weakening of the family structure in recent decades, due to social changes such as the lower birth rate, the availability of divorce, and geographical migration in search of work. In the south, however, the family is as strong as ever.

A CHILD-FRIENDLY COUNTRY

Do not worry about taking babies or young children to the Italian lakes, as they will be made very welcome. Children keep very late nights and are not excluded from any family activities. Waiters traditionally make a huge fuss of small children who come to their restaurants and will prepare special portions for them. Older children will find plenty to occupy themselves and will enjoy the theme parks and boat trips.

Below: *A skilfully carved door – typical of the rich artwork in the churches of northern Italy.*

Food and Drink

Although few people would actually choose a holiday in northern Italy because of its food, one of the joys of visiting the area is to sample its cuisine and its wines. To be precise there is no such thing as typically Italian food, because there are a vast number of regional variations. Another popular misconception is that Italian food is all pasta and pizza. These do, of course, figure prominently on menus, but there are also some fine regional fish and meat dishes.

Food

Although many hotels provide an international-style **breakfast**, the average Milanese does not make a big thing about this meal, which is likely to be a quick coffee and a *brioche* taken standing at a bar.

Lunch, however, is a different matter. Many workers will take a long lunch with four courses (although others will prefer to have a light lunch and save the big meal for the evening). The meal starts with the *antipasti* (literally 'before the pasta'). Similar to the French hors d'oeuvres, *antipasti* may be served buffet-style on a long table, often placed near the door of the restaurant to tempt diners in. Here a variety of items are on offer, including seafood, hams, mushrooms and salad from which you can make up your own assortment, known as *antipasto mista*.

The second course is known, confusingly, as the *primo piatto*. A soup is always on offer and this will either be a thick country soup or a thin minestrone on which Parmesan cheese can be sprinkled. As the Lombardy Plain is a rice-growing area, a risotto is an alternative choice. These are often coloured yellow with saffron and may come with vegetables, meat or seafood. The third choice will involve pasta. There are said to be over 350 pasta shapes, but the most common are spaghetti, tagliatelle, lasagna, the meat-stuffed ravioli, and cannelloni. There are almost as many sauces to accompany the pasta, while Parmesan cheese is usually offered as a topping. Don't expect the waiter to come around with a pepper grinder – this only happens in Italian restaurants abroad!

Below: *Pasta comes in a vast variety of forms, often with imaginative sauces.*

The main course is the *secondo piatto* and will be a meat or fish dish accompanied by a modicum of potatoes and vegetables. Regional specialities include *Cotoletta alla Milanese*, which is a veal slice dipped in egg and fried in breadcrumbs. Chicken (*pollo*), pork (*maiale*), beef (*manzo*)

and lamb (*agnello*) are other meat choices. Another local speciality for those with strong stomachs is *busecca*, which is tripe with white beans. The fish is likely to be of the freshwater variety from the lakes to the north, and could include carp, trout or perch. Among the seafood, sea bass (*spigola*), red mullet (*triglia*) and swordfish (*pesce spada*) are often on the menu.

Above: *A visit to an Italian market is a highly recommended holiday experience.*

To complete the meal there will **cheese**, **desserts** or **fresh fruit**. Apart from the well-known blue-veined *gorgonzola* and *bel paese*, there is a whole host of local cheeses from all over the country. Italian desserts can be a delight or a disappointment, but you cannot go wrong with Italian ice cream, particularly in Milan, which considers itself a specialist ice cream making area.

Visitors preferring a pizza should head for one of the specialist **pizzerias**, where the food is cooked in the traditional oven. The pizzas are usually thin and cooked to age-old recipes – don't expect any exotic toppings such as sweet corn or pineapple.

Drinks

Italy produces more wine than any other country in the world and much of it is from the Lombardy area. Probably the best-known wines are the light red (*rossi*) Valpollicellas and Bardolinos and the crisp white (*bianco*) Soaves grown to the east and south of Lake Garda. To the west of Lake Maggiore are the good quality red wines that include the full-bodied Barolo and the fragrant Barbaresco. Much of the wine exported from northern Italy in the past has

Above: *Among the many Italian spirits is the daunting grappa.*

been of only moderate standard but in more recent years higher quality wines have been produced. It is a good idea to try local wines – ask for *vino locale* or *vino della casa*. The Italians are certainly not wine snobs and frequently keep their lighter red wines in the fridge during the summer. Often their stronger white wines are not chilled at all.

Fortified wines include the usual *cinzano*, *martini* and *campari*. A wide variety of **spirits** are on sale. A popular local firewater is *grappa*, which is drunk for effect rather than taste. Good local brandies include *stock* and *Vecchia Romagna*. Widely drunk **liqueurs** include *strega* (often taken with ice), the apricot-flavoured *amaretto*, cherry *marascino* and the aniseed-tasting *sambuca*.

Beer (*birra*) comes in bottles or draught and is of the lager type. A small bottle is a *pícola* and a larger bottle is known as a *media*. There are also darker beers available. Known as *birra nera*, they are sweeter and heavier and resemble English bitter. The local beers include Peroni, Moretti and Dreher, which are all excellent. If you don't ask for them you will probably be given foreign imported beers, which will be more expensive.

There are plenty of **soft drinks** to choose from, including a wide variety of fruit juices. Fizzy drinks include the ubiquitous cola and the thirst-quenching lemon soda. Tap water is usually drinkable, but the Italians themselves drink vast amounts of bottled mineral water (*aqua minerale*), which comes either sparkling (*con gas*) or still (*naturale*).

Tea and Coffee

The Italians are enthusiastic coffee drinkers, and it comes in a bewildering variety. It is always made in an espresso machine – instant coffee is rarely an option. The choice is usually between a small black *espresso* or a larger white *cappuccino* (don't expect a topping of chocolate grains). Other possibilities are a longer, weaker coffee (*Americana*), a long coffee with a dash of milk (*macchiato*), and a long milky coffee (*latte*). Many Italians like a drop of spirit in their drink – this is called *caffè corretto*. A popular choice in summer is to take coffee cold (*caffè freddo*). If it is topped with crushed ice and cream, you have *caffè granita*.

Tea (*tè*) is much simpler. It comes either with lemon (*con limone*) or milk (*con latte*), but in summer cold tea (*tè freddo*) is also popular.

Sport and Recreation

Of the spectator sports, **football** (*calcio*) is almost like a religion. The Italian League is divided into four divisions, the most prestigious of which is called Serie A. Matches are played in the winter months, usually on Saturday afternoons at the San Siro Stadium (*see page 47*). Other popular spectator sports have been imported from America and include **basketball** and **baseball**. Also keenly followed is **motor racing**, and an annual Grand Prix is held at Monza just north of Milan. **Cycling**, too, is popular with both riders and spectators, and the weekend roads are full of recreational and competitive cyclists.

Northern Italy and the lakes provide a venue for a number of recreational activities. There is a long **skiing** season in the Alps, which can easily be reached from Milan. In the summer the mountains are popular for **hiking** and **rock climbing**. The lakes are used for a variety of water sports. The northern end of Lake Garda is one of the world's prime **windsurfing** locations and it also provides challenging sailing conditions. **Canoeing** has boomed in recent years, particularly on the white-water stretches of the rivers leading into the lakes.

Personal fitness is not something that interests the majority of Italians, but a number of fitness and leisure centres have recently sprung up in Milan. Here it is very important to look good and the leisure centre gives the opportunity to show off the latest designer sportswear.

WATER SPORTS ON THE LAKES

The Italian lakes provide plenty of opportunity for water sports. There are a number of shingle beaches that provide safe **swimming** and **snorkelling**. Many types of craft can be hired, from **pedaloes** to **jet skis**, while **water-skiing** is popular in many areas. The northern parts of the lakes are often windy and are ideal for **sailing**. The northern end of Lake Garda is one of the prime **windsurfing** areas in Europe.

Below: *Sunday morning is the traditional time for chess in Bergamo Alta's main square.*

2
Milan

It is said that 'anyone who understands Milan understands Italy'. Milan is a microcosm of Italian life, far more so than sleepy Florence, historic Rome or lovely Venice. Milan is Italy's industrial and commercial capital, its second largest city, a world centre for fashion and high finance, and the focus of the country's media. But it's more than just a business city – its historic core, centred on the Duomo or cathedral, boasts a fine collection of medieval churches, art galleries, museums and palaces.

Milan is nothing like the somnolent south of Italy. A long afternoon siesta is considered a waste of time, for the Milanese are too busy making money. Milan's traditional industries include vehicles, textiles, clothing and chemicals, but in recent years the service industries have become dominant. Milan will host EXPO, the world's largest trade fair, in 2015. This industrial success has drawn immigrants, not only from southern Italy, but from many parts of the world, including Africa and Asia. Milan has always been a melting pot for other cultures and today the recent immigrants give the city a cosmopolitan feel. It is estimated that almost 16% of Milan's inhabitants are foreign born. Although central Milan has lost population in recent years, its metropolitan district has grown enormously and it is estimated that nearly half a million people commute into the city daily, putting a great strain on the transport services and causing congestion on the roads.

Milan's inhabitants may work hard but they also know how to enjoy their leisure. The city has 50 cinemas, almost as many theatres and some of the best discos and

Opposite: *Milan's Duomo, where a lift takes visitors to the roof to view the city.*

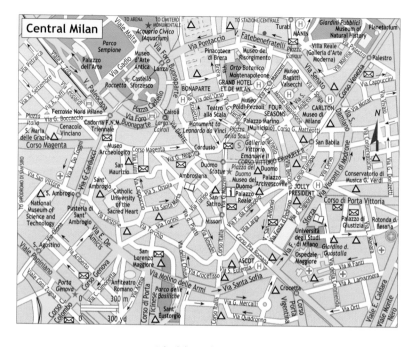

Central Milan

The average January temperature in Milan is 1.9°C (35°F) and winters can be raw. Precipitation is light, but there is some snowfall in most years. Fog can linger for days on end. The average July temperature is 24.8°C (76°F) and it is even higher in August, when the humidity can be trying. Thunderstorms can be expected in late summer. May and September are the most pleasant months for sightseeing.

nightclubs in the country. During weekends, the Milanese stream out northwards to the lakes, where many of the city's flat-dwellers have villas and boats.

Milan's road system, which is a combination of concentric ring roads and radiating avenues, owes much to its ancient past. The inner ring road (*convallazione interna*) encloses much of the medieval city, where most of the historic sights can be seen. The 19th-century industry extended out to the canal ring (*cerchia dei navigli*), which has largely been filled in. Postwar development has spread towards the outer ring road (*circunvallazione esterna*). Most visitors, however, spend their time in the historic core, where most of Milan's attractions can be reached on foot.

PIAZZA DEL DUOMO

The heart of Milan is the Piazza del Duomo, or Cathedral Square (Metro 1, 3, Duomo). It is always throbbing with activity, with tourists feeding the pigeons and taking photographs, businessmen striding purposefully towards their offices, and the youth of Milan simply hanging out with their friends. Surrounding the square is a fine array of 19th-century arcaded buildings with their ground floors providing welcome cafés. On the north side of the square is the neo-Renaissance **Galleria Vittorio Emanuele II**, while on the south side is the rather ugly **Palazzo dell' Argengario**, which is now the conveniently sited **tourist office** (open 08:00–19:00 Monday–Saturday; tel 02 7252 4300). At the western end of the square is the bronze equestrian **Statue of Victor Emmanuel II**, the work of Ercole Rosa, which was unveiled in 1896. The statue depicts the king at the Battle of San Martino in 1859, while the sides of the massive plinth show the triumphant entry of the Piedmont troops into Milan after the Battle of Magenta (1859). The only jarring note about the piazza is the western end, where commercial buildings covered with neon advertisements somewhat ruin the atmosphere. This area is due for redevelopment, so hopefully improvements are on the way. One aspect of the Piazza del Duomo that the visitor will **not** see – because it underground – is the remains of the Basilica of St Tecla, which was unearthed during an archaeological dig in 1942.

The Duomo ★★★

Dominating the piazza, of course, is the Duomo or cathedral. As you emerge from the metro, you have a breathtaking view of the west front, with its pink-fringed marble and forest of pinnacles and statues. The sheer size of the cathedral is also impressive. It is claimed that the Duomo is the third largest cathedral in the world after Seville in Spain and St Peter's in Rome. It is also the only Gothic cathedral of any note in Italy.

The Duomo was begun in 1386 by Gian Galeazzo Visconti. The cathedral itself took another 500 years to complete. The main spire, with its golden Madonna, was added in the 18th century, and it was left to Napoleon to complete the west façade in 1813. Even in the 20th century, work was being carried out on the roof and the five bronze doors on the façade.

> **FACTS ABOUT THE DUOMO**
>
> **Length:** 158m (520ft).
> **Width:** 66m (215ft).
> **Central nave:** 17m (55ft) wide; 48m (157ft) high.
> **Interior height of dome:** 68m (220ft).
> **Distance from statue of the Madonna to the ground:** 108m (355ft).
> **Main façade:** 66m (200ft) wide; 56m (180ft) high.
> **Tallest spire:** 108m (355ft) high.
> There are 135 **spires**, 2245 statues, and 96 **gargoyles**.

Below: *In the Piazza del Duomo this imposing equestrian statue of Victor Emmanuel II faces the cathedral.*

THE NAIL OF THE HOLY CROSS

Stand in the choir of the Duomo and look up into the vaulting. A small red light marks a niche that contains a nail reputed to come from Christ's cross. The nail is in the shape of a horseshoe and was found by St Helena. It eventually came into the possession of Sant'Ambrogio. San Carlo Borromeo carried the nail in the procession during the plague of 1576. Each September 14, the Bishop of Milan is carried heavenwards on a small platform with invisible pulleys (it must seem like a miracle!) to collect the nail and show it to the people of Milan.

The most photographed part of the Duomo is the ornate west front or **façade**. Six huge vertical buttresses divide this triangular shape into five sections, each of which is capped with a range of pinnacles.

The initial impression on entering the **interior** is one of gloom, but on becoming accustomed to the light it is apparent that there are five aisles supported by 52 pillars (said to represent the weeks of the year). The capitals on each pillar are, unusually, decorated with statues of the saints. The exceptional stained glass varies in age from 15th century to modern, and casts a delicate light.

Let us take an anticlockwise walk around the interior of the cathedral. On the floor at the west end is a **meridian** placed there by the Brera astronomers in 1786. Along the south aisle you can appreciate the stunning stained glass. In the north transept there is a gruesome **Statue of St Bartholomew**. Dating from 1562, it shows the saint, having been flayed alive, carrying his own skin!

Walk over towards the altar and take the door that leads down to the **crypt**. For a small entrance charge admittance is gained to the room where an octagonal Baroque vault contains the remains of San Carlo Borromeo, the 16th-century Bishop of Milan. Returning to ground level, walk along the choir aisle, noting the funerary **Monument to Gian Giacomo Medici**. At this stage look at the vault above the choir where a small red light marks the niche where a nail allegedly from Christ's cross is kept.

Entering the ambulatory, don't miss the **southern sacristy door**, which dates from 1393 and has some superb carvings and inscriptions. You now reach the **apse**, which is generally considered to be the most beautiful part of the cathedral. There are

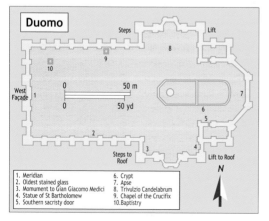

Duomo

Steps

Lift

West Façade

1. Meridian
2. Oldest stained glass
3. Momument to Gian Giacomo Medici
4. Statue of St Bartholomew
5. Southern sacristy door
6. Crypt
7. Apse
8. Trivulzio Candelabrum
9. Chapel of the Crucifix
10. Baptistry

Steps to Roof

Lift to Roof

N

three magnificent windows
with delicate tracery and some
fine 19th-century glass. The
ambulatory now leads to the
north transept, which is dominated by the monumental
early 13th-century **Trivulzio
Candelabrum**, attributed to
French goldsmith Nicholas de

Verdun. The enormous 4.87m (16ft) candelabrum has
seven branches and sits on a decorated stone base.

Above: *Palazzo Reale
was once the seat of the
Visconti family.*

The route has now returned to the west end. Before
leaving, take the steps down to the octagonal **baptistry**
where Sant'Ambrogio is reputed to have baptized St
Augustine in AD387.

A tour of the Duomo would not be complete without a
visit to the **roof terraces**. Fortunately, the vast number of
stairs can be avoided by using the lift (small charge) on
the north side of the cathedral. The roof gives an opportunity to study the statues, spires and buttresses in detail.
There are also fine views over the city's rooftops and it is
even possible, on a clear day, to see the Alps in the
distance. The Duomo is open daily from 07:00–18:30.

Palazzo Reale ★★

Just to the southeast of the Duomo is the Palazzo Reale,
a building with a chequered history. When Milan was a
comune in the 11th and 12th centuries, the Palazzo
was the town hall. Later it was the seat of the Visconti
family, but when the front part of the building was
removed to make way for the cathedral, the Dukes of
Milan moved to the Castello Sforzesco. The palace later
became the residence of both the Spanish and Austrian
governors. After unification, the building was renamed
the Palazzo Reale (Royal Palace). It was handed over to
the city authorities in the 20th century.

Civico Museo d'Arte Contemporanea (CIMAC) ★

The second floor of the Palazzo Reale houses Milan's
modern art museum. Its paintings and sculptures include

> ## MILAN'S ASTOUNDING POPULATION GROWTH
>
> Earliest population figures
> available show that from the
> 13th to 15th centuries Milan
> had a population of around
> 200,000, making it the largest
> city in Europe. At the time of
> the 1630 plague the figure
> had dropped right down to
> 60,000. Thereafter there was
> a gradual recovery until the
> end of the 19th century when
> there was a massive spurt in
> population numbers. By 1923
> it had reached 850,000, and
> in the post-World War II
> period it neared 1,400,000,
> making Milan the second
> largest city in Italy and 10th
> largest in Europe. Greater
> Milan today has 3,780,000
> inhabitants. What has caused
> this startling growth? The
> answer is **economic migra-
> tion**. Milan's thriving industry
> has attracted migrants looking
> for work from many areas of
> southern Italy and other parts
> of the world including North
> Africa and Asia.

work by Klee, Picasso, Modigliani and Matisse. Open 10:00–13:00 and 14:30–18:30 Mon, Wed–Fri; 10:30–18:30 Sat and Sun; closed Tue.

Museo del Duomo ★★

(Metro 1, 3, Duomo)

A wing of the Palazzo Reale is occupied by the Museo del Duomo. Among its collections are paintings, sculptures, stained-glass windows and a host of religious objects from the cathedral. A star exhibit is a wooden model of the Duomo dating from 1519. The Museo del Duomo is open from 09:30–12:30 and 15:00–18:00; closed on Monday.

The Galleria Vittorio Emanuele II ★★★

(Metro 1, 3, Duomo)

This stylish shopping arcade has four 'arms', the south and north arms connecting the Piazza del Duomo with the Piazza della Scala. The Galleria was built between 1865 and 1877 to the design of Giuseppe Mengoni, who sadly fell to his death from scaffolding shortly before the arcade was opened. The Galleria is entered through a squat 'triumphal arch', which leads to the central dome, made of iron and glass, and considered to be an engineering triumph in its day. The Galleria is claimed to be the most exclusive shopping arcade in the country and is filled with fashion outlets, bookshops and restaurants. The elite of Milan like to be seen eating here after attending a performance at La Scala. Beneath the dome is Il Savini, considered to be the most exclusive restaurant in Milan. Amazingly, the diners at Il Savini have to look across to an American fast-food chain – an unfortunate juxtaposition.

PIAZZA DELLA SCALA

The north arm of the Galleria leads into the Piazza della Scala. In the centre of the square is Pietro Magni's **Monument to Leonardo da Vinci**, erected in 1872. On the corners of the plinth are Leonardo's pupils, Boltraffio, Salaino, Oggiono and da Sesto. Between their figures are reliefs showing the fields in which Leonardo excelled – anatomy, hydraulic engineering, painting and architec-

WHAT'S IN A NAME?

How did Milan get its name? The obvious answer is that it derives from either the Celtic 'midland' or the Roman *Mediolanum*, meaning 'in the middle of the plain' – Milan lies in the middle of the Plain of Lombardy between the Alps and the Apennines. Some authorities, however, claim that the name comes from *scrofa semilanuta*, the half-woolly bear, which was the city's emblem in pre-Roman times.

ture. Between the monument and Galleria lies the **Palazzo Marino**, a 16th-century building, now the City Hall.

La Scala ★★★
(Metro 1, 3, Duomo)

On the other side of the square, opposite Palazzo Marino, is the world's most famous opera house – **La Scala**. The name is derived from the Church of Santa Maria alla Scala that once stood on the site. The opera house was financed by the Austrian Empress Maria Theresa and opened in 1778. All the world's best-known conductors and opera singers have performed at La Scala. After refurbishment it re-opened in 2004, appropriately with an opera by Salieri, which had not been performed there since La Scala's opening in 1778. For ticket information, call Infotel (tel: 02 7200 3744, open 09:00–18:00). Tickets can be bought on the day from the Central Box Office beneath Piazza del Duomo.

Museo la Scala ★★

The museum is located just to the left of the main doors of La Scala. There is a fascinating collection of opera memorabilia, including musical scores, sets, and paintings of several famous performers. The entrance ticket includes a visit to the auditorium, providing that no rehearsal is taking place. The museum is open from 09:00–12:30 and 13:30–17:00 daily. Closed on Monday.

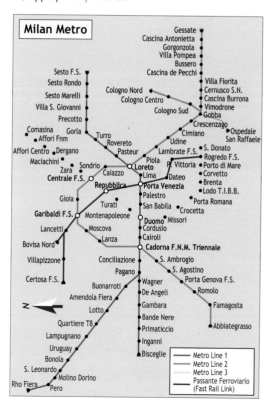

Milan Metro

GIUSEPPE VERDI
(1813–1901)

Born in Parma, Verdi moved to Milan at a very early age and spent most of his life in the city. He failed to gain entrance to the conservatoire, which ironically now bears his name. He is known almost entirely for his operas, most of which had their debuts at La Scala. They included *Rigoletto* (1851), *La Traviata* (1853), *Aïda* (1871) and *Otello* (1887). Verdi made his home in the Grand Hotel et de Milan, where he died in what is now suite 107.

Church of Santa Maria delle Grazie ★★★
(Metro 1, 2, Cadorna; 1, Conciliazione)

Few visitors to Milan would wish to miss the opportunity to see Leonardo da Vinci's painting of the *Last Supper*. Head for the Church of Santa Maria delle Grazie. Da Vinci's masterpiece is in the refectory, but first look around the church. The exterior is largely brick and is distinguished by the hemispherical dome on a cubic base. Santa Maria delle Grazie was built between 1463 and 1490 by Guiniforte Solari in a style described as a 'Gothic Renaissance transitional'. Ludovico el Moro later commissioned Bramante to make alterations, and the architect replaced the original apse with one in Renaissance style. Find time to visit the charming Great and Little Cloisters. The latter leads to the sacristy, which is often used today for art exhibitions.

The *Last Supper*, which is located in the refectory, was painted by Leonardo for Ludovico el Moro between 1495 and 1497, and covers the entire rear wall of the refectory, measuring 9m (30ft) by 4.5m (14ft). It depicts the moment just after Christ said: 'One of you will betray me'. The painting began to deteriorate almost immediately and it has had some controversial restoration over the centuries. Getting to actually see *The Last Supper* is quite a challenge. Visits should be booked by telephone (02 8942 1146) at least a week in advance and even longer during the summer and at weekends. Alternatively, use the website (www.cenacolovinciano.it). In addition to the entrance cost, there is a small booking fee. Viewing times are Tue–Sun, tel: 0815 1845. Don't dismiss the painting on the opposite wall of the refectory. This is Donato da Montafano's *Crucifixion*, which dates from 1495 and was commissioned by the Dominicans.

National Museum of Science and Technology ★★
(Metro 2, Sant'Ambrogio)

Just a stone's throw from Santa Maria delle Grazie is another location for da Vinci fans – the National Museum of Science and Technology. It is housed in the 16th-century

Left: *Da Vinci's Last Supper, on the refectory wall of the Church of Santa Maria delle Grazie.*

Monastery of San Vittore, which, after the monasteries were suppressed, became a military hospital and later a barracks. Badly damaged during World War II, it was restored soon afterwards and became the museum in 1947. The collections occupy a number of buildings, and there are sections on transport, metallurgy, physics, optics, acoustics, printing, cinema photography and astronomy. The **Leonardo da Vinci Gallery** attracts people by the score and his inventions are well displayed. There is a Leonardo self-portrait engraved on a glass panel, and a room dedicated to his drawings and models, some of which can be worked by visitors. The museum is open 09:30–17:00 Tuesday–Friday; 09:30–18:30 on Saturday and Sunday; closed on Monday (www.museoscienza.org).

THE CASTELLO SFORZESCO AREA
(Metro 1, Cairoli-Cadorna; 2, Lanza-Cadorna)
To the northwest of the Duomo the pedestrianized Via Dante, with its open-air cafés, leads to the Largo Cairoli, a large square ringed by distinguished 19th-century buildings. In the centre of the square is an equestrian statue of Giuseppe Garibaldi by Ettore Ximenes, erected in 1895. From here the tree-lined Via Foro Buonaparte stretches in a semicircle around the Piazza Castello and the Castello Sforzesco.

Castello Sforzesco ★★★
This complex of brick buildings and towers, which in the past formed a formidable defensive fortress, now contains a series of excellent museums.

The castle has a long and fascinating history. It was built in 1368 by the Viscontis purely as a fortress, but later

---

PAINTING THE LAST SUPPER

Fresco is a technique where the paint is put onto 'fresh' (*fresco*) mortar, which in drying binds the coloured pigment so that the painting becomes part of the wall itself. When Leonardo painted *The Last Supper* he tried a different technique, using tempera over a double layer of plaster. This proved faulty as the fresco could not withstand the dampness of the wall it was painted on and very soon it began to decay. Experts have tried heating the wall from behind, but this was unsuccessful. The fresco has been 'restored' so many times over the centuries that it is highly probable that little of Leonardo's original paintwork survives.

Above: *Statues and other works of art abound at the Castello Sforzesco.*

THE EDICT OF MILAN

In AD313 in Milan the Emperor Constantine made a proclamation granting religious tolerance for Christianity within the Roman Empire. The Edict assured Christians of their legal rights and directed the prompt return of their confiscated property. As a result of the Edict, Milan became the capital of western Christendom. A bronze statue of the Emperor Constantine (a copy of a Roman original) can be seen in the courtyard of the Basilica of San Lorenzo, fittingly located between the church's portals and the line of Roman columns. It is, h owever, doubtful whether Constantine himself ever became a Christian, although the Church claimed that he was baptized on his deathbed.

became the ducal palace. During the short-lived Ambrosian Republic it was partially demolished, but rebuilt almost immediately by the Sforzas. Under Ludovico el Moro it evolved into a glittering Renaissance palace, in which Leonardo da Vinci and Bramante the architect worked. During the times of Spanish and Austrian occupation it reverted to the role of fortress. It was badly damaged during the Napoleonic era, but restored to its original 15th-century magnificence by Luca Beltrami in the 1890s. The castle was further damaged by bombs during World War II, necessitating more restoration in the postwar years.

The castle takes the shape of a square, with massive walls pockmarked with holes at regular intervals. Once used for scaffolding, they now provide homes for some of Milan's ubiquitous pigeons. The main façade facing the Largo Cairoli has a round tower at each corner. These towers reach 31m (100ft) high and show the emblem of the snake, the symbol of the Sforza and Visconti families. Once water cisterns, the towers were given a military makeover in Beltrami's reconstructions. In the centre of the façade is the **Filarete Tower**, named after its designer. In 1521, it collapsed when the gunpowder that was stored there exploded. Beltrami rebuilt it from Filarete's plans.

Pass the ornate computerized fountain and enter the main gateway under the Filarete Tower. This leads into the enormous Piazza D'Armi, the Sforza military training ground. Cross this courtyard and pass through a gateway. To the right is the Ducal Court containing the **Sforza Castle art galleries**. The first of these is the **Civic Museum of Art**, which is mainly given over to sculpture and tapestries. The prize exhibit is Michelangelo's *Rondanini Pietà*. The unfinished sculpture shows Mary struggling to hold up the body of the crucified Christ. On the other side of the courtyard in the upper storey is the **Pinacoteca**, which has a comprehensive collection of art from the 15th–18th centuries, including work by Bellini, Titian, Canaletto and a number of Lombard artists.

On the opposite side of the castle is the arcaded **Roccetta Courtyard**, which was always the last refuge in the event of a siege. The museum here has a collection of ancient Egyptian artefacts and local archaeological items. The castle is open 09:00–17:30 daily and the museums 09:00–17:30 Tuesday–Sunday. Free admission to the castle, but you have to pay for a combined ticket for the museums.

Continuing through the castle and over the moat, you reach the **Parco Sempione**. Once the Sforza family's hunting grounds, the park was remodelled in the late 19th century by Emilio Alemagna in what was considered to be typically English style. Today, the park covers about 47ha (116 acres) and includes a number of lakes between the mature trees. Almost hidden among this leafiness is the **Monument to Napoleon III**, dating from 1881 and brought here in 1927 from its original site at the Senate building. Nearby is the **Acquario Civico**, which has a good collection of mammals and fish. It is very popular with Italian schoolchildren. The aquarium is open 09:30–17:30 daily.

On the opposite side of the park is the **Palazzo dell' Arte**. Built in 1933, it is the permanent venue for the Milan Triennale, and stages other exhibitions of art, fashion and design.

At the far end of the park is the **Arco della Pace**. Standing 25m (82ft) high, its construction began in 1807 as a triumphal arch in celebration of Napoleon's victories. On Napoleon's fall from power, work stopped on the arch and it was not resumed until 1826, when Francis I of Austria dedicated it to Peace.

For information on the Castello Sforzesco area, *see* www.milanocastello.it

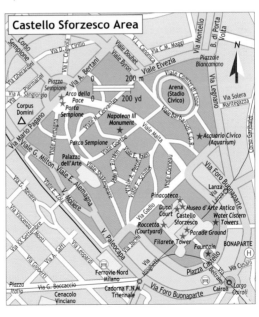

Castello Sforzesco Area

ALESSANDRO MANZONI (1785–1873)

One of Milan's most famous residents, Manzoni wrote what is considered to be Italy's greatest novel, *I Promessi Sposi* (The Betrothed), describing life in Milan in the 17th century. In the novel he used a form of Italian that everyone could understand, stirring feelings for unification. His former home, **Casa Manzoni**, in Via Morone, is now a museum and the seat of the National Centre for Manzoni Studies. The house also contains the Lombard History Society's collection of over 40,000 books.

Below: *The Milan fashion shows are renowned the world over.*

THE BRERA QUARTER

(Metro 1, 3, Duomo; 2, Lanza)

The Brera area is one of the liveliest and most atmospheric parts of Milan. The winding, cobbled streets are full of cafés, art galleries and antique shops, while students from the Academy of Fine Art add to the colourful ambience. A good time to visit the quarter is on the third Saturday of each month when a flea market is held in the Via Brera.

Pinacoteca di Brera ★★★

The focus for most visitors to the Brera area will be the Pinacoteca di Brera, one of Italy's top art galleries. It is located in a palace that dates from 1773, although it is on the site of a much earlier monastery. Entry is via a rectangular courtyard with a double arcade of slender paired columns. In the centre of the cobbled courtyard is a bronze statue of Napoleon, who was largely responsible for getting together the original collection from suppressed churches. The collection has since been augmented by donations. The paintings are mainly Italian and 90 per cent of those displayed are of a religious nature.

Particularly important are Bramante's eight frescoes, Tintoretto's *Rediscovery of St Mark's Body*, the *Pietà* by Bellini, several Raphaels including *The Marriage of the Virgin*, and *Virgin With Child* by Piero della Francesca. Don't miss the foreshortened *Dead Christ* by Mantegna. The gallery is on the first floor and reached by the steps from the courtyard. The Brera is open 08:30–19:15 Tuesday–Sunday; closed on Monday (www.brera.beniculturali.it).

THE FASHION DISTRICT

(Metro 1, Duomo)

Via Monte Napoleone, Via Manzoni, Via Sant'Andrea and Via della Spiga enclose the Quadrilatero d'Oro, Milan's famous fashion district. Here are the shops of some of the top international fashion designers interspersed with aristocratic palaces, tearooms and antique shops. Names such Armani, Gucci, Versace, Chanel and Cardin ensure that this district is a Mecca for serious shoppers and spenders.

Just to the northeast of the fashion district are the **Giardini Pubblici**, Milan's public gardens. They cover some 17ha (42 acres) and were originally laid out in 1782 by Piermarini, who used the grounds of suppressed monasteries. Within the public gardens are the city's **Planetarium** (open according to the programme with guided tours) and the **Museum of Natural History**, which has a good collection of fossils (including dinosaurs), minerals and insects. Open 09:00–18:00 Monday–Friday; 09:30–18:30 on Saturday and Sunday.

Above: *Magnificent window displays can be found in the Quadrilatero d'Oro.*

CA' GRANDE

(Metro 1, 3, Duomo; 3, Missori)
Southeast of the Duomo is the Casa Grande or Ospedale Maggiore. This former hospital was built in the mid-15th century for Francesco Sforza, who planned to centralize the city's many hospitals. It has a magnificent arcaded central courtyard, which separated the men's and women's quarters. Since 1952 Ca' Grande has been the home of the Liberal Arts faculty of Milan's State University.

OTHER MUSEUM HIGHLIGHTS

There are over 50 museums and galleries in Milan. Some have already been described. Here is the pick of the remainder. Remember that most museums are closed on Sunday afternoons and all day on Monday. In theory all state museums should be free to all EU citizens under 18 and over 65 – but in practice this may not be the case.

FASHION AND FRAUD

Anyone strolling around the Quadrilatero d'Oro – the Golden Quadrangle – will have little doubt that Milan regards itself as the fashion capital of the world. Not only are there shops with household names such as Versace, Gucci, Armani, Benetton and many more, but the Italians strolling around the street dress themselves in the latest fashion. The Milanese like to *fare bella figura* or cut a fine figure – even the local footballers look like male models. Unfortunately the fashion world was caught up in the fraud and corruption allegations of the 1990s, and two of the leading figures have been assassinated – Gianni Versace in Florida and Maurizio Gucci in Milan.

Museo Poldi Pezzoli ★

(Metro 3, Montenapoleone)

Located on Via Manzoni, this museum is only a short walk from the Piazza della Scala. As well as some highly regarded artwork including paintings by Mantegna, Bellini and Canaletto, there are displays of glassware, clocks, porcelain and tapestry. Open Tue–Sun 10:00–18:00 (www.museopoldipezzoli.it).

Above: *The Milan metro is cheap, effective and the best way to get around the city.*

Museo Archeologico ★

(Metro 1, 2, Cadorna)

Based in a former monastery located at corso Magenta 15, the archaeological museum has some interesting collections from prehistoric, Etruscan and Roman times. Open Tue–Sun 09:00–17:30; closed on Monday.

Ambrosiana ★★

(Metro 1, 3, Duomo; 1, Cordusio)

On Piazza Pio XI – just to the west of the Duomo – the Ambrosiana is a huge library and art gallery, set up by Federico Borromeo, cousin of the better-known bishop. The library contains over 750,000 books and priceless manuscripts, including some of Leonardo's sketchbooks. The superb art collection includes Leonardo's *Portrait of a Musician*, Caravaggio's impression of a basket of worm-eaten fruit (thought to be the first still life painted in Italy), and works by Tintoretto, Botticelli and Titian. Open 10:00–17:30; closed on Monday (www.ambrosiana.it).

Pusterla di Sant'Ambrogio ★

(Metro 3, Duomo)

Set in one of the medieval city gates at via Carducci 41, the museum has a collection of ancient weapons and criminological artefacts. Open 10:00–13:00 and 15:00–19:00 daily; closed on Monday.

USING THE METRO

Using Milan's underground railway system or **metro** could not be simpler. Maps of the metro show that there are three lines – Line 1 coloured red, Line 2 coloured green and Line 3 coloured yellow (plus the Passante high-speed link, coloured blue). Cheap tickets can be bought from newsstands and tobacconists and are valid for 75 minutes anywhere on the system. Trains are generally clean and safe and you can reach 90 per cent of the places mentioned in this chapter by using the metro (*see* map on page 35).

Museo Bagatti Valsecchi ★

(Metro 3, Montenapoleone)

At via Santo Spirito 10, in the former house of the two Bagatti Valsecchi brothers, the collection gives a good indication of the tastes in art and furniture in the late 19th century. Rooms are devoted to tapestries, ivory work and paintings, along with a superb collection of furniture that children would have used in the 15th to 17th centuries. Open Tue–Sun 13:00–17:45; closed Mon (www.museobagattivalsecchi.org).

Museo del Risorgimento ★

Set in the Palazzo Moriggia, via Borgonuovo 23, the museum covers the course of the unification movement from the 1700s to 1870. Open 09:00–18:00; closed on Monday (www.delrisorgimento.mi.it).

MORE CHURCHES

There are enough historic churches in central Milan to keep an enthusiast busy for a week. Some have already been mentioned. The following are all well worth a visit:

Basilica of San Lorenzo Maggiore ★★

(Metro 3, Missori)

The basilica, sometimes called 'alle Colonne', is just south of the city centre near the old Porta Ticinese gateway. In front are 16 Corinthian columns dating from the 2nd or 3rd century, originally belonging to an unidentified temple. This is Milan's oldest church, dating back to the 4th century, and its design is unlike any work of the Lombard architects. It suffered from many fires in the Middle Ages and had to be rebuilt after 1573 when the dome collapsed. The 5th-century Cappella di Sant' Aquilino has superb mosaics and the imposing statue of Emperor Constantine that marks the church's Roman connections. Open daily 07:30–12:30 and 14:30–18:30.

Sant'Ambrogio ★★★

(Metro 2, Sant'Ambrogio)

Milan's best-known church can be found at the end of Via

THE AMATEUR BISHOP

Ambrose (Ambrogio) was a Roman governor sent to Milan in 374 to oversee the election of a new bishop. This was at a time of some theological turmoil, following the Arian controversy. Ambrose made an eloquent speech calming the crowds, who suddenly took up the chant 'Ambrose Bishop'. Although he had not even been baptized, he converted to Christianity immediately and in just over a week he had been made Bishop of Milan. He proved to be extremely successful at preserving the unity of the Church and establishing good relations between the Church and the Empire. Such was the reputation of this amateur bishop that he became the patron saint of Milan, and people from the city are still known today as *Ambrosiani*.

San Vittore next to the 12th-century gate, the **Pusterla di
Sant'Ambrogio**. The building is dedicated to St Ambrose,
the city's patron saint, who founded the church in 379. It
has been enlarged and rebuilt many times, but what we
see today dates mainly from the 1080s. Sant'Ambrogio is
widely considered to be the finest example of Romansque
architecture in northern Italy and its pure architecture has
been retained, with the round arches found throughout
the complex of buildings. The interior of the basilica is
basically severe, with the red-brick vaulting setting off the
white walls. An exception to this austerity is the golden
altarpiece or *paliotto*, a 9th-century masterpiece by
Volvinio, composed of four silver and gold panels
encrusted with pearls and precious stones. Notice, too,
the 11th-century pulpit that is placed above a Romano
Christian sarcophagus. The remains of St Ambrose are to
be found in the crypt, along with those of Saints Gervasio
and Protasio. The upper section of the portico (designed
by Bramante) contains the **Museo della Basilica di
Sant'Ambrogio**, which displays vestments, manuscripts,
frescoes and even what is claimed to be the saint's bed.
The museum is open 10:00–12:00 Monday, Wednesday–
Friday; 15:00–17:00 Saturday and Sunday; closed on
Tuesday. Next to Sant'Ambrogio is the **Catholic University of the Sacred Heart** located in the former
Benedictine monastery. The university was founded in
1921 and the building retains two of Bramante's cloisters.

Below: *Part of the lavish
Lombard-Romanesque
interior of Sant'Ambrogio,
showing the gilded and
bejewelled altarpiece.*

San Satiro ★★

(Metro 1, 3, Duomo)

Tucked in between tall buildings
along the Via Torino is the little
Renaissance gem of San Satiro. It was
built largely by Donato Bramante in
1478 on the site of a 9th-century
church. Bramante found that space
was tight, so he built an exceptionally
large nave and then relied on perspective and optical illusions to
achieve effect. He created the illusion

of an apse by using *trompe l'oeil* decoration. Other features to note are the octagonal baptistry and the newly restored Cappella della Pietà. Outside, the brick-built 9th-century campanile is the oldest in Lombardy.

Sant'Eustorgio ★
(Metro 2, Stazione Genova)

Some way south of the historic centre and close to the *navigli* (canals), Sant'Eustorgio was built in the 11th century to house the relics of the Magi, which were taken to Milan by Bishop Eustorgius. In 1162, Frederick Barbarossa destroyed the building and took the relics to Cologne (they were not returned until 1903). The church was rebuilt in 1190, with the addition of a bell tower topped with a cone-shaped cusp. This is Milan's tallest bell tower and the first to have a clock. The simple façade gives little indication of the delights of the interior, which has so many art treasures it is almost like a museum. Not to be missed is the Portinari Chapel, which was originally commissioned by a Milanese banker. In the entrance is the magnificently carved raised tomb of St Peter the Martyr, built by Giovanni di Balduccio and dating from the mid-14th century. The other joy of the chapel is in the frescoes by Vincenzo Foppa that adorn the walls and ceiling. They were not discovered until 1878 when building work was taking place. Most of the artworks can be seen in the string of chapels of varying ages on the south side of the church.

San Maurizio ★
(Metro 1, 2, Cadorna)

This church, in Corso Magenta, was begun in 1503 for a closed order of Benedictine nuns, and the design had strict divisions between the public and the nuns. The exterior of the church is of little interest, but the interior has some superb frescoes attributed to Leonardo da Vinci's follower Bernardino Luini. They have been dated at around 1530 and are probably the artist's last work. In

Above: *Milan's taxis are always white in colour. They can only be boarded at official taxi ranks.*

Above: *Stazione Centrale, Milan's main railway station, has an impressive façade built in the time of Mussolini.*

one of the chapels Luini has painted scenes from the life of St Catherine, including the *Decapitation of St Catherine*. It is believed that the face of the saint is actually a portrait of Countess Bianca Maria di Challant, who was actually beheaded herself in the courtyard of the Castello Sforzesco in 1516.

FURTHER OUT

A number of places in Milan that are well worth a visit are some way from the city centre and will require transport to reach them.

Stazione Centrale ★

(Metro 2, 3, Centrale)

The Central Station was completed in 1931. It defies architectural definition and is really a political and ideological statement, reflecting Mussolini's obsession with making the trains run on time. Faced with light grey Aurisina stone, the façade alone is 207m (679ft) wide, and the roof is topped with winged horses. Inside the station there is a flight of steps leading to a concourse with a booking office, shops and a tourist information office. The platforms are spanned by massive glass and steel vaulting. An estimated 300,000 people use the station daily, but probably few appreciate the fact that a large number of Italian Jews left here for their extermination at Auschwitz towards the end of World War II.

Pirelli Building ★

(Metro 2, 3, Centrale)

Opposite the station is the elegant Pirelli Building. Built in the 1960s, it was Milan's first skyscraper and was built as the head office of the Pirelli organization. It is 124m (400ft) high and today acts as the headquarters of the Lombardy Regional Government.

The tower experienced a dramatic incident in 2002 when a light aircraft crashed into the building, reminding Milanese of New York's 9/11 drama. The pilot died, along with two office workers, but the building remained intact.

SORTING OUT YOUR TRAINS

The Italian State Railways (*Ferrovie dellos Stato*) provide an excellent service with fares at bargains rates. There are many types of train and their varying speeds will affect journey times. *EuroCity* are international express trains, while *InterCity* trains provide a luxury service between Italian cities. *Expressos* are long-distance trains, which, despite their name, can be slow because they stop at many stations. The slowest trains are the *diretto* and the *locale*.

Cimitero Monumentale

This cemetery has, somewhat bizarrely, become a tourist attraction. It is the burial ground of the great and good of Milan, each trying to outdo the other with the magnificence of their funerary monuments, hiring the best available sculptors for the task (*see* panel, this page).

San Siro Stadium ★

(Metro 1, Lotto)

This stadium, at via Piccolomini 5, is now officially known as the Meazza, after a highly regarded footballer who played for both of Milan's teams – Inter and AC. Originally built in 1926, the stadium was modernized in the 1950s and again in 1990 when a roof was added. It now has a ground capacity of 85,000. Guided tours of the stadium take place daily from Monday–Saturday, except on days when matches are held. Also in the complex are a horse-racing track and a trotting stadium.

The Navigli ★★

To the southwest of the city centre are the remains of the once extensive canal system. First constructed in the 12th century, the canals linked Milan with the network of north Italian waterways. The canals brought Canoglia marble to the city to build the Duomo, along with fruit and vegetables from the countryside plus coal and salt from the ports. In the opposite direction went handmade goods such as textiles. Many of the canals were filled in during the 1930s, but it is interesting to note that Milan was Italy's 10th largest port as late as the 1950s. The area around the canals was once a staunch working-class area and it is still possible to see the old wash houses, the *Vicolo dei Lavandai*, that lined the canals. Today, however, the area has been gentrified. Real estate values have jumped and the old blocks of flats now command high prices, while boutiques and antique shops line the waterfront. The Navigli area also claims to have the trendiest restaurants in Milan. There is a popular antique market on the canal side on the last Sunday of the month during the summer, and a flea market each Saturday.

CIMITERO MONUMENTALE

It is hard to think of a cemetery as a tourist attraction, but Milan's *Cimitero Monumentale* is just that. The monuments to Milan's great and good include a pyramid, a life-size crucifiction and a sculpted recreation of *The Last Supper*. In the centre of the cemetery is a huge neo-Gothic temple, containing the tomb of writer Alessandro Manzoni and busts of Verdi and unification figures Cavour and Garibaldi. The *cimitero* is a long way from a metro station, so you will need a taxi to get there, but don't miss it.

Below: *The Pirelli Building, one of Milan's few skyscrapers, is a symbol of the city's postwar reconstruction.*

Milan at a Glance

Climatically, it is best to avoid Milan in winter when a raw fog can settle over the city for days on end, while August can be very hot and humid and many places close down for this period. **Spring**, early **summer** and **September** are the most comfortable times for visiting. Opera fans will need to come to the city in winter as the La Scala season begins in December.

Visitors arriving by **train** will find themselves at the Stazione Centrale, from where there are connections by metro, bus and taxi to other parts of the city. **Air** travellers will land at either **Linate Airport**, a few kilometres northeast of the city, or, more likely, at **Malpensa Airport**, 50km (30 miles) northwest of the city. Shuttle buses run regularly from both airports to Stazione Centrale. Visitors arriving by car will use the *autostrada*, but be warned that traffic levels in the city are high and a car is a dubious advantage. It is advisable to use the ATM parking areas on the outskirts of the city and then use public transport. Remember that there is a congestion charge for all vehicles entering central Milan.

Milan's **taxis** are white in colour, cheap and widely used by the business com-munity. They can't be hailed, however, and must be picked up at authorized taxi ranks. Check that the meter is on. For a radio taxi ring 02 8585 or 02 6767. **Scooters**, **mopeds** and **cycles** are a good way of getting around if you are confident in the aggressive traffic. Cyclists should beware of the tramlines. The **integrated public transport system** in Milan, involving buses, trams, trolley buses and the metro, is cheap and efficient, although often crowded. Trams and buses are yellow in colour. Tickets must be bought before board-ing – available at newsstands and tabacconists. The **metro** has three lines – no. 1 is shown on maps in red, no. 2 is green and no. 3 is yellow. In addition there is the short Passante line, which is a fast rail link and shown on some maps in blue. Metro tickets are only valid for 75 minutes. Tourist tickets are good value and there are also weekly and monthly passes.

As Milan tends to cater for business travellers rather than tourists, its accommodation is largely of the expense account type and prices are notoriously high. There is little acceptable accommodation in the budget range, which tends to cater for newly arrived immigrants to the city and cannot really be recommended. Hotels cluster around the Central Station and the Piazza della Repubblica, or near Fiera di Milano, the trade fair centre. Book in advance, as rooms tend to be snapped up, particularly during trade fairs and fashion weeks. The tourist offices provide a free hotel reservation service.

LUXURY

Four Seasons, via Gesù 8, tel: 02 77088, fax: 02 7708 5000, www.fourseasons.com/milan Generally reckoned to be the best hotel in town, with prices and service to match. Set in a converted monastery in the middle of the fashion district. **Grand Hotel et de Milan**, via Manzoni 29, tel: 02 723 141, fax: 02 8646 0861, www.grandhoteldemilano.it Historic hotel with Art Nouveau public rooms and antiques in bedrooms. Commendable restaurant. **Principe di Savoia**, piazza della Repubblica 17, tel: 02 62301, fax: 02 659 5838, www.hotelprincipedisavoia. com Lavish hotel with garage and rooftop pool. Elegant rooms and own airport shuttle.

MID-RANGE

Manin, via Manin 7, tel: 02 659 6511, fax: 02 655 2160, www.hotelmanin.it Quiet location opposite Giardini Pubblici. Friendly service. **Una Hotel Scandinavia**, via Fauché 15, tel: 02 336 391; fax: 02 3310 4510. New hotel close to the trade fair centre, good restaurant.

Milan at a Glance

Madisson, via Gasparetto 8, tel: 02 6707 4150, fax: 02 6707 5059. Friendly bed and breakfast in a side street a short walk from the Stazione Centrale.

BUDGET

Youth Hostel

Milan's Youth Hostel, **Piero Rotta**, is located at Viale Salmoiraghi, tel: 02 39026 7095 . Large modern building in the suburbs near the San Siro Stadium. Open 07:00–09:00 and 15:30–00:30. There is a 00:30 curfew so you may not reserve ahead; arrive early.

Camping

There are two camp sites close to the city:
Città di Milano, via G. Airaghi 61, tel: 02 4820 0134. Take the metro 1 to De Angeli and then bus 72.
Autodromo, Parco di Monza, tel: 02 3938 7771. Located in a park near the motor racing circuit, this camp site is only open in the summer months.

WHERE TO EAT

Milan offers just about every kind of food you care to think about, such as local cuisine, food from other regions of Italy, bland international dishes and food from other countries including Chinese, Indian, Japanese and South American. One thing is certain: it will be more expensive than anywhere else in Italy, but still reasonable by London or New York standards.

LUXURY

Savini, Galleria Vittorio Emanuele II, tel: 02 7200 3433. Has been serving classic Milanese delicacies since 1867; remains one of the top restaurants in the city.
La Scaletta, piazza Stazione Porta Genova 3, tel: 02 5810 0290. Fresh ingredients in creative recipes. One of the best restaurants in Milan.
Aimo e Nadia, via Monte-cuccoli 6, tel: 02 416 886, www.aimoenadia.com Family restaurant; consistently high standards.

MID-RANGE

Trattoria Toscana Il Cerchio, via Galvani 15, tel: 02 670 0738. Popular and homely trattoria close to the Stazione Centrale.
Ponte Rosso, ripa di Porta Ticinese 23, tel: 02 837 3132. Excellent food in this friendly family establishment along-side the Naviglio Grande.
I Malavoglia, via Lecco 4, tel: 02 2953 1387. Good Sicilian food in a friendly atmosphere. Closed Monday.

BUDGET

There are any number of American fast-food outlets in Milan, where it is possible to eat cheaply. Pizzerias are also inexpensive, while many trattorias can be equally suitable for the budget-conscious. *Tavola Calda* (hot tables), where meals are taken standing up at the counter, are also affordable options.

SHOPPING

Shopping in Milan can be a very enjoyable activity – providing you have a deep pocket. Most shopoholics head for the Quadrilatero d'Oro, the fashion centre of Milan, but shops throughout the city tend to be stylish, and window shopping can be almost as gratifying as actually buying. **Department stores** are not a common feature in Italy, but Milan has three – the classy La Rinascente whose restaurant has a superb view of the pinnacles of the Duomo; Coin on the Piazza Cinque Giornate; and Upim in Piazza San Babila. Milan also has a number of lively **street markets**, selling everything from antiques to the clothes worn by fashion models.

USEFUL CONTACTS

Tourist Information Centres: Tourist information is provided by the **Azienda di Promozione Turistica (APT)**. They have information about the city including free maps, hotel lists and information on cultural events. They are usually willing to book hotel reservations ahead.
The main APT office is at via Marconi 1, at the side of the Duomo. Open 08:30–20:00 Mon–Fri, 09:00–13:00 and 14:00–19:00 Sat, 09:00–13:00 and 14:00–17:00 Sun; tel: 02 7252 4301, fax: 02 7252 4350, www.provincia.milano.it/turismo

3
Excursions from Milan

Milan is a handy centre for visiting a number of ancient cities and abbeys on the Plain of Lombardy. In many cases these towns flourished during the Dark Ages or the Middle Ages, but since then they have been left behind by Milan's determined growth. Fortunately this has meant that the towns have retained their old cobbled streets, ancient buildings and medieval atmosphere. **Bergamo**, for example, has a superb Old Town set up on a hill and protected by fortifications. **Pavia**, to the south of Milan, has retained its old Roman street plan and has an imposing Visconti castle and an ancient university. **Cremona**, away to the east, has a magnificent cathedral. It was the birthplace of Monteverdi and is noted for its manufacture of violins. The longest of the trips is to **Mantua**. Surrounded by lakes and swamps, the city is famous for its atmospheric squares. It was ruled by the wealthy Gorzaga family for centuries and they encouraged artists such as Andreas Montegna to base themselves in Mantua under their patronage. There are also two fine abbeys to visit. One, the **Abbey of Chiaraville**, is within Milan's city boundaries. The other, the **Certosa di Pavia**, just north of Pavia, is an ebullient mixture of Gothic and Renaissance styles. After Milan's Duomo, it is the most important monument in the region.

Fortunately, all the places mentioned above can easily be reached from Milan using public transport such as bus or train, although the use of a car would definitely be more convenient.

SWITZERLAND
Lake Maggiore
Lake Como
Lake Garda
Bergamo
Monza
MILAN
Brescia
Verona
Pavia
Torino
Cremona
Mantua (Mantova)
ITALY
Genova
Bologna

DON'T MISS

★★★ Certosa di Pavia: Visconti Charterhouse – Lombardy's top monument after Milan's Duomo.
★★★ The Città Alta, Bergamo: the Venetian Empire's fortified hill town.
★★★ The Palazzo Ducale, Mantua: the stronghold and palace of the Gonzaga family.
★★ The Palazzo Tè: Federico Gonzaga's country retreat.
★★ The Basilica di San Michele Maggiore: the best of many Romansque churches.
★★ Monza's Duomo: beautiful cathedral containing the Iron Crown of Italy.

Opposite: *Bergamo – one of many ancient cities within easy reach of Milan.*

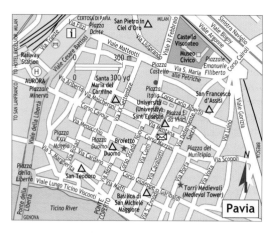

Pavia

Chiaraville Abbey ★★

Once surrounded by water meadows, the abbey and its grounds have been swallowed up by the suburbs of Milan, but this does not detract from this impressive complex. The abbey was founded by French Cistercian monks in the mid-12th century. The bell tower was added in 1349 and it has a small church on either side. The huge main tower, which also dates from 1349, is a landmark for miles around. It has a range of double, triple and quadruple lancet windows and a vast number of small marble columns. Also worth seeing are the superb frescoes, the choir stalls and the rebuilt cloisters. Napoleon closed the monastery down in 1798 and it fell into disrepair. In recent years, however, the abbey has been restored and given back to the monks. The Abbey of Chiaraville can be reached by the number 13 tram from the Duomo, or from the nearest metro station, Corvetto, on line 3. It is open 09:00–12:00 and 14:00–17:00; closed on Monday.

Monza

This small town of around 120,000 people is probably best known for its Grand Prix motor-racing circuit, but there is much more to see, including an impressive cathedral, the Duomo.

Located some 15km (9 miles) to the northeast of Milan, Monza was the place where the Lombard kings were crowned. The dominating building in the town is the **Duomo**, which dates from the 13th century, having been built on the site of a church that was set up by the Lombard Queen Theodolinda. A small remnant of this ancient church, depicting the queen and her family, can be seen above the main door of the cathedral. The façade, composed of green and white marble with a stunning rose window, is linked to a brick campanile dating from 1609. There is much to appreciate in the interior of the Duomo. Look for Theodolinda's Chapel to the left of the High Altar. As well as containing the queen's tomb, the chapel has some superb frescoes. The Duomo's most cherished relic is the **Iron Crown of Italy**, used to crown numerous Lombard kings, holy Roman emperors and, more recently, Napoleon. The jewel-encrusted gold crown has a rim of iron, said to have been made from one of the nails of the Cross. The cathedral museum is also worth visiting. One of its exhibits is Theodolinda's processional cross, given to her by Gregory the Great.

Parco di Monza ★

Monza's other main attraction is the **Parco di Monza**, on the north side of the town. The park covers some 800ha (1976 acres), of which about 15 per cent is taken up with the motor-racing track and grandstands. In the middle of the park is Archduke Ferdinand of Austria's **Villa Reale**, built between 1776 and 1780 by Giuseppe Piermarini. The landscape around it is very much on English lines, with scattered trees, lakes and even a grotto. In 1805, Napoleon's viceroy in Italy expropriated the park, and handed it over to the people. Today, there are several sports available in the park, including golf, tennis, polo and swimming. Bicycles can be hired and there is a jogging track. Monza can be reached in 20 minutes by bus from Milan's Stazione Centrale.

PAVIA

The small town of Pavia is some 35km (22 miles) south of Milan and although it is rather somnolent today, this has not always been the case. Having been occupied by the Romans and the Goths, it became the capital of the Lombard Empire until it was finally eclipsed by Milan in the 11th century. Both Charlemagne and Barbarossa were crowned in Pavia, while one of its most famous denizens was Lanfranc, who became the first Archbishop of Canterbury after the Norman Conquest. Under the

> ### THE IRON CROWN OF ITALY
>
> The museum in the Duomo at Monza contains the Iron Crown of Italy. The 'iron' is in fact claimed to be the 'true nail' used to attach Jesus to the cross. It came to Monza via Queen Helena, who gave it to her son the Emperor Constantine. He had the nail beaten out into a strip that formed the rim of his jewel-encrusted crown. Over the centuries, more than 40 kings and holy Roman emperors have used the crown at their coronations. One of the most recent was Napoleon, who used the iron crown at his coronation in Milan Cathedral in 1805.

Below: *Italian restaurants use a variety of methods to attract diners.*

Viscontis, Pavia became an intellectual centre and it was during this era that the university (probably the oldest in Italy) was founded.

The Duomo ★★

Head for the historic centre, which is partly pedestrianized and still retains its old Roman street plan. Dominating the core of the town is the rather stolid looking Duomo in Lombard Renaissance style. Work began on the cathedral in 1488 and Bramante, Leonardo, Amadeo and many others had a hand in its design. Its huge 19th-century dome, the third largest in Italy, towers above the rooftops. It was once accompanied by the Torre Civica, but this collapsed in 1989, killing four people.

The Basilica di San Michele Maggiore ★★★

Far more attractive than the Duomo is the Basilica di San Michele Maggiore, a fine Romanesque church dating back to 661. A major reconstruction took place in the 12th century after damage from a lightning strike. Some decorative sculpture can be seen, both on the frieze on the sandstone façade and on the capitals of the main columns in the interior. Also look for the Romanesque mosaic in the presbytery.

There are a number of other churches of interest in Pavia, including the 12th-century **San Teodoro**, the 13th-century **San Francesco d'Assisi**, the Romanesque **San Pietro in Ciel d'Oro** with its gold ceiling, **Santa Maria del Carmine** dating back to 1390, and **San Lanfranco** with a memorial to the Archbishop of Canterbury.

The Ponte Coperto ★

The River Ticino in Pavia is straddled by an attractive covered bridge, the **Ponte Coperto**. The original

Below: *Pavia University has much of architectural interest, including a cloistered courtyard.*

medieval covered bridge was just to the east, but this was destroyed during World War II.

Castello Visconteo ★

On the opposite side of the town is the **Castello Visconteo**. Built in 1360, it was partially destroyed in the Battle of Pavia in 1525. Three sides of the castle

survive and they now house the **Museo Civico**, which contains an excellent archaeological section. The art gallery has some important works by Italian and Dutch painters. The museum is open 10:00–12:00 and 14:30–16:00 Tuesday–Sunday, closed on Monday.

Above: *The Ponte Coperto or Covered Bridge spans the River Ticino in Pavia.*

The University ★

Much of the northeastern part of the historic core of Pavia is taken up by the University. Within its campus are three of the remaining medieval towers for which the town was once famous, plus the crypt of the demolished 12th-century Church of Sant'Eusebio.

The Certosa di Pavia ★★★

The Certosa or Charterhouse is located 10km (6 miles) north of Pavia on the road to Milan. It can be reached by bus or train from Milan. It was built by Gian Galeazzo Visconti in the 1390s as a family mausoleum. Many of the architects and masons working on Milan's cathedral also spent time on the Certosa, but the main input was from Giovanni Antonio Amadeo, who was responsible for the design of the façade. The building shows a transition in styles from the Gothic to the Renaissance and is considered to be the most important monument in Lombardy after Milan's Duomo. The Certosa became a Carthusian monastery, but this was suppressed by Napoleon. In 1968 a group of Cistercian monks took over the monastery and maintain the old traditions, including

---

THE LATE LAMENTED MILLE MIGLIA

Although Grand Prix motor racing is alive and well, one popular race that has fallen by the wayside is the **Mille Miglia**. It was a race for sports cars over one lap of 1000 miles over public roads. It started from Brescia to the north of Milan and went along the Adriatic coast to Rome and back through the Apennines. In 1955 it was won by an Englishman, Stirling Moss, at an average speed of 158.5kph (98.5mph). Two years later, perhaps not surprisingly, the race was discontinued as it was considered too dangerous.

Above: *The view over the roofs of Bergamo from the Torre Civica.*

a vow of silence. A few of the monks are released from this vow in order to take guided tours around the Certosa. A highlight of the tour is the stunning façade of the church, which has more than 70 statues of saints and prophets. The interior has some impressive groin vaulting, a massive metalwork screen, marble mosaics on the floors, and beautiful stained-glass windows. The north transept contains the tomb of Ludovici el Moro and his wife Beatrice d'Este – brilliant work by Cristoforo Solari – while the south transept has the tomb of Gian Galeazzo Visconti. The tour leaves the south transept and enters the Little Cloister, with its terracotta decorations. From here there is a good view of the church's octagonal tower and cupola. This leads to the arcaded Great Cloister, with 122 arches supported by marble columns. The cloister is surrounded by the monks' comfortable cells – each has its own bedroom, study, chapel and walled garden. The tour ends in the refectory, which has ceiling frescoes by Bergognone and an elaborately carved pulpit, from where prayers are read to the silent diners. The Certosa is open 09:00–11:30 and 14:30–17:30 Tuesday–Sunday, although closing times may vary between summer and winter.

BERGAMO

Lying some 51km (31 miles) northeast of Milan, Bergamo can easily be reached by train, or by car using the Autostrada Serenissima, although parking can be very difficult. Bergamo was an independent city-state or *comune* during the 12th century, but after 1329 it came under Visconti control. Then, for the next 350 years, it was an outpost of the Venetian Empire – which explains the large number of statues of Venetian lions to be seen around the city. Bergamo is divided into two parts – the hilltop settlement of **Città Alta**, ringed by Venetian defensive walls, and **Città Bassa**, which spreads across the plains below. Bergamo has a proud military history, producing the famous Venetian *condottiere* Bartolomeo Colleoni and raising the largest contingent of any city for Garibaldi's Red Shirts.

Città Bassa

Life in the modern lower town centres around the main square, Piazza Matteotti. Here we find tree-lined arcades or *senterione* with their popular cafés, and the **Teatro Donizetti**, named after the locally born opera composer. In Lower Bergamo there is an excellent art gallery, the **Pinacoteca dell'Accademia Carrara**. It is housed in an old palace in Via San Tomaso and is one of the top galleries in northern Italy. Works by Botticelli, Bellini and Titian are complemented by international artists such as Van Dyck and Brueghel. It is open Tuesday–Sunday 09:00–13:00 and 14:30–17:30. Admission is free on Sundays.

Città Alta

The Viale Vittorio Emanuele II leads to the lower station of the funicular railway that takes you up into the heart of the Città Alta. From the upper station it is just a short walk to the charming **Piazza Vecchia**, which is surrounded by a wonderful collection of medieval and Renaissance buildings. In the centre of the square is a low-slung fountain protected by rather badly eroded Venetian lions. On Sunday mornings, tables are set up in the square for chess competitions. Dominating the piazza is the 12th-century **Torre Civica**, some 52m (170ft) high. Steps or the lift lead to the belfry, affording panoramic views over the roofs of Bergamo and also the surrounding countryside. The belfry has a 15th-century clock, and a huge bell still tolls 180 times at 22:00 for the nightly curfew. At the upper end of the Piazza Vecchia is the 12th-

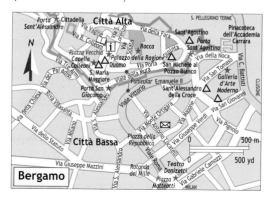

Below: *A lion, symbol of the Venetian empire, guards the entrance to Bergamo's Basilica of Santa Maria Maggiore.*

century **Palazzo della Ragione**. A sloping covered stairway leads to the upper floor, which has a stone balcony and a Lion of St Mark in relief. The palace can only be visited when it is staging an exhibition.

The arches under the palace lead to the smaller, more intimate **Piazza Duomo**. Immediately ahead is the **Basilica of Santa Maria Maggiore**. Although much of the exterior of this church is hidden by other buildings, it is clear that it is one of the finest Romanesque churches in northern Italy. The delicate porch, built by Giovanni da Campione in 1360, is guarded by more Venetian lions. The interior is quite stunning, graced by some superb Flemish tapestries. Donizetti's tomb is tucked away against the west wall. Head for the presbytery where there are wonderful tarsias (inlaid woodwork) showing Old Testament scenes. Open Monday–Saturday 09:00–12:30 and 14:30–18:00.

In comparison, the nearby 15th-century **Duomo** is something of an anticlimax, but worth looking around for its artworks. On the other side of the Basilica of Santa Maria Maggiore is another gem – the **Colleoni Chapel**. Dating from the 1470s, the chapel was designed by Amadeo for the tomb of the *condottiere* Bartolomeo Colleoni, and the sacristy of the basilica was knocked down to accommodate it. The incredibly ornate façade is built of polychromatic marbles and is a riot of lateral and rose windows, columns and balustrades leading up to the lantern-crowned dome. The interior of the chapel is equally impressive. On the top of Colleoni's tomb is an equestrian statue, while on another wall is the captain's daughter's tomb. Excellent paintings by Tiepolo line the dome. The chapel is open Tue–Sun 09:00–12:00 and 14:30–18:30.

The Città Alta also has several interesting churches, a Civic Archaeology Museum, a Natural History Museum with a life-sized reconstruction of a mammoth, a botanical garden, and two small museums devoted to Donizetti. If a picnic is the order of the day, then head for the **Rocca**. This is a ruined section of the old defensive fortifications, which has now been converted into shady gardens with fine views over the city and the surrounding plain.

Above: *The dome of Santa Maria Maggiore – Bergamo's finest church.*

CREMONA

The town of Cremona sits on the north bank of the River Po, to the southeast of Milan. It can be reached by train in around two hours. If you come by car, head for the Via Villa Glori car park, where you can exchange your vehicle for a bicycle for the day.

As with most of the towns of the Lombardy Plain, Cremona has had a chequered history. It was founded by the Romans but after the decline of their Empire it was repeatedly sacked by the Goths and Huns. Under the Lombards it became an independent *comune*. Later it came under the control of Milan's great dynasties, the Viscontis and the Sforzas, before becoming successively ruled by the Venetians, the Spanish and the Austrians. Among Cremona's famous sons are Virgil the Roman poet, Stradivarius the violin-maker and Claudio Monteverdi, one of the founders of opera as an art form.

Life in Cremona centres around the large but elegant **Piazza del Comune**, which is dominated by the imposing 112m (370ft) **Torrazzo**. Built around 1250, it is reputedly the tallest bell tower in Italy. It is open 10:30–13:00 and 15:00–18:00 Tuesday–Sunday, April–October. From November–February it is open from 15:00–18:00 on Saturdays only. There are 502 steps to the top, but the climb is well worth the effort for the exceptional views.

Alongside the tower, and linked to it by a portico, is the **Duomo**. The original church on the site was destroyed by an earthquake in 1117 and rebuilt by the Comacini masons, salvaging the original main door. The Duomo was originally a basilica, but when Gothic became the flavour of the day the two transepts were added. Recent restoration has revealed some primitive frescoes. Also of interest are the Flemish tapestries, the twin pulpits, and the beautiful choir stalls inlaid with views of Cremona. Also in the Piazza del Comune are the **Battistero di San Giovanni** dating from 1167 and the **Loggia dei Militi** which has an outdoor pulpit used by the popular preachers of the time. Behind the loggia is the **Palazzo del Comune**. It dates from 1206 and is now the town hall.

Cremona is, of course, famous for its violins. The industry was started in the 16th century by the Amati family and followed on by Guarneri and Stradivarius. Today more than 50 violin-makers keep up the tradition. A comprehensive view of the subject can be enjoyed at the **Museo Stradivariano** in Via Pedestro, with more memorabilia at the **Museo Civico**, which also has a good section on archaeology. The School of Violin and Viola Makers also has a museum of stringed instruments at the **Palazzo dell'Arte**. Cremona has a clutch of fine churches, the best of which is 11th-century **Sant'Agata** in Corso Garibaldi, with some impressive frescoes.

MANTUA (MANTOVA)

Although it is a two-hour train journey from Milan, Mantau is well worth the effort of getting there. Its setting is unpromising – in the middle of a flat plain and almost completely surrounded by water where the River Mincio has swollen out into three lakes: Lago Superiore, Lago di Mezzo and Lago Inferiore. Influenced by the water, Mantua's climate can be raw and foggy in winter and hazy and humid in the summer.

Mantua had an uneventful history until it became an independent *comune* under the influence of the Gonzaga dynasty, which for three centuries ensured a peaceful way of life. The Gonzagas were enthusiastic

---

HOME-GROWN FIREWATER

Those wishing to have a drink for effect rather than for taste will find that **grappa** fits the bill. This colourless spirit gains its name from the *graspa*, the detritus of the grapes after the wine has been fermented. These dregs are then distilled to make grappa. It is produced in **Bassano di Grappa**, halfway between Lake Garda and Venice, but is available all over northern Italy. Its acquired taste being such, it is probably not surprising that it was used as a medicine in the Middle Ages!

sponsors of art and encouraged promising painters to take up residence in their court. The most important of these was Andrea Mantegna. After the Gonzagas' fall and the Austrian occupation, it was downhill all the way for Mantua, with the majority of the Gonzagas' art treasures scattered around the art galleries of Europe. Today, it has spawned some ugly Fascist-era suburbs and some nasty industrial estates on the outskirts, yet the centre of the town is virtually unspoiled, with four interconnecting cobbled squares and a host of restored palaces and churches, making this one of the gems of northern Italy.

Most of the monumental buildings are found in the northeast corner of the town. As you approach from the Lago di Mezzo, where cars can be parked, you reach the imposing **Castello di San Giorgio** guarding the entrance to the town. The castle was built between 1395 and 1400 during the time of Francesco I Gonzaga (open Tue–Sun 08:45–19:15, tel: 037 224 832, www.mantovaducale.it). Opposite the castle on the right-hand side of the road is the House of Rigoletto, with a statue of the court jester in the garden.

You now approach Mantua's largest square, the **Piazza Sordello**. Almost the whole of the southeast side of the square is taken up with the façade of the **Palazzo Ducale**, the home of the Gonzagas. The huge complex is almost like a city in itself, with streets, courtyards, gardens and over 500 rooms covering 34,000m²

> ### TOILETS
>
> Public toilets are almost non-existent in Italy. Where they can be found, they may be in a less than hygienic condition. Do what the Italians do – slip into the nearest bar or even hotel foyer and use their facilities. This is standard practice and will not cause offence.

Below: *Mantua's main square, the busy Piazza Sordello.*

(366,860 sq ft). When the building was ransacked in 1630, it is said that it took 80 carriages to take away the 2000 works of art. There are three main structures – the original **Corte Vecchia**, the 14th-century **Castello**, and the **Corte Nuovo**. Visits are by guided tour only and they take about 1½ hours. The highlights of the tour are the **Camera degli Sposi**, containing Mantegna's frescoes of the Gonzaga family, and the private **apartments of Isabella d'Este**, which include some miniature rooms, once thought to be for the dwarfs whom she collected to cheer her up! The Palazzo Ducale is open 08:45–19:15 Tuesday–Sunday; June–September until 23:00.

Opposite the Palazzo Ducale on the corner of Piazza Sordello is the **Duomo** (Cattedrale San Pietro). Built in the 13th century, the façade is neoclassical, the side facing the square is Gothic, and other parts of the exterior, including the bell tower, have Romanesque elements. The interior is more interesting, having been rebuilt by Giulio Romano after a fire in 1545. It has a nave and four broad aisles divided by elegant fluted columns (open 07:00–12:00 and 15:00–19:00). On the other side of the square are the **Bonacolsi Palaces** from pre-Gonzaga times. Rising from their crenellated roofs is the notorious **Torre della Gabbia**, said to contain an iron torture cage in which prisoners were suspended over the city.

An archway leads through to the **Piazza Broletto**, where we find the town hall containing the **Museo Tazio Nuvolari**, dedicated to a local hero who was a racing driver. Another portico marks the entrance to the charming **Piazza dell'Erbe**, lined with arcaded cafés and stalls. Sunk slightly below the level of the square is Mantua's oldest church, the 11th-century **Rotonda di San Lorenzo**, said to be modelled on the Church of the Holy Sepulchre in Jerusalem. It has been sympathetically restored during recent years and it is possible to see some 12th- and 13th-century frescoes (open 10:00–12:00 and 14:30–16:30).

Below: *The Rotonda di San Lorenzo, Mantua's oldest church.*

Dominating the nearby **Piazza Mantegna** is the **Basilica di Sant'Andrea**, designed by Alberti. The façade takes the form of a triumphal arch, while the interior is based on the traditional design of an Etruscan temple with a single barrel-vaulted nave and numerous high-arched side chapels. The tomb of Andrea Mantegna

Above: *A wedding scene at the Basilica di Sant'Andrea in Mantua.*

is in the first chapel on the left. The dome, which was completed in 1782, rises to 80m (262ft). Under the dome is an octagonal balustrade, which is immediately above the crypt. This houses two sacred reliquaries said to contain the blood of Christ and given to St Andrew by Longinus, the Roman centurion who pierced Christ's side with a lance.

On the southern outskirts of Mantua is the summer residence of the Gonzagas, the **Palazzo Tè**. It was built by Federico Gonzaga as a retreat from the Palazzo Ducale where he could see his horses and his mistress, Isabella Boschetta, who was not approved of by Federico's mother. The word *tè*, incidentally, comes from *tejeto*, meaning drainage canal. The complex was designed by Giulio Romano and it is considered to be his greatest work. The main attraction for visitors is the series of rooms with extraordinary frescoes, trompe l'oeil and paintings, showing that Romano was given full permission to shock and amaze. Many of the classical frescoes are erotic, even vaguely pornographic, but never dull. The **Sala dei Cavalli** has portraits of the best horses from the Gonzaga stable; the **Sala di Psyche** has frescoes showing the wedding banquet of Cupid and Psyche; and in the **Sala dei Giganti** there is a remarkable fresco showing Jupiter's rage towards the Titans who had dared to climb Mount Olympus. The Palazzo Tè is open Monday 13:00–18:00, Tuesday–Sunday 09:00–18:00.

A VARIETY OF PASTA

A pasta course is an essential part of an Italian meal, but the pasta itself and the sauces that go with it vary tremendously. There are said to be over 100 varieties of pasta, depending on its shape. It can, for example, be flat, tubular, straw-like, twirled, conch-like, rolled or filled. It can also vary in its ingredients, with flour, eggs, oil and salt forming the basics. The sauces to accompany the pasta change according to the region.

Excursions From Milan at a Glance

All the cities mentioned in this chapter are on the Plain of Lombardy, which is notorious for its days of raw fog in the winter and the heat and humidity in the summer. Choose spring and autumn for the most comfortable sightseeing weather. Local saints' days are always enjoyable times to visit, but accommodation may be hard to find on these occasions.

All the historic towns mentioned are within easy reach of Milan. A **car** can give flexibility and convenience; the efficient *autostrada* system allows distances to be covered quickly. Visitors wishing to use public transport will find that all the towns are linked with Milan by **rail** and in many cases by **bus**.

All the towns described have compact historic cores, where most of the sites can easily be visited on foot. Indeed, in many cases cars may be banned. Otherwise, **taxis** are readily available.

Cheaper hotels tend to be booked up with immigrant workers and few can be recommended. Hotels close to Milan can be fully booked well in advance during trade fair weeks.

LUXURY

Hotel de la Ville, viale Regina Margherita 15, Monza, tel: 039 39421, fax: 039 367 647, www.hoteldelaville.com The town's top hotel with a view overlooking the park.

Moderno, viale Vittorio Emanuele II 41, Pavia, tel: 0382 303 401, fax: 0382 25225, www.hotelmoderno.it Close to the railway station.

Excelsior San Marco, piazza della Repubblica 6, Bergamo, tel: 035 366 111, fax: 035 223 201, www.hotelsanmarco.com One of the best hotels in town with air-conditioned rooms and a reputable restaurant.

Impero, piazza della Pace 21, Cremona, tel: 0372 413 013, www.hotelimpero.cr.it An Art Deco palace provides a wonderful setting for this hotel.

San Lorenzo, Piazza Concordia 14, Mantua, tel: 0376 220 500, fax: 0376 327 194, www.hotel sanlorenzo.it Delightful setting overlooking the Piazza dell'Erbe. Leisure facilities.

MID-RANGE

Excelsior, piazza Stazione 25, Pavia, tel: 0382 28596, fax: 0382 26030, www.excelsior. pavia.com Comfortable hotel in a handy location.

San Vigilio, via San Vigilio 15, Bergamo, tel/fax: 035 253 179, www.sanvigilio.it Marvellous position near the top of the western funicular.

Duomo, via Gonfalonieri 13, Cremona, tel: 0372 35242. A short walk from the Piazza del Comune. Good restaurant.

ABC, piazza Don Leoni 25, Mantua, tel: 0376 323 347. Rooms round a courtyard. Close to station.

BUDGET

Aurora, viale Vittorio Emanuele II 25, Pavia, tel: 0382 23664, fax: 0382 21248. Has showers in all rooms. Close to station.

Astoria, via Bordigallo 19, Cremona, tel: 0372 461 616, fax: 0372 461 810. Popular, near the Piazza del Comune.

Peter Pan, citadella Piazza Giulia 3, tel: 0376 392 637. Mantua's only cheap hotel, a few minutes' walk across the lake.

Bed and Breakfast

Bergamo has a thriving B&B scene in some atmospheric locations (www.bedand bergamo.it).

Youth Hostel

The only one is in Bergamo: **Youth Hostel**, via G. Ferraris 1, Bergamo, tel: 035 361 724. Out of town – take no. 14 bus.

Camp Sites

Three handily placed sites: **Ticino**, via Mascherpa 10, Pavia, tel: 0382 527 094. Open April–November. No. 4 bus from the railway station.

Parco al Po, Via Longo Po Europa, Cremona, tel: 0372 21268, fax: 0372 27137. Open May–September. Take the no. 1 bus from the railway station.

Corte Chiara, Porto Mantovano outskirts, Mantua, tel: 0376 390

804. Open May–September. This is a small site, so booking is essential.

Eating out in the historic cities of the Plain of Lombardy is generally cheaper than in Milan, but there is not the wide range of international cuisine. Local and regional specialities are the order of the day, such as the notorious Spezzatino di Mantua – donkey stew. Restaurants with outside tables in the main squares of the towns are likely to be more expensive than those in side streets.

LUXURY

Ceresole, via Ceresole 4, Cremona, tel: 0372 30990. High-class Cremonese cuisine.
L'Aquila Nigra, via Vicolo Bonacolsi 4, Mantua, tel: 0376 366 751, www.aquila nigra.it All Mantua's local specialities in a frescoed dining room near the Palazzo Ducale. Closed Mondays.
Da Vittorio, via Giovanni XXIII 21, Bergamo, tel: 035 218 060. One of Italy's top restaurants. Specializes in seafood. Closed Wednesday.
Hotel de la Ville's Derby Grill, viale Regina Margherita 15, Monza, tel: 039 382 581. The best food in Monza.
Locanda Vecchia Pavia, via Cardinal Riboldi 2, Pavia, tel: 0382 304 132. Ancient restaurant next to the cathedral, serving local dishes in nouvelle cuisine style.

MID-RANGE

Vesuvio, piazza Libertà 10, Cremona, tel: 0372 434 858. Reasonably priced local food.
Pavesi, Piazza dell'Erbe, Mantua, tel: 0376 323 627. Friendly restaurant, one of several in the atmospheric little square. Local specialities. Closed on Thursdays.
Al Garibaldini, via S. Longino 7, Mantua, tel: 0376 328 263. Restaurant in a characterful house in the historic core. Closed on Wednesdays.
Taverna del Colleoni, Piazza Vecchia, Bergamo, tel: 035 232 596. Atmospheric restaurant in the old square, serving classical Italian food. Closed on Mondays.
Antica Osteria del Vino Buono, Piazza Mercato delle Scarpe, Bergamo, tel: 035 247 993. Friendly *osteria* next to the upper funicular station. Closed on Mondays.
Dell'Uva, piazza Carrobiolo 2, Monza, tel: 039 323 825. Reasonably priced regional food in the centre of town.
Antica Osteria del Previ, via Milazzo 65, Pavia, tel: 0382 26203. Closed Monday. On the bank of the Ticino River. Noted for its frogs' legs, snails and river fish.

BUDGET

Head for pizzerias and small trattorias for budget food.
Fragoletta Antica Osteria, piazza Arche 5, Mantua, tel: 0376 323 300. Little ambience, but great cooking. Closed on Mondays.

Pizzeria Cremonese, piazza Roma 39, Cremona. Pizzas plus local dishes.
La Colombina, borgo Canale 12, Bergamo, tel: 035 261 402. Terrace restaurant serving local specialities. Closed on Mondays.
Piedigrotto, corso Libertà 15, Mantua, tel: 0376 327 014. Good traditional pizzas. Closed on Wednesdays.

There are **APT Tourist Information Offices** in the following towns:
Cremona: Piazza del Comune, opposite the Duomo. Open 09:00–12:00 and 15:00–18:00 Monday–Saturday, 09:45–12:00 Sunday, tel: 0372 23233, www.aptcremona.it Apart from maps and brochures, they have a list of violin-makers' workshops.
Mantua: Piazza Mantegna 6, tel: 0376 432 432, www.turismo.mantova.it Open daily 09:00–19:00. They have a useful map of the town with information on the major sites.
Bergamo: viale Vittorio Emanuele II 20. Open 09:00–12:30 and 14:00–17:30 Monday–Friday, tel: 035 210 204, website: www.apt.bergamo.it Another office in Bergamo Alta is at Vicolo Aquila Nera 2, off the Piazza Vecchia, and it is open all year round, tel: 035 242 226.
Pavia: via F. Filzi 2, tel: 0382 22156. Open 08:30–12:30 and 14:00–18:00 Monday–Saturday, www.apt.pavia.it

4
Lakes Maggiore, Orta and Varese

Lake Maggiore stretches for 64km (40 miles) from north to south, making it the second largest of the northern Italian lakes. The lake is fed by the **River Ticino** from the north and the **River Toce** from the northwest. It is drained in the south by the Ticino, which runs in a large arc to the west of Milan, before joining the Po at Pavia. The most northerly one-fifth of Lake Maggiore is in the Swiss Canton of Ticino, with the stylish **Locarno** its main town. The western shore of the lake is in Piedmont, but the eastern shore comes under the administration of Lombardy.

The Romans called Maggiore *Lacus Verbanus* after the verbena plant that grows prolifically around its shores. Maggiore had close links with dynastic families such as the **Viscontis** and the **Borromeos**. The latter still own large tracts of land and islands in the area. In the 19th century, Lake Maggiore was an important and enjoyable part of the **Grand Tour**, and writers, artists and musicians, such as Goethe, Byron and Toscanini, frequently visited the lake. Queen Victoria stayed at Baveno and English tourists have been coming to Lake Maggiore ever since.

The leading resort on the lake is **Stresa**, which overlooks the enchanting **Borromean Islands**, an essential excursion for all visitors. A road encircles the lake and it is possible to drive its 162km (100 miles) in a day, but most visitors would want to take longer to enjoy Lake Maggiore's charms. To the west of Maggiore is the smaller **Lake Orta**. Its main attraction is the town of **San Giulio** and the island of the same name. East of Maggiore are a clutch of smaller lakes, the largest of which is **Lake Varese**.

DON'T MISS

★★★ **Borromean Islands:** Isola Madre, Isola dei Pescatori and Isola Bella should be on everyone's itinerary.
★★★ **Orta San Giulio** and **Isola San Giulio:** the village and island are star attractions.
★★ **Stresa:** an important and well-situated resort.
★★ **Statue of San Carlo Borromeo:** enormous 23m (75ft) statue of one of Milan's best-known archbishops.
★★ **Villa Taranto:** early 20th-century gardens near Pallanza.
★ **Sacro Monte:** 21 chapels with over 350 statues.

Opposite: *Lake Maggiore, with the Borromean Islands, viewed from Stresa.*

THE SWISS NORTH

The northern 20 per cent of Lake Maggiore is in Swiss territory, where the main town is **Locarno**. Once under the control of Milan, it fell into Swiss hands in 1512 and has remained there ever since. Locarno has a sheltered south-facing position and it has developed over the years as a health resort. The **Locarno International Film Festival** is held in the town every August. It has a popular **casino** in Lago Zorsi 1 (open 12:00–02:00 Sunday–Thursday; 12:00–04:00 Friday–Saturday). The town is distinguished by pleasant public gardens, elegant squares and galleried shops. The 14th-century **Castello Visconti** was partially destroyed by the Swiss and its remains now house a small museum containing a strange mixture of archaeological artefacts and modern art (open April–October 10:00–12:00 and 14:00–17:00 Tuesday–Sunday). It is also worth taking the cable car to the **Church of Madonna del Sasso**, which dates from 1480. Its altarpiece displays the *Flight Into Egypt*, by Bramantino. A chair lift then leads up to **Cimetta di Cardado** at a height of 1671m (5482ft), from where there are spectacular views along the lake.

Below: *The waterfront at Locarno is backed by wooded hills.*

Separated from Locarno by the reedy delta of the River Maggia is the small town of **Ascona**. Once a small fishing port, it is now growing as a resort with a strong German influence and attracting a lively artistic community. Just offshore is a group of small islands known as the **Isoli di Brissago**, the largest of which has some subtropical gardens and a 16th-century church. The town of **Brissago**, after which the islands were named, is the last settlement before the Italian border is reached. Brissago is a minor health resort, but ironically the town is dominated by its huge tobacco factory.

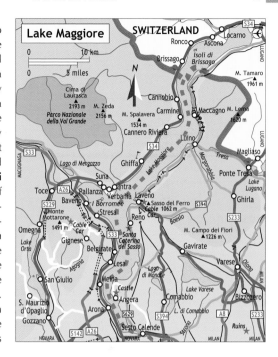

Lake Maggiore

SWITZERLAND

THE PIEDMONT SHORE OF LAKE MAGGIORE

The first settlement of any size on the Piedmont shore is the medieval town of **Cannobio**. With small squares, cobbled alleys and an attractive lake frontage, it is a pleasant place to stop for a few hours, particularly on a Sunday when there is a quayside market. The main place of historic interest in Cannobio is the **Santuario della Pietà**, a church built to house the miraculous picture of the dead Christ, which was once said to have shed real blood (*see* panel, page 71). A scenic excursion from Cannobio is up the valley behind the town, leading to a spectacular gorge and the little church of **Santa Ana**. The narrow mountain road eventually reaches the **Val Vigezzo**, the valley followed by the spectacular Domodossola–Locarno railway.

As the road approaches **Cannero Riviera**, a group of

FACTS ABOUT LAKE MAGGIORE

Length:
64km (40 miles).
Average width:
4.8km (3 miles).
Maximum depth:
372m (1220ft).
Water area:
215km² (84 sq miles).

Above: *A ferry runs from the town of Intra, on the western arm of Lake Maggiore, to Laveno.*

small, low rocky islands can be seen close to the shore. Capped with ruined castles, they were once the haunt of a group of extremely bloodthirsty brigands, who were eventually dealt with by the Viscontis. Cannero is almost a mirror image of Cannobio, with cobbled streets, picturesque houses and an attractive little harbour. The next stop is **Ghiffa**, which once had an important hat-making industry, but the factory, once the largest in Italy, closed in 1981. You can, however, learn about the industry at the local **Hat Museum** (open 15:30–18:30 Saturday and Sunday throughout the year).

A minor conurbation has been formed at a fork in the lake. The towns of Intra, Pallanza and Suna were merged in 1939 to form **Verbania**. The most industrial of the three is Intra, which gets its name from its situation between two streams. A car ferry, the only one on Lake Maggiore, runs across to Laveno, the journey taking 20 minutes (for information, tel: 03 233 1480). Pallanza has an attractive lake frontage with parks and gardens, including a string of exuberant fountains, backed by restaurants and bars. It is worth visiting the **Church of San Leonardo**, which is close to the waterfront. This dates back to the 16th century and its 65m (213ft) bell tower is an imposing landmark. Back in the town, in Piazza Cavour is the **Museo del Paesaggio**, a museum of landscape painting set in an old palace. There are also some sculptures and some local archaeological finds (open 10:00–12:00 and 15:30–18:30 Tuesday–Sunday April–October). Just offshore is the **Isolino di San Giovanni**, the fourth and smallest of the Borromean Islands and the only one that cannot be visited.

It was a favourite hideaway of Arturo Toscanini, the conductor. A major attraction at Verbania is the **Villa Taranto** (*see* panel, page 72). The villa itself is not open to the public, but is widely used for congresses and conferences – the EU prime ministers met there recently. The gardens are open daily from 08:30–18:30 or sunset, April–October (www.villataranto.it).

Between Verbania and the Via Vigezzo is the **Parco Nazionale della Val Grande**, a true wilderness and the least inhabited area of the Alps. Although the park only rises to just over 2000m (6500ft) there are spectacular views of the Alps to the north. There are barren peaks, steep-sided gorges, bubbling streams and forests at lower levels, along with a vast array of Alpine flowers. This is good hiking country for the experienced mountain enthusiast, but there are few trails and only a small number of spartan huts.

A small arm of Lake Maggiore leads northwest to meet the road from the Simplon Pass. The road runs close to the small reed-fringed **Lago di Mergozzo**, once part of the main lake but cut off by silt deposits from the river. The lakeside road now swings back southeastwards towards the resort of **Baveno**, made popular by

THE SANTUARIO DELLA PIETÀ

Back in 1522 a picture of the dead Christ being taken down from the cross was hanging in a house in Cannobio when a strange thing occurred – Christ's wounds in the picture began to bleed. Shortly afterwards Cannobio was spared when all the towns around were decimated by the plague. San Carlo Borromeo decreed that this was a miracle and ordered that a church should be built to house the picture, which was put in an elaborate frame. It can be seen today in the Santuario della Pietà – although, oddly, there is no sign of any blood stains on the picture.

Left: *Stresa's hotels and restaurants are among the best in the Italian lake area.*

VILLA TARANTO

The villa was built in 1875, but by the turn of the century it had become derelict. Both the villa and the land were bought in 1931 by a Scots captain, Neil McEacharn. He spent the next 10 years creating the finest botanical gardens in northern Italy. Covering some 20ha (65 acres), they contain over 20,000 species of plants, including Amazonian lilies, maples, bottle brushes, monkey puzzles, handkerchief trees and many more. The gardens are particularly attractive in late spring, when the azaleas and rhodo-dendrons are in full bloom. As McEacharn had no des-cendants, he left the gardens and villa to the Italian state.

Below: *Stresa's lake shore is graced by elegant hotels and attractive gardens.*

Queen Victoria, who stayed here at the Villa Clara (now known as the Castello Branca). The town is backed by a huge pink cliff, marking the granite quarries that supplied the material for Milan's Galleria Vittorio Emanuele II and the Basilica of St Paul's in Rome. Graceful villas line the road and shoreline, while in the centre of the town the 11th-century church of **Santi Gervasio e Protasio** in the main square has a 12th-century façade and a Romanesque bell tower. It is worth seeking out Baveno's most photographed building, the **Casa Morandi**, with its highly original exterior stairways.

STRESA

Without doubt, Stresa is the most attractive town on Lake Maggiore, its popularity having increased considerably after the opening of the Simplon Tunnel in 1906. Its string of large and elegant hotels along the lake shore are widely used by tour parties and for conferences. Lush gardens and villas line the shore from where there are stunning views of the Borromean Islands. The old town centre focuses on the triangular **Piazza Cadorna**, with its pavement cafés and boutiques. From here cobbled alleyways lead in all directions. Among Stresa's attractions are the **Villa Pallavicino**, a botanical garden and animal park to the south of the town (open 09:00–18:00 from March–October), and **Villa Ducale**, with a small museum and connections with the Catholic philosopher, Antonio Rosmini (open daily 09:00–12:00 and 15:00–18:00).

EXCURSIONS FROM STRESA

Just north of Stresa, a cable car climbs up to **Monte Mottarone**, 1491m (4891ft), from where there are superb views of the

lake and away to Monte Rosa and other Alpine peaks. The cable car runs at half-hourly intervals, from 09:30–17:30, taking 18 minutes to reach the top station. From here, there are a number of hiking routes, and mountain bikes can be hired. It is also possible to drive up to Monte Mottarone via a toll road, passing en route the **Giardino Alpinia**. These Alpine rock gardens are a must for keen botanists (open from 09:00–18:00 Tuesday–Saturday, April–October; 09:00–18:30 Sundays and holidays). Also en route, in the hamlet of Gignese, is quite an unusual **Umbrella Museum**, devoted to the history and making of umbrellas, once an important industry in these parts (open 10:00–12:00 and 15:00–18:00 Tuesday–Sunday, April–September).

Above: *The Alpine village of Macugnaga is easily reached from Stresa.*

Macugnaga ★★

A coach trip to Macugnaga, Alpine village and ski resort, is a very popular excursion from Stresa. The route initially follows the Dossola River past the Candoglia marble quarries and then heads west into the Anzasca Valley through some spectacular scenery. Many more quarries are seen near Castiglione and these have supplied the marble steps for the United Nations building in New York. The valley becomes increasingly narrow and eventually the village of **Macugnaga** is reached. With its wooden chalets, Alpine cattle and the backdrop of the snow-

SAN CARLO BORROMEO (1538–84)

Charles Borromeo was undoubtedly the most influential and distinguished churchman of his day. He was a cardinal by the age of 22 and became Archbishop of Milan when he was 26 – a startling rise up the career ladder helped by a push from below by his uncle, Pope Pius IV. San Carlo did, however, fulfil a strong disciplinary role in the church, saving sacred church music and ending the somewhat comfortable life of the clergy. In doing so he made enemies, and survived an assassination attempt in Milan Cathedral. But he was a courageous man and risked his life comforting the victims of the plague. He was canonized in 1610 and his feast day is on 4 November.

Above: *Isola dei Pescatori is notable for its fine fish restaurants.*
Opposite: *Terraced gardens with statues and exotic plants form the eastern end of Isola Bella.*

capped peaks of **Monte Rosa** reaching up to 4638m (14,136ft), this is a totally different world to Lake Maggiore. Macugnaga is a popular ski resort, and a cable car and chair lift lead up to the slopes above the tree line. The village itself has a pretty square with a tourist office and a number of restaurants and bars. The church is worth a visit. Although plain on the exterior, with a short copper spire, the interior is flamboyant and ornate, more in the Spanish style – which is perhaps not surprising as the Spaniards occupied the valley for 200 years.

The Hundred Valleys Line ★★

Another excursion from Stresa that will particularly appeal to the railway enthusiasts is the trip along the **Vigezzo Valley**. A train is taken to Domodossola, where a change is made to a light railway. This runs along the Vigezzo, a route known as the **Hundred Valleys** because of the vast number of tributaries that join the main valley. The line ends up at **Locarno**, where there is time for shopping before taking the lake steamer back to Stresa, making a magnificent day out.

THE BORROMEAN ISLANDS

The Borromeo family became the rulers of this part of northern Italy in the 15th century and still own much of the area today, including the four little islands that occupy the northwest arm of Lake Maggiore. **Isolino di San Giovanni** is privately owned and not accessible to visitors, but the other three islands form the major tourist attraction in the whole of the Italian lakes. All three are readily accessible by ferry and motor launch from Stresa, Baveno and Pallanza. A night trip around the islands when they are floodlit is a memorable experience.

Isola Madre

This is the largest island and the nearest to Pallanza. It is open to the public from mid-March to late September 09:00–17:30. There are superb informal gardens that are particularly attractive in late spring, with azaleas, rhododendrons and hydrangeas, plus a host of specimen trees, dominated by a huge 300-year-old weeping silver cupressus. There is a small aviary, and white peacocks and ornamental pheasants strut around at will. Guided tours are available around the 16th-century villa, which has a collection of paintings and is the home of the Borromeo family's puppet theatre (see panel, page 74). There is a small restaurant near the landing stage.

Isola dei Pescatori ★★★

This island was once a working fishing village and it is still possible to see the occasional fishing net hanging up to dry and a few of the distinctive fishing boats with their curved roofs and large lights. Most of the fishing now takes place at night in the quieter northern part of the lake. Take time to wander around the picturesque cobbled alleys and sample a fish lunch at one of the

ROCK AND STONE

The area to the northwest of Lake Maggiore is renowned for the quality of its building stones. Very noticeable from the lake is the pink cliff behind the town of **Baveno**. This is the granite quarry that supplied the stone for La Scala Opera House and the Galleria Vittorio Emanuele II in Milan. On the eastern side of the Dossola Valley are the **Baveno** marble quarries that supplied the material for Milan's Duomo. They are still open today but are only allowed to provide marble for repairs to the cathedral – and nowhere else. The **Anzasca Valley** has a whole string of quarries that supply fine marble all over the world, including that used for the steps of the UnitedNations building in New York.

A Giant of a Man

Just outside the lakeside town of **Arona** is the enormous statue of **San Carlo Borromeo**. Commissioned by Federico, a nephew of San Carlo, it was designed by Cerano in 1614 and erected in 1624. Made of copper, the statue is 23.4m (77ft) in height and rests on a stone plinth 11.7m (38ft) high. The head has a circumference of 6.50m (21ft), the eyes are 0.5m (1.6ft) wide, the nose is 0.85m (2.8ft) long and the thumb is 1.4m (4.5ft) long – surely the greatest saint ever!

lakeside restaurants. The 11th-century (but much renovated) little church is also worth a visit, along with the immaculately kept adjacent cemetery.

Isola Bella

This is the nearest of the islands to Stresa and tends to be the most crowded. In the 17th century Carlo III Borromeo decided that he would convert what was a flat rocky island into a paradise for his wife Isabella. He commissioned the architect, Angelo Crivelli, to carry out the transformation. Tons of earth were brought from the mainland to create a garden of ten terraces in the formal Italian style, with fountains, grottoes and statues of gods and cherubs, complemented by exotic shrubs and trees. The gardens culminate at the eastern end of the island with a huge ornate terrace looking like the bridge of a liner – just a little 'over the top'. A sumptuous **palazzo** (open 09:00–17:30 mid-March to late September) was also built, with a number of impressive rooms. You can see, for instance, the bedroom where Napoleon and Josephine slept in 1797, rooms devoted to arms, medals and musical instruments, a library, a room full of 16th-century Flemish tapestry, and six grotto rooms decorated with shells, stones and volcanic material. Best of all is the richly decorated Great Hall. Many of the rooms have valuable paintings and frescoes, while nearly all have the most dazzling Murano glass chandeliers. Try to join a tour, as the guides are famously witty.

SOUTH OF STRESA

There is ribbon development along the lake shore south of Stresa, with the settlements of **Belgirate**, **Lesa**, which has a ruined medieval castle, and **Meina**. The first town of any size, however, is

Left: *Part of the historic town of Arona, protected by a Borromeo fortress.*
Opposite: *The massive statue of San Carlo Borromeo towers over the southern end of Lake Maggiore.*

Arona. A strategic route centre and market town, it was protected by a Borromeo fortress, or *rocca*, but it is now in ruins as it was dismantled by Napoleon. Head for the attractive little Piazza del Populo, where the 15th-century Casa del Podestà has an arched portico. Also in the square is the 16th-century church of Madonna di Piazza. Two other churches that are worth a look are Santa Maria, which has a Borromeo family chapel, and Santi Martiri, with delightful 16th-century stained-glass windows. Most people come to Arona, however, to see the enormous **Statue of San Carlo Borromeo**, the famous 16th-century Archbishop of Milan (*see* panel, page 76).

THE LOMBARDY SHORE OF LAKE MAGGIORE

Although far quieter than the Piedmont side of the lake, the eastern shore does, however, have plenty to see.

Angera

Opposite Arona is the small town of Angera, dominated by the **Rocca di Angera**, a castle built initially by the Lombards on Roman foundations. Considering that it was fought over by the Franks, the Torrianis and the Viscontis before finally being taken by the Borromeos, it is in remarkably good condition. There are a number of frescoes inside, mainly glorifying the victories of the Viscontis, plus an unusual doll museum (*see* panel, this page). The castle and museum are open 09:00–17:30 daily Easter–October.

ANGERA'S DOLL MUSEUM

The castle at Angera near the southern point of Lake Maggiore has seen much fierce fighting. It was successively a stronghold of the Lombards, the Viscontis and the Borromeos. It comes as a surprise, therefore, to see that this now houses, of all things, a **doll museum**, with a comprehensive collection of Italian dolls ranging from the late 18th century through to the modern dolls of today. As well as viewing the immaculately preserved items, it is also possible to buy dolls from one of Italy's finest doll-makers.

Santa Caterina del Sasso

A few kilometres north of Angera is the former Dominican monastery of **Santa Caterina del Sasso**. Perched on a cliff face 18m (59ft) above the water, it can only be seen from the lake and is a regular stop for boats. If arriving by car, be prepared for a series of steep steps from the car park to the monastery. The original chapel to Santa Caterina had a monastery added in the 13th century. The monastery was suppressed by Joseph II of Austria in 1770 and was deserted for two centuries, but after a 15-year period of restoration it was reopened in 1987. There are numerous frescoes to see, varying in age from the 14th to the 17th centuries, but it is the setting that will appeal most to visitors. Open daily April–October 08:30–12:00 and 14:30–18:00.

Laveno

Around the headland from the monastery is the port of **Laveno**. The only natural harbour on the lake, it was an important Roman settlement and later an Austrian naval base. Today, its car ferry runs across to Intra on the Piedmont side of the lake. Laveno was well known for its ceramics industry, but this finally closed down in 1980. You can, however, visit the **Ceramics Museum** (open 10:00–12:00 and 14:30–18:00 Friday, Saturday and

Sunday, all year) which is full of items such as bizarrely decorated toilet seats and bidets. If you are in Laveno at Christmas time, don't miss the floodlit underwater nativity scene set up by local divers. The more adventurous could take the chair lift up to **Sasso del Ferro**. At 1062m (3483ft), it provides fine views of the lake and the Alps.

Luino

The next place of any size is **Luino**. It has a long history going back to Roman days but in more recent times it was famous as the place where, in 1848, Garibaldi's small band of men defeated an entire Austrian detachment, thereby speeding up the unification of the country. Luino is believed to have been the birthplace of Bernardino Luini, the most important of Leonardo's followers. One of his frescoes can be seen in the **Oratorio di Santi Pietro e Paolo**. The sleepy town really comes to life on Wednesdays when the weekly market, claimed to be the largest in Europe, is held in Piazza Garibaldi.

Maccagno

The only other settlement of any size before you reach the Swiss border is **Maccagno**. It is actually one of the oldest settlements on the lake, but very quiet today. It makes a good base for walks in the nearby Val Veddasca, which can be followed all the way into Switzerland.

LAKE ORTA

The most westerly of the Italian lakes, Lake Orta is also one of the smallest, measuring just 13.5km (8.5 miles) in length. It is the only lake that is wholly in Piedmont, and its outlet river, the Nigoglia, is the only one that runs north-

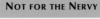

NOT FOR THE NERVY

There are a number of chair lifts and cable cars around Lake Maggiore, taking visitors effortlessly up to higher altitudes to appreciate the wonderful scenery. The most exciting, without doubt, is the lift from Laveno to the peak of Sasso del Ferro. The visitor does not travel in a chair, but in a two-person yellow bucket, which rises over the woods, meadows and rocks to the 1062m (3485ft) peak. If this is not enough for the more adventurous traveller, parascending and paragliding are on offer at the top of the bucket lift.

Opposite: *The Rocco di Angera, built by the Lombards, today houses a doll museum.*
Below: *Regular passenger boats run from Omegna to link all the settlements along the shores of Lake Orta.*

wards towards the Alps rather than southwards to join the Po. The package tour industry has not homed in on Lake Orta to any great extent, although it is a popular day-trip destination. The main attraction on the lake is the small town of Orta San Giulio and the Island of San Giulio just offshore.

There are a number of attractive villages around Lake Orta, including **Pettenasco**, with a pretty lakeside frontage, **Armeno**, famous for producing an extraordinary number of chefs, and **Gozzano**, with its 4th-century bell tower. At **Vacciago** there is a 17th-century villa that was the home of the artist Antonio Calderara (1903–78). His house now contains the **Collezione Calderara** (open 10:00–12:00 and 15:00–18:00 Tuesday–Sunday May–October), which includes not only Calderara's work but also paintings by a host of other artists. Nearby is **San Maurizio d'Opaglio**, once the household tap-making capital of Italy (see panel, page 83).

Lake Orta

Omegna

The only town of any size on Lake Orta is **Omegna**, located on the Nigoglia River at the northern end of the lake. An industrial town with a strong metalworking tradition it sees few tourists despite having an attractive tree-lined waterfront backed by graceful houses with pretty wrought-iron balconies. There is also a pleasant square looking over the river and the remains of a bridge that is possibly Roman. There is a lively

lakeside market here
on Thursdays.

Although you can
drive around the lake
to visit Orta San Giulio,
it is far more enjoyable
to take the lake steamer
from Omegna, stopping
at several lakeside vil-
lages en route.

Orta San Giulio ★★

This small lakeside town is a gem of a place. A dimin-
utive square, **Piazza Morta**, is right next to the main
landing stage and surrounded by bars and *gelaterie*. In
among these pavement cafés is the little town hall, the
Palazzo della Comunità. It is decorated with frescoes
dating back to 1582 and has an arcaded loggia. An outside staircase leads to the upper floors and a tiny
campanile. Leading back from the square are narrow
alleyways full of restaurants, craft shops and boutiques.
Look, too, for the tower of **Villa Crespi**, the house of a
newspaper owner who employed Turkish stonemasons.
Prayers from the Koran can be seen on the tower of the
villa, which is now a hotel. A steep cobbled road leads
up to the yellow frontage of the **Church of Madonna del
Sasso**, which dates from the 15th century, although it
had a major restoration 300 years later. The interior is
noteworthy for its strangely sloping nave floor and its
impressive frescoes. On the right-hand side of the
church, a steep lane leads up to **Sacro Monte**, the sacred
hill with a collection of 21 chapels dedicated to St
Francis of Assisi. Even if the chapels are of little interest,
it is worth the walk for the stupendous views over the
lake and island of San Giulio. Sacro Monte has recently
been designated a UNESCO World Heritage Site.

Isola San Giulio ★★★

Every 15 minutes or so, boats leave from the landing
stage at Piazza Morta for Isola San Giulio. Dominating

Above: *The town
hall (Palazzo della
Comunità) on the
Piazza Morta in Orta
San Giulio.*

> ### THE STORY OF
> ### SAN GIULIO
>
> In the 4th century, Giulio, a
> Roman missionary, decided
> that the island on Lake Orta
> would be an ideal base for
> his work. The local inhabit-
> ants, however, refused to
> row him to the island as they
> believed it to be the haunt of
> dragons and other nasty
> beasts. Undeterred, Giulio
> went across the water in the
> wind, standing on his cloak
> and using his staff as a rud-
> der – surely the world's first
> windsurfer! Not surprisingly,
> the dragons fled on seeing
> such extraordinary behaviour
> and Giulio was able to settle
> on the island and devote
> himself to converting the
> Orta natives to Christianity.

Right: *A steep, cobbled road leads to the Church of Madonna del Sasso, from where there are fine views of Lake Orta and Isola San Giulio.*

ORTA'S SACRED MOUNTAIN

The idea of **sacri monti** – sacred hills – was brought to Italy by a Franciscan friar, Bernardino Caimi, after his pilgrimage to Jerusalem. Orta's **Sacro Monte** was begun in 1591 and dedicated to St Francis. It took over 200 years to build the 21 chapels with their 376 statues and over 900 frescoes. The route passes through shady woods and provides superb views over the lake and Isola San Giulio. People found that this was an excellent picnic spot and this eventually encouraged a small bar and restaurant to open, so that the Sacro Monte is now a very popular weekend venue.

the island is the **basilica** (open 09:30–12:00 and 14:00–18:45 daily, reduced hours in winter) which was originally built around the 9th century on the site of the hermit San Giulio's cell. Much of the present church dates from a major rebuilding in the 11th century. Of great interest is the large black pulpit decorated with mythical beasts. There are also some 15th-century frescoes (they were evacuated to the Vatican during World War II) and a large vertebra in the sacristy, said to come from one of the dragons that San Giulio chased off the island, but in all probability it is a whale bone. A cobbled alleyway runs around the island, much of which is taken up with the monastery, but there are a few private houses, a restaurant and a shop.

LAKE VARESE AND AROUND

West of the city of Varese and southeast of Lake
Maggiore are a trio of small lakes. The largest is **Lake
Varese**, some 9km (5.5 miles) long and surrounded by
low rolling hills and forests. Sadly, the lake is badly
polluted, so that swimming and some water sports have
been banned, while the fishing industry has all but dis-
appeared. In the south of the lake is the tiny **Isolino
Virginia**, which is largely made up of the remains of
pile-built lake dwellings going back to Neolithic times.
Artefacts collected from the site can be seen in the
museum in Varese. The two smaller lakes, **Lake
Comabbio** and **Lake Monate**, also have examples of
Bronze-Age pile dwellings.

The city of **Varese** has ancient origins, but today its
parks and gardens give it a 'garden city' atmosphere. It
is increasingly becoming a dormitory suburb of Milan
and its hotels take the overflow of visitors when Milan
holds its trade fairs. It has a small amount of light industry, particularly shoe-making. There is much to see in
Varese. Pride of place goes to the **Palazzo Estense**, a
mid-18th-century Baroque palace, surrounded by extensive gardens. Once the home of the Duke of
Modena, it is now the city's town hall. Nearby is the
Villa Mirabello, which houses the **Musei Civici**, with a
jumbled collection of
local archaeology,
paintings and natural
history. Also of interest
here is the **Basilica of
San Vittore** with its
neoclassical façade
and some mildly inter-
esting artwork. Next to
the basilica is Varese's
landmark, the 72m
(236ft) **Campanile del
Bernascone**, which is
capped with an onion-
shaped dome.

MUSEUM OF TAPS

There are some strange
subjects for museums in
the Lake Maggiore region.
The Umbrella Museum at
Gignese, the Chimney
Sweep Museum at Santa
Maria Maggiore and the Hat
Museum at Ghiffa readily
spring to mind. Probably the
most bizarre is the Tap
Museum – Museo de la
Rubinetta – at San Maurizio
d'Opaglio. The area was
once famous for the manu-
facture of bathroom fittings,
particularly luxury items
such as the gold taps much
favoured by wealthy Arabs.
Today, the industry has
largely moved to Brescia, but
the memorabilia can still be
seen in the Museum of Taps.

Below: *An attractive
flower-bedecked corner
of the pretty town of Orta
San Giulio.*

Lakes Maggiore, Orta and Varese at a Glance

BEST TIMES TO VISIT

In **winter** many of the attractions and monuments close from October–March. In **summer** the popular resorts can get overcrowded and the roads jammed with cars. The best time to visit is in late **spring**, when the azaleas and rhododendrons are in bloom and the botanical gardens are looking their best. **September** is also a good time as the high summer temperatures have dropped and the crowds have gone.

GETTING THERE

Trains from Milan's Stazione Centrale stop at Arona and Stresa, while the service from Milan's Porta Garibaldi serves the eastern side of Lake Maggiore. Trains from Switzerland arrive via the Simplon Tunnel to Domodossala or via the Swiss town of Bellinzona. The **road** route from Milan is simple, using the A8 and the A26 *autostradas*.

GETTING AROUND

Roads follow the shores of both Lake Maggiore and Lake Orta and a car is convenient for getting to many of the attractions. **Railways** run along the east and west of Lake Maggiore, but not the northern shore. **Lake steamers**, mostly run by *Navigazione Lago Maggiore*, link all major resorts, although services are cut considerably in winter. Hydrofoils provide an especially quick link. The only car ferry across the lake runs from Intra to Laveno.

WHERE TO STAY

There is a wide range of accommodation – from some of the most luxurious hotels around, down to humble *pensiones* and camp sites. All are likely to be fully booked during peak season, particularly those hotels that are popular with tour groups. Pre-booking at this time of the year is strongly recommended.

LUXURY

Grand Hotel des Iles Borromées, corso Umberto 167, Stresa, tel: 0323 938938, www.borromees.it It would be hard to better this lakeside edifice in terms of service, facilities and ambience.
Bristol, corso Umberto I 73, Stresa, tel: 0323 32601, fax: 0323 33622, www.zaechera hotels.com Another luxurious lakeside hotel, with indoor and outdoor pools and gym.
La Palma, corso Umberto I 1, Stresa, tel: 0323 32401, fax: 0323 933 930, www. hlapalma.it Modern hotel with pool across the road by the lake. Good restaurant.
Dino, via Garibaldi 20, Baveno, tel: 0323 922 201, fax: 0323 924 515, www.jpmoser.com Luxury hotel with a private lakeside beach.
Majestic, via Vittorio Veneto 32, Pallanza, tel: 0323 509 711, fax: 0323 556 379, www.grandhotelmajestic.it Comfortable older-style hotel with excellent facilities and private beach.

MID-RANGE

Sasso Moro, in hamlet of Arolo di Leggiuno, 7km (4.3 miles) south of Laveno, tel: 0332 64730, www.varesehotels.it Quiet hotel with a fine waterside location.
Park Hotel Paradiso, via Guglielmo Marconi 20, Ghiffa, tel: 0323 59548, fax: 0323 59878. Small hotel in Art Nouveau villa with pool and good views.
Rigoli, via Piave 48, Baveno, tel: 0323 924 756, fax: 0323 925 156. Lakeside; stunning views in all directions.
Cannero, 28821 Cannero Riviera, tel: 0323 788 046, fax: 0323 788 048, www.hotel cannero.com Rooms with balconies overlooking the lake. Swimming pool. Good restaurant.
Pironi, via Marconi 35, Cannobio, tel: 0323 70624, fax: 0323 72184, www.pironi hotel.it Comfortable hotel in 15th-century palace.
Dell'Angelo, Piazza Grande, Locarno, Switzerland, tel: 41 91 751 8175, fax: 751 8256, www.hotel-dell-angelo.ch Large rooms, roof terrace and cheap pizzeria.

BUDGET

Pensione l'Isola, via Rebolgiane 68, Laveno, tel: 0332 666 031. Reasonably priced, in the centre of town.
Elena, piazza Cadorna 15, Stresa, tel: 0323 31043, fax: 0323 33339. Excellent budget choice in the main square. Large rooms with balconies.

Lakes Maggiore, Orta and Varese at a Glance

Orsola, via Duchessa di Genova 45, Stresa, tel: 0323 31087. Comfortable, good value, close to train station.
Olina, via Olina 40, Orta San Giulio, tel: 0322 905 656, fax: 0322 905 645. A rare cheap option in this popular town. Good reasonable restaurant.

There are plenty of **camp sites** around and they include:
Lido, on the lakeside at Arona, tel: 0322 243 383.
Parisi, via Piave 50, Baveno, tel: 0323 923 156. Open Apr–Sep.
La Residence, Cannobio, close to the river. Open Mar–Oct. Also has some rooms in a nearby villa.
Lido, waterfront at Maccagno, tel: 0332 560 250.

WHERE TO EAT

Some of the best restaurants are in the main hotels, but the food is often bland and international. The towns around the lakes have few 'foreign' restaurants, such as Chinese or Mexican. Most serve Italian regional food, with an emphasis on traditional local fish dishes.

LUXURY
Taverna del Pittore, piazza del Popolo 39, Arona, tel: 0322 243 366. One of the top restaurants on Lake Maggiore, with fine views from its terrace over the lake and the Rocca. Bring a bulging wallet.
Centenario, lungolago Motta 17, Locarno, Switzerland, tel: 41 91 743 8222. Top restaur-

ant noted for its gourmet food.
L'Emiliano, corso Italia 52, Stresa, tel: 0323 31396. Nouvelle cuisine, imaginative dishes and very expensive.

MID-RANGE
Campanile, via Montegrappa 16, Baveno, tel: 0323 922 377. Classic pasta dishes.
Torchio, via Manzoni 25, Stresa, tel: 0323 503 352. Good value game dishes.
Verbano, Isola dei Pescatori, tel: 0323 30408. Good fish restaurant on the east of the island overlooking Isola Bella.
Osteria dell'Angelo, piazza Garibaldi 35, Pallanza, tel: 0323 556 362. Well known for its imaginative risottos.
Lo Scalo, Piazza Vittorio Emanuele II 32, Cannobio, tel: 0323 71480. Traditional Piedmontese recipes; terrace overlooks lake.

BUDGET
For the standard cheap meal go to **Panini** bars, which offer sandwiches in different types of bread. **Pizzerias** are another option. Many bars in the main resorts offer cheap snack food.

SHOPPING

Most resorts have a street market on one day of the week. Bargains can be found in leather goods and shoes.

TOURS AND EXCURSIONS

The numerous **cable cars** and **chair lifts** are popular with tourists. Nobody should leave Lake Maggiore without visiting

the **Borromean Islands**, which are easy to reach by ferry. Favourite excursions with tour operators are to the Alpine village of **Macugnaga** and the **Hundred Valleys** rail trip.

USEFUL CONTACTS

A list of **Tourist Information Offices** is shown below. Most are run by APT, others by local municipalities. For more information visit the website: www.lagomaggiore.it
Stresa, via Canonica 8, tel: 0323 31308. Open 10:00–12:30 and 15:00–18:30. They will give details of the Stresa International Festival of Classical Music.
Baveno, pizziale Dante Alighieri 14, tel: 0323 924 632.
Cannobio, via A. Giovanola 25, tel: 0323 71212.
Luino, viale Dante 6, tel: 0332 530 019.
Orta San Giulio, Via Panoramica, tel: 0322 905 614.
Varese, via Carrobbio 2, tel: 0332 252 412.
Locarno, Lago Zorzi 1, tel: 41 91 791 0091.
Ascona, Casa Seradine, tel: 41 91 791 0090.

USEFUL WEBSITES

www.maggiore.ch
www.borromeoturismo.it

FERRY SERVICES

Navigazione Lago Maggiore, tel: 0322 232 200, www.navigazionelaghi.it
For details of ferry times, tel: 0322 46651, www.stresa.org (Lake Maggiore Tourist Board).

5
Lakes Como and Lugano

Lake Como, which is also known by the Roman name of Lario, is the third largest lake in Italy, stretching for around 50km (32 miles) from north to south. It is also believed to be the deepest lake in Europe, glaciers having scoured it out to a depth of 410m (1345ft). The lake takes the form of an inverted Y, its three arms known as Como, Lecco and Cólico. Lake Como is the only northern Italian lake to have a major city on its shore, the ancient town of Como, with its defensive walls largely intact, historically guarding the north–south and east–west routes.

Como is generally considered to be the most attractive and romantic of the northern lakes. Picture-perfect lakeside villages, sumptuous villas such as **Villa Carlotta** and **Villa d'Este**, and exotic gardens prolific with blooms attracted English poets including Wordsworth, Shelley and Byron. Royalty followed and Lake Como soon began to be an important part of the 19th-century Grand Tour.

Today, unfortunately, Como is also the most crowded of the lakes. In the summer its waters are dotted with a wide variety of crafts from sailboards to hydrofoils, while the perimeter roads can be clogged with traffic. Como is the nearest of the northern lakes to Milan, and the Milanese arrive in hordes at the weekends and during the holiday month of August. Yet somehow the essential attractiveness of Lake Como is never quite ruined by the crowds, and it remains a fabulous holiday destination.

DON'T MISS

★★★ Villa Carlotta: 18th-century neoclassical lakeside villa at Tremezzo.
★★★ Como's Duomo: the magnificent cathedral shows transitional architecture from Gothic to Renaissance.
★★ Villa d'Este: 16th-century villa at Cernobbio, now a luxury hotel.
★★ Bellagio: often described as the prettiest village on the Italian lakes.
★ Funicular to Brunate:. superb views over Como and the lake from the top of the funicular railway at Brunate.

Opposite: *The Villa d'Este has a long history and is now a luxury hotel.*

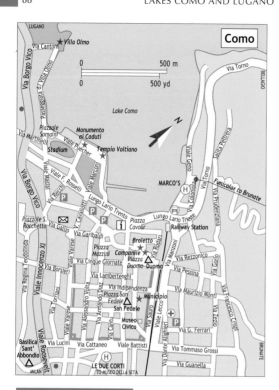

COMO

The city of Como, at the tip of the southwest arm of the lake, has had a long and eventful history. The first settlement was probably in the Bronze Age, but it became important during Roman times, when Julius Caesar brought settlers to the site. The Romans recognized the strategic importance of Como and linked it by road to Milan. It later came under the rule of the Viscontis and then the Sforzas, when it became very prosperous, its wealth based on silk and other textiles. The Spanish rule marked a period of decline, but it picked up later during the Habsburg and Napoleonic occupations. Como was prominent during the Risorgimento, and after Garibaldi defeated the Austrians at the Battle of San Fermo, his troops were received enthusiastically in the city.

Today Como has a population of 100,000 and its prosperity is based on textiles, engineering and tourism. Despite some industrial suburbs, its historical core is attractive, with a street plan intact from the days of the Roman *castrum* and its medieval walls in good condition.

Life in the city today centres on the **Piazza Cavour**, which opens out onto the lakeside promenade with its gardens and landing stages, enabling boat passengers to disembark in the heart of the city. It is a lively square, backed by hotels and cafés. From Piazza Cavour, Via Plinio leads inland to **Piazza Duomo**, with the cathedral, Broletto (the striped marble town hall) and a Campanile.

LAKE COMO'S CLIMATE

Lake Como has a mild, almost frost-free climate that enables a variety of exotic plants to grow and thrive. The **summer** can be hot, particularly in August, when thunderstorms are not uncommon. **Spring** is the best time of the year for sightseeing, with many plants and shrubs in full flower. **Winds** can occasionally be strong, with the *breva* blowing northwards from midday to sunset, while the *tivà* blows south during the night and the early morning.

The Duomo

Como's magnificent cathedral was begun in 1396 and completed in 1744. It is regarded as a superb example of the transition from Gothic to Renaissance. The east end is pure Renaissance, with green-roofed apses, matching the Baroque dome that was added by Filipo Juvarra in 1744. The flat western façade is largely Gothic, its polished marble setting off the long narrow windows and numerous statues. On either side of the main west door are statues of the Elder and Younger Plinys who were both born in Como (but in the days when the Roman Empire was pagan). The statues were the work of the Rodari brothers, who were also responsible for the ornate north door (facing the Broletto) known as the Porta della Rana or Frog Door.

The interior is equally interesting, with three Gothic aisles sitting happily with the Renaissance transepts and choir. Don't miss the hanging tapestries between four columns of the nave. They date from the 16th and 17th centuries and originated in Tuscany and Flanders. Note also the rose window with fine stained glass, the paintings by Gaudenzio Ferrari and Bernardino Luini, and the Romanesque lions near the main entrance, which were retained from an original church on the site that was demolished to make way for the cathedral. The Duomo is open daily 09:00–18:30. Entry is free.

Attached to the north side of the Duomo is the **Broletto** or **Town Hall** which dates from 1215. Though two of its arches were removed when the cathedral was built, there is still much to admire, including the triple-arched windows. Alongside the Broletto is the **Campanile**, made contrastingly of rough-hewn stone.

Piazza San Fedele ★

Head deeper into the old town of Como to the cobbled **Piazza San Fedele**, the site of the old corn market. Dominating the square is the 10th-century **Basilica of San Fedele**, built on the site of a pagan temple to Jupiter but named after the saint who brought Christianity

PLINY AND PLINY

The famous Romans, Pliny the Elder and Pliny the Younger, were both natives of Como. Pliny the Elder was a notable Latin prose writer who became a government servant. His most famous work was his *Natural History*, a comprehensive book dealing with the world's geography, bioloagy, geology and medicine. He died inhaling the fumes from the eruption of Vesuvius at Pompeii. Pliny the Younger was the nephew and adopted son of Pliny the Elder. He was also a prose writer and became a Roman senator. Although both were pagan, their statues can be found on either side of the west door of Como's cathedral.

Below: *The cafés in Como's Piazza Duomo are convenient for viewing the cathedral.*

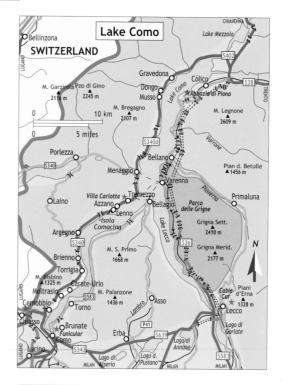

Lake Como

to the area. Much of the work on the basilica was carried out by the **Maestri Comocini**, the area's famous master builders and stonemasons. One of the best features of San Fedele is the exterior of the apse, with its upper arcade and round windows decorated with Romanesque bas-reliefs. Como's other fine church is the Romanesque **Sant'Abbondio**, built in the 11th century and boasting some colourful 14th-century frescoes.

Museums

A short walk from San Fedele is the **Museo Civico**, housed in two palaces. The **Palazzo Olginati** has the Risorgimento museum, with plenty of Garibaldi memorabilia, while the **Palazzo Giovio** keeps the local collection of archaeology and art. Open 09:30–12:30 and 14:00–17:00 Tuesday–Saturday; 10:00–13:00 Sunday.

A rather special museum is the **Tempio Voltiano** in the lakeside park. The circular building was erected in 1927 to house the instruments and papers of Como's famous self-taught scientist, Alessandro Volta, who gave his name to the electrical measurement (*see* panel, page 93). The museum is open 10:00–12:00 and 15:00–18:00 Tuesday–Sunday, April–September; 10:00–12:00 and 14:00–16:00 Tuesday–Sunday, October–March.

The **Museo della Seta**, located in Via Vallegio to the south of the historic centre of Como, charts the history of the city's silk industry. Open 09:00–12:00 and 15:00–18:00 Tuesday–Friday.

FACTS ABOUT LAKE COMO

Como is the third largest of the Italian lakes. It has the longest shoreline of all the lakes and is one of the deepest lakes in Europe, having been scoured out by glacial action.
Length: 50km (32 miles).
Maximum width: 4.4km (2.7 miles).
Area: 148km² (55 sq miles).
Perimeter: 170km (106 miles).
Maximum depth: 410m (1345ft) near Argegno.

Villa Olmo ★

At night, you can't miss the floodlit **Villa Olmo**. In formal neoclassical style, it was built on the site of a monastery in the late 18th century. Its manicured formal gardens are open to the public (09:00–19:00 in winter, 08:00–23:00 in summer). A couple of the rooms in the villa can be visited (09:30–12:00 and 15:00–18:00 Monday–Saturday) if they are not being used for conferences.

The Funicular to Brunate ★★

Do not leave Como without taking the funicular to Brunate. The service runs every 30 minutes from the lakeside station to the hill village. For superb views over Como and the lake, walk down the road from the upper station for 100m (110yd), or take the panoramic footpath in the opposite direction for 500m (666yd). Brunate is also a good starting point for hikes in the surrounding hills. A clutch of cheap restaurants and pizzerias alongside the upper station make this a good lunchtime stop.

Above: *The Villa d'Este is a luxury hotel with magnificent landscaped gardens.*

THE WESTERN SHORE OF LAKE COMO

The suburbs of Como extend along the western shore to **Cernobbio**, the third largest town on the lake. Although there is light industry on the outskirts, Cernobbio has a pleasant waterfront leading back to a small square, the site of a popular market on Wednesdays and Saturdays. There is also a lakeside lido nearby. Cernobbio is the start of a 130km (80-mile) trek through the mountains along the western shore of Como known as the **Via dei Monte Lariani**. The town is best known, however, for its sumptuous villas, which include **Villa Erba**, now an exhibition and conference centre, **Villa Il Pizzo** with its beautiful gardens, and the world-famous late 16th-century **Villa d'Este**, now a luxury hotel.

> **FROM VILLA TO LAVISH HOTEL**
>
> The **Villa d'Este** at Cernobbio was built in 1568 as the summer residence of Cardinal Tolomeo Gallio, who was Pope Gregory XIII's Secretary of State. It remained in the family's hands until the 19th century when it became the home of Caroline of Brunswick, exiled wife of the Prince of Wales (who was later George IV). In 1873 Villa d'Este became a luxury hotel, and over the years it has accommodated a long list of royalty and celebrities, from the Duke of Windsor and Mrs Simpson to Greta Garbo and Madonna.

The road north passes along one of the most attractive stretches of Lake Como, with a series of tunnels and glimpses of the blue waters of the lake and the far shore. There is a string of villages including **Moltrasio**, where the Villa Passalacqua was a favourite stop for the composer Bellini; **Carate-Urio**, above which is the 10th-century **Santuario de Santa Maria**, giving fine views across the lake; **Torrigia,** and **Brienno**.

Eventually you will reach **Argegno**. It is a pleasant village, with lakeside cafés and wooden-beamed houses almost covering the stepped alleyways running between them. The Val d'Intelvi, inland from Argegno, is drained by the River Telo, which rushes under an old bridge believed to be of Roman origin. A winding narrow road follows the valley inland and over the hills to Lake Lugano. Try the *funvia* that runs up to the hamlet of Pigra at a height of 881m (2890ft), giving stunning views over the lake.

THE TREMEZZINA

The next stretch of the lake is known as the Tremezzina, a sheltered area with lush vegetation and a gentle climate. Offshore is Como's only island, **Isola Comacina**. Full of ruined churches, its only inhabitants are a small colony of artists. It can be reached by ferry, but its only restaurant, the Locanda den'Isola, is one of the priciest around the lake. The first village of the Tremezzina is **Lenno**, where Pliny the Younger had a villa. He wrote that he could fish from his bedroom window. The next village, **Azzano**, has more recent historical fame, for it was here that Mussolini and his mistress were executed by partisans in 1945.

The main resort of this stretch of the lake shore is the romantic **Tremezzo**, which looks across towards Bellagio at the junction of the three arms of Lake Como. A string of opulent palaces and villas, many of which have been converted into hotels, line the shore. One of these, the **Villa Carlotta**, is one of the main tourist attractions of the Italian lakes. It was built in the 18th century in neoclassical style by Marchese Giorgio Clerici and in the following century came into the hands of Princess Carlotta of the Netherlands. The interior of the villa is full of fascinating works of art, but it is the gardens, with their azaleas, rhododendrons and camellias, that will probably leave a more lasting impression. Villa Carlotta is open 09:00–11:30 and 14:00–16:30 daily 15 March to 31 October; 09:00–18:00 daily April to September.

Menaggio, the next resort, is the busiest of the towns on the western shore. A car ferry connects it to the eastern shore at Varenna, while a road leads westward to Lugano and Switzerland just 12km (7.5 miles) away. Menaggio is a lively resort with a good beachside lido, golf course, stylish shops, attractive harbour and a number of good hotels.

After a string of small hamlets, the town of **Musso** is reached. It is defended by a castle built on the Sasso di Musso, which was once the home of Il Medighino, a member of the Medici who terrorized the lake for many years during the 16th century. The quarries in the hills behind Musso provided the marble for Como's Duomo and also the Arch of Peace in Milan. Just north of Musso is **Dongo**, the place where Mussolini was captured by partisans in 1945 while attempting to flee to Switzerland in a German lorry.

The last town of any size on the western shore is **Gravedona**. The oldest town on the lake after Como, it has two main monuments. The **Palazzo Gallio** was built in 1586 for Cardinal Tolemeo Gallio and today it operates as the offices of the local council. The **Church**

ALESSANDRO VOLTA (1745–1827)

Volta was born in Como, where he became a schoolteacher. He published several papers on electricity and magnetism, and as a result of his skill he was made Professor of Physics at Padua University. He is best known for inventing the voltaic pile, which was the first example of an electric battery of primary cells, and also for his development of the theory of current electricity. When he retired, he returned to Como, where there are a street and a square (with his statue) named after him. The pupose-built **Tempio Voltiano** (see page 90) on the lake shore contains an exhibition of his manuscripts and apparatus.

Opposite: *The Villa Carlotta was named after a Dutch princess. Don't miss its fine gardens.*
Below: *The waterfront at Menaggio, the tourist resort on the western shore.*

of **Santa Maria del Tiglio** dates from the 12th century and is believed to have been built over the remains of an earlier Roman church. It has an attractive aisled nave where you will find a 6th-century mosaic floor and some frescoes dating from the 12th–14th centuries. There is also an ancient wooden crucifix.

At the extreme northern end of Lake Como is the tiny **Lake Mezzola**, measuring just 3km by 2km (2 miles by 1.25 miles). Once part of the main lake, it became detached by the build-up of silt and boulders deposited by the rivers Mera and Adda. The surrounding reed beds and marsh land provide a haven for wildfowl.

THE EASTERN SHORE OF LAKE COMO

The first village of any size and the last northerly stop of the lake steamers is **Cólico**, but this has little to detain visitors. Just to the south, however, is a small lagoon known as the **Lago di Piona**, and on the finger of land that encloses the lagoon is a restored 11th-century abbey, the **Abbazia di Piona**. The abbey was taken over by the Cistercians in the early years of the 20th century and today it is open daily to visitors from 08:00–19:00. The abbey has some particularly attractive mid-13th-century cloisters and an imposing campanile.

Further south is **Bellano**, the home of the Boldini family who were credited with introducing the silk industry to the Como region. Bellano seems to successfully combine a little light industry with a tourist trade. Its most impressive monument is the **Church of San Nazzaro and San Celso**. Dating from the 14th century, it has a fine rose window and a superb marble façade. Look out too for the 16th-century *Madonna and Child*, possibly by Luini.

Behind the town is a deep gorge or *orrido*, where the River Pioverna comes crashing down the valley. It is accessible by steps and rope walkways.

Varenna ★★

A short distance south of Bellano is Varenna, one of the most picturesque towns on the lake. The houses are strung out along the base of the hills and the old quarter, in particular, is an attractive maze of narrow lanes, alleyways and arches. On the hill above the town is a ruined castle, which is believed to have been the last home of the Lombard Queen Theolinda. A more recent denizen of the town was Pirelli, who founded the tyre firm.

There are two churches of interest. The **Oratorio di San Giovanni** goes back to the 10th century and is one of the oldest surviving churches on the lake. **San Giorgio** is in Romanesque style and its exterior is graced by an elegant campanile and a fresco of St Francis. Inside are some more frescoes and an altarpiece by Pietro Brentani.

There are a number of magnificent lakeside villas in Varenna, most of which have become hotels or conference centres. The most famous are **Villa Cipressi**, with terraced gardens going right down to the lakeside (open 09:00–20:00 in summer and 09:00–18:00 in autumn and spring), and **Villa Monastero**, built on the site of a Cistercian monastery and used today by the government as a scientific centre; its gardens are well worth a visit (open April–October 09:00–19:00 daily, www.villa monastero.it). Varenna also boasts the **Museo Ornitologico**, which concentrates on the birds that have been seen around the lake. Open 15:00–18:00 Tuesday, Thursday and Saturday, June–September; 10:00–12:00 Sunday. Varenna is also an important ferry centre – a car ferry runs to Tremezzo and steamers to Bellagio, Villa Carlotta, Menaggio and most of the other lakeside resorts.

Above: *Picturesque Varenna on the eastern shore of Lake Como.*
Opposite: *Lakeside Bellano, once an important silk-producing centre.*

> ### CENTRE OF SILK PRODUCTION
>
> In the 17th century, the production of silk moved from Milan to Como and within a short time the area was providing fine silk to the royal courts in many parts of Europe. The mulberry bushes, on which silkworms were raised, were a common sight along the lake. In the 19th century disaster struck when an epidemic wiped out all the Como silkworms. The industry survived by importing raw silk from China. Today, the industry flourishes, producing 80 per cent of Europe's silk, and is the major source of the fine silk fabrics that the Milan fashion industry demands. The development of the industry can be seen in the **Museo della Seta** (Silk Museum) near Como.

Below: *Bellagio, with its many lakeside cafés, is usually considered to be the most attractive of Lake Como's resorts.*

THE LECCO ARM

The southeasterly arm of Lake Como is also known as the **Lago di Lecco**. It is the least developed part of the lake, with few settlements and fiord-like scenery. The small town of **Mandello del Lario** is backed by the **Grigna** mountain range, which rises to 2410m (7906ft). Mandello's main claim to fame these days is that it is the headquarters of the Moto Guzzi motorcycle firm, who run the **Museo del Motocicio** in Via Parodi. There are daily guided tours Monday–Friday at 15:00 (www.motoguzzi.it). Of more ancient interest is the **Church of San Lorenzo**, which dates back to the 9th century.

Lecco

At the southern end of the lake is the industrial town of Lecco. With a population of 46,000, it is the second largest town on Lake Como. Despite the commercial activity, there is much of historical interest. It is believed that there was a settlement here in prehistoric times and the remains of its fortifications go back to the 6th century. Lecco was taken over by the Viscontis, who built the **Ponte Vecchio** (or Ponte Azzone Visconti) in 1336. The bridge has recently been restored. Lecco was the birthplace of **Alessandro Manzoni**, the famous Italian novelist, and his best-known work, *I Promessi Sposi* ('The Betrothed'), was set in the town. His childhood home, the **Villa Manzoni** in Via Amendola, is now a museum (open 09:30–17:30 Tue–Sun). Manzoni fans can also check out the statue of the author in the town's main square.

The town museum is in the 18th-century **Palazzo Belgiojosa** in Corso Matteotti (open 10:00–12:30 and 14:30–17:30 Tue–Sun, www.museilecco.org). Just south of the Ponte Visconti is the old fishing quarter of **Pescarenico**, often described as the last genuine fishing village on the lake. Certainly there are plenty of the

traditional boats and drying nets to see. For a good view over the town and the lake, take the cable car to **Piani d'Erna** at 1328m (4360ft). This is a good start for hiking trails into the surrounding mountains.

Bellagio

Arguably the most beautiful town in Italy, Bellagio sits prettily on the tip of the triangle of land between the two southern arms of Lake Como. Its leafy promenade is backed by attractive villas and restaurants, and leading from here is a maze of stepped and cobbled alleyways. It is worth walking up to the crest of the peninsula where Pliny the Younger had a villa and from where there are stunning views in all directions. There is good lake swimming to be had at the lido at the end of the promenade. **Villa Melzi** dates from 1810 and has some attractive gardens. Liszt composed some of his works here. The 16th-century **Villa Serbelloni** is perched on the hill above the town. Once popular with European monarchs, it is now owned by the Rockefeller Foundation, and JF Kennedy was once a guest here. The villa is not open to the public, but there are guided tours of the gardens, which have to be booked at the tourist office on Piazza della Chiesa. Before leaving Bellagio, take a look at the 12th-century **Church of San Giacomo**, which has a painting in the sacristy by Foppa and a pulpit with carvings of the Apostles.

LAKE LUGANO

Lake Lugano is situated largely in the Ticino canton of Switzerland, except for part of the western shore, the northeastern arm and the little enclave of Campione,

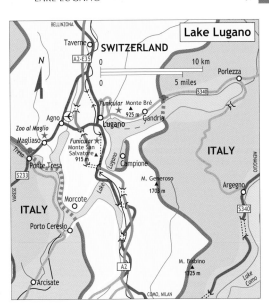

A SHORT-LIVED REPUBLIC

During medieval times the three towns of **Dongo**, **Sorico** and **Gravedona** formed the **Tre Pievi** (or three parishes) **Republic**, with the larger Gravedona as capital. The republic at one time ran a 'pirate ship' that terrorized the northern end of the lake. The republic itself was later terrorized by the inquisitor, Peter of Verona, as they had a stated policy which doubted that the pope was Christ's representative on earth. The feisty republic in revenge hacked Peter to death, but within a few years the three parishes had been taken over by the forces of Como.

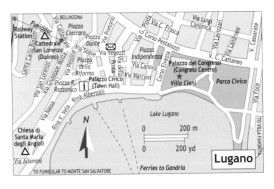

Opposite: *The charming little Church of Santa Maria degli Angioli, dating from the early 16th century.*

which are Italian. Lake Lugano is narrower and more remote than the other lakes and has fewer developments around its shore. It does, however, have the sophisticated major city of Lugano.

The first lakeside town encountered when arriving at Lake Lugano from Lake Como, just 12km (7.5 miles) to the east, is **Porlezza**. It is a pleasant enough place, although it has little in the way of monuments, apart from a ruined church. After crossing the Swiss border, the first place of any size is **Gandria**, which has an interesting **Customs Museum**, illustrating the battle against smuggling that has gone on over the centuries. The museum is open 14:30–17:30 daily, Easter to October. From Gandria a funicular leads up to **Monte Brè** at a height of 925m (3035ft), providing superb views of the Alps and the lake.

LUGANO

Elegant Lugano has been Swiss since it was taken from Milan in 1512, but its language and flavour are still very much Italian. It has a beautiful lakeside setting, with a tree-lined promenade leading to the **Parco Ciani**. Here is **Villa Ciani**, which houses the town's art collection. Further along the lake shore at Castagnola is **Villa Favorita**, which once displayed the Thyssen-Bornemisza Old Masters art collection. These are now in Madrid and Barcelona, but it is still possible to see the family's extensive watercolour collection. Villa Favorita is open 10:00–17:00 Friday, Saturday and Sunday, April–June; 10:00–17:00 Tuesday–Sunday, July–October.

Back in Lugano, life revolves around the charming main square, **Piazza della Riforma**. On the south side of the square, flanked by fountains, is the neoclassical **town hall**. This is the location of the Tourist Information Office.

Pedestrianized streets with fashionable shops lead away from the square. The **Duomo**, dedicated to San Lorenzo and dating from 1517, has a gracious Lombard-Venetian façade with richly carved portals. The interior has some 14th-century frescoes. More impressive than the cathedral is the **Church of Santa Maria degli Angioli**, which was built by the Franciscans in 1510. The simple interior has a large olive-wood altar and four side chapels, but it is dominated by a huge crucifixion scene with life-sized figures, painted around 1529 by Bernardo Luini, the pupil of Leonardo da Vinci. Less attractive is the lakeside model of the Chiesa San Carlo, made in wood by the unemployed. Funicular fans could take the trip from Lugano's southern suburb of Paradiso to the top of **Monte San Salvatore**, which rises to 915m (3001ft). There is a restaurant at the top and hiking trails lead off in a number of directions.

OTHER LAKESIDE PLACES

On the eastern shore is the Italian enclave of **Campione**, with a popular municipal casino. In the west, the short River Tresa drains Lake Lugano, feeding into Lake Maggiore. On either side of the river lies the town of **Ponte Tresa**, one half in Switzerland, the other half in Italy. Nearby at **Magliaso** is the popular **Zoo al Maglio**, with over a hundred species of mammals. The zoo is open 10:00–17:00 daily, with extended closing in the summer months. One of the most attractive villages on the lake is **Morcote**, located at the tip of the peninsula that leads south from Lugano. The **Church of Madonna del Sasso** has some superb 16th-century frescoes, while the lakeside **Parco Scherrer**, with its statues set among some exotic trees and shrubs, is a peaceful place to spend an hour or so. Across the lake from Morcote, set in a fairly wide bay, is the transport centre of **Porto Ceresio**.

> ## A LITTLE BIT OF ITALY IN SWITZERLAND
>
> The enclave of **Campione** on the eastern shore of Lake Lugano has been part of Italy since it was bequeathed to the church of Sant'Ambrogio in Milan in 777. In the Middle Ages it was famous for its master builders, the **Maestri Campionesi**, whose skills can be seen in many of the cathedrals of northern Italy. Today Campione is better known for its **casino**, which has been fleecing the Swiss of their francs since 1917.

> ## FACTS ABOUT LAKE LUGANO
>
> Four-fifths of Lake Lugano is situated in Switzerland, one-fifth in Italy.
> **Maximum length:** from northeast to southwest is 36km (22 miles).
> **Maximum width:** 2km (1.25 miles).
> **Largest town:** Lugano.
> **Population:** 40,000.

Lakes Como and Lugano at a Glance

Avoid July and August, which are hot and crowded. In winter many monuments and attractions are closed. Late spring is best; September is also good as the crowds have gone and the temperatures have moderated.

The nearest international **airports** are Milan Linate and Milan Malpensa. The cities of Como and Lugano can be reached by **road** using the A2/A9 *autostradas* from Milan. Lecco and the eastern side of Lake Como can be accessed using the N36. Road routes from Switzerland to the area use the St Bernard and St Gotthard tunnels and passes. Como, Lecco and Lugano are all linked to Milan by **rail**.

The most pleasant way to get around the lakes is by **boat**. Craft include car ferries, steamers, hydrofoils and hire boats. **Roads** run round Lake Como and for much of the shore of Lake Lugano. A **railway** runs the full length of the eastern shore of Lake Como, and there is also a link between Como and Lugano.

Expensive hotels around lakes Como and Lugano can be booked up well in advance in high season. Budget accommodation can be hard to find, but the larger towns of Como and Lecco have possibilities.

LUXURY

Villa d'Este, via Regina 40, Cernobbio, tel: 031 3481, fax: 031 348 844, www. villadeste.it World-famous luxury with a long list of celebrity clients. Facilities include wonderful gardens and a swimming pool that 'floats' in the lake.
Grand Hotel Villa Sebelloni, via Roma 1, Bellagio, tel: 031 950 216, fax: 031 951 529, www.villasebelloni.com Luxurious villa in glorious gardens. Wide range of leisure facilities. Closed in November.
Grand Hotel Tremezzo Palace, Tremezzo, tel: 0344 42491, fax: 0344 40201. Comfortable 19th-century lakeside hotel situated next to Villa Carlotta.
Hotel Bellevue au Lac, riva Caccia 10, Lugano, Switzerland, tel: 41 91 543 333. Comfortable large hotel with pool and sun terrace.
Le Due Corti, Piazza Vittoria 12/13, Como, tel: 031 328 111, fax: 031 328 800. Hotel in a former monastery, with rooms around the old cloisters.

MID-RANGE

Du Lac, via del Pristino 4, Varenna, tel: 0341 830 238, fax: 0341 831 081. A 19th-century lakeside house with fabulous views from the rooms.
Florence, piazza Mazzini 46, Bellagio, tel: 031 950 342, fax: 031 951 722, www.hotel florencebellagio.it Small traditional hotel on the lake shore.
Marco's, via Coloniola 43, Como, tel: 031 303 628, fax: 031 302 342, www.hotel

marcos.it Small, comfortable hotel. Rooms with balconies.
Bella Vista, Menaggio, tel: 0344 32136, fax: 0344 31793, www.hotel-bellavista.org Lakeside hotel, comfortable rooms, good facilities.
Washington, via San Gottardo 55, Lugano, Switzerland, tel: 41 91 966 4136, fax: 967 5067. Attractive gardens and a recommended restaurant.

BUDGET

La Griglia, via Milano 15, Argegno, tel: 031 821 147, fax: 031 821 562. On lake front, Como's western shore.
Suisse, Piazza Mazzini 23, Bellagio, tel: 031 950 335. Looks tatty on the outside, but has a good restaurant.
Villa Marie, via Regina 30, Tremezzo, tel: 0344 40427. Clean, small hotel on the lake shore close to Villa Carlotta.

Youth Hostels

Villa Olmo, via Bellinzona 2, Como, tel: 031 573 800, www.ostellionline.org Open Mar–Nov. Has laundry facilities and rents out bikes.
Ostello La Primula, via IV Novembre 86, Menaggio, tel: 0344 32356, www.menaggio hostel.com Open mid-Mar to mid-Nov. Good meals, rents out bikes and gives discounts on local attractions.

Camp Sites

There are a number of official camping grounds around Lake Como and Lake Lugano. Try **Lido** at Menaggio (tel: 0344

31150, open May–Sep), and **Serenella** at Gravedona (tel: 0334 89452, open Apr–Sep).

Many of the so-called best restaurants are in the large hotels, but their food tends to be international. Plenty of restaurants serve local specialities, including fish from the lake. For budget eating try local trattorias and pizzerias.

LUXURY

Locanda del Boschetta, via Boschetta 8, Lugano, Switzerland, tel: 41 91 542 493. One of Lugano's best restaurants, noted for its Ticino specialities.

Bilacus, Salita Serbelloni 9, Bellagio, tel: 031 950 480. Often claimed to be Bellagio's best restaurant. Beautiful terrace for alfresco eating.

Imbacadero, piazza Cavour 20, Como, tel: 031 270 166. Hotel restaurant with tables on the square and local cuisine.

Vecchia Varenna, via Scoscesa 10, Varenna, tel: 0341 830 793. Summer eating on terrace facing the lake. Local specialities. Closed Mon.

MID-RANGE

Trattoria del Gino, via Camozzi 16, Menaggio. Simple local food, good tourist menu.

Restaurante Teatro Socialle, via Maestri Comocini 8, Como, tel: 031 264 042. Reasonably priced menu in this theatre restaurant near the cathedral.

Silvio, via Carcano 12,

Bellagio, tel: 031 950 322. Specializes in local dishes, particularly lake fish.

BUDGET

La Scuderia, piazza Matteotti 4, Como. Cheap pizzeria near bus station. Closed Thursday.

Caffe Nova Comum, Piazza Duomo 2, Como, tel: 031 260 483. A great pleace to sip a cappuccino while admiring the façade of the cathedral.

La Grotta, salita Cernaia 14, Bellagio. Excellent for cheap, tasty pizzas. Closed Monday.

Ostello La Primula, *see* Where to Stay. You do not have to be a hosteller to use the superb value restaurant of this hostel.

The best shopping centre around Lake Como is undoubtedly the city of **Como**, where good bargains can be had in leather goods, fashion clothing, watches and jewellery. **Lugano** also has some fashionable shops, although prices are more expensive than in Italy. Chocolates and leather goods are particularly noteworthy. All the lakeside towns have **open-air street markets** on one day of the week.

Many tour destinations on the lake shore can be reached independently by using service government-operated boats (tel: 031 579 211, www.navigazione laghi.it). The most popular site is **Villa Carlotta**. Other commonly visited places include

Isola Comacina and the villages of **Bellagio** and **Varenna**. On Lake Lugano, the main excursion is to the village of **Marcote**. For **seaplane tours** of the lake contact **Aero Club Como**, tel: 031 574 495, www.aeroclubcomo.com

Tourist Information Offices: **Como**, Piazza Cavour. Open 09:00–13:00 and 14:30–18:00 Mon–Sat Oct–May, 09:30–12:30 Sun; same hours Mon–Sat Jun–Sep, 14:30–18:00 Sun; tel: 031 269 712; website: www.lakecomo.org

Cernobbio, largo L. Visconti 4, tel: 031 510 198.

Menaggio, Piazza Garibaldi 3, tel: 0344 32924.

Varenna, Piazza San Giorgio, tel: 0341 830 367, www.varenaitaly.com

Bellagio, Piazza della Chiesa, tel: 031 950 204

Lecco, Via N. Sauro, off Piazza Garibaldi, tel: 0341 362 360, www.bellagiolakecomo.com

Lugano, Palazzo Civico (Town Hall), Riva Albertolli, tel: 41 91 913 3232, www.lugano-tourism.ch

Lake Transport Information: Lake Lugano, tel: 091 971 5223. Lake Como, tel: 031 579 211.

www.lakecomo.org
www.lagodilugano.it
www.lakelugano.ch

Navigazione Lago Maggiore, tel: 031 579 211.

6
Lake Garda
and Verona

G arda is the largest of the northern Italian lakes and, indeed, the largest lake in Italy, measuring 50km (31 miles) from north to south. Scenically, Lake Garda presents contrasts. The north of the lake is narrow, steep-sided and fiord-like, while the south of the lake is wider, with rolling hills forming the shoreline. A glacier was responsible for scouring out the lake and also for depositing low hills of moraine in the south. Weather-wise, Garda is milder than the other lakes, with the south having what borders on a Mediterranean climate, enabling citrus fruit, olives and vines to grow in profusion. Spectacular thunderstorms can occur in late summer, particularly in the mountainous north of the lake. Strong winds in the afternoon, especially around Tarbole, make this area one of the world's prime windsurfing locations.

The shores of Lake Garda are also full of historical interest. The area of prehistoric rock engravings near the Punta San Vigilio provides the earliest evidence of human occupation. Lake Garda also has more Roman remains than any other part of northern Italy, with important villas at Sirmione and Desenzano. Later the Scaligeri dynasty of Verona built a number of castles around the lake shore. There are particularly fine examples at Sirmione and Malcésine.

Today, Lake Garda is the most popular of the northern Italian lakes and is the most orientated towards mass tourism. The lake is particularly attractive to German and Austrian visitors, who pour over the Alps in their thousands. During the summer months, the

DON'T MISS

*** Gardaland: outstanding theme park near Peschiera.
*** The Roman Arena: at Verona; once the haunt of gladiators, now the unusual venue for summer operas.
** Scaligeri castles: distinctive lakeside castles at Sirmione, Malcésine and Riva.
** Il Vittoriale: house and gardens of poet and eccentric Gabriele d'Annunzio.
* Piramidi di Zone: curious geological formations in the form of earth pinnacles topped with boulders.

Opposite: *An exciting roller coaster ride at the Gardaland Theme Park.*

LAKE GARDA'S CLIMATE

The **winter** climate of Garda is milder than that of the other lakes, at around 6°C (43°F). It also has warmer **summer** weather, so that the southern part of the lake in particular has a semi-Mediterranean climate. **Rainfall** is light but the northern part of the lake has some spectacular thunderstorms in the late summer. The best months (weather-wise) for touring are May, June and September.

Below: *Lake Garda has many attractive lakeside resorts with opportunities for water sports.*

water can be congested with boats and the roads can be blocked with vehicles. There are a number of **golf courses** around the southern shores of the lake and it is here that we find several **theme parks**. **Gardaland**, the area's answer to Disneyland, is a particular favourite with children, while there are no fewer than three aquaparks. Yet, despite this popularity, Lake Garda is certainly not spoiled. It has a longer tourist season than the other lakes and even in the winter it can be a most attractive place to take a holiday.

LAKE GARDA'S WESTERN SHORE

The **Gardesana Occidentale** or western shore of Lake Garda forms one of the most spectacular drives in Italy. Initially the scenery is fairly tame and gives no indication of the delights to come. The rolling hills form a region known as the **Valtenisi**, with a few old villages such as **Padenghe**, **San Felice** and **Moniga**, the latter with a delightful little port and castle. Near **Manerba** a rocky headland capped by a ruined *rocca* protrudes into the lake. The fortress looks out over the water towards **Isola di Garda**, the largest island on the lake. The island once had a monastery, but this fell into ruins and the island is now the home of a magnificent private villa.

Salò

It is unfortunate, perhaps, that Salò's main claim to fame is that it was the headquarters of Mussolini's puppet republic set up by the Germans towards the end of World War II. Today Salò is an attractive town located on a wide bay fringed by a delightful promenade. It has a 15th-century Gothic **Cathedral** and although the interior is rather gloomy, there are

Left*: The lakeside resort of Salò was the headquarters of Mussolini's puppet government towards the end of World War II.*

some fine paintings to admire, including a *Madonna and Saints* by Romanino. There are two museums of interest. Attached to the town hall is the **Museo Civico Archeologico**, with artefacts from the local area. The **Museo del Nastro Azzuro** (the Blue Ribbon Museum) in Via Fantoni is dedicated to prominent Italian military figures and their weapons and uniforms from the period 1797–1945. Open all year, 16:00–18:00 Saturday, 10:00–12:30 and 17:00–19:00 Sunday. The ancient city gate, the **Torre dell'Orologio**, is also worth a glance.

The scenery dramatically improves north of Salò, where the **Gardone Riviera** claims to have the best climate in the whole of the Italian lake area. Benefiting from the mild winters are parks and public gardens, particularly the **Giardino Botanico Hruska**, which displays over 8000 plants varying in origin from Alpine to Mediterranean (open 09:00–12:00 and 14:00–18:00 from March to October).

Il Vittoriale ★★

On the hillside above Gardone is the villa known as Il Vittoriale (The Victory), the former home of **Gabriele d'Annunzio**, the poet and eccentric. He was given the villa by Mussolini in 1925 and d'Annunzio turned it into an extraordinary museum that illustrates the bizarre nature of the man. The house is kept in the semidarkness that d'Annunzio preferred. As well as a library of price-

less books, the tour reveals such macabre items as the coffin that the poet used to lie in to meditate, and his pet tortoise embalmed in bronze after it had died from overeating. The gardens are also full of interest, with an open-air theatre and d'Annunzio's mausoleum.

The writer's coffin is flanked by those of his followers and war comrades. Nearby is the World War I warship, the *Puglia*, which was hauled up the hillside to its final resting place. Also on display is the aircraft from which d'Annunzio dropped propaganda leaflets over Vienna, and two of the cars that the poet drove flamboyantly into battle. Not surprisingly, this bizarre place is one of Lake Garda's major attractions. Potential visitors should be aware that Il Vittoriale is so popular that at peak periods numbers may be restricted and it is necessary to arrive well before the opening time to be sure of getting a ticket (open daily 08:30–20:00 Apr–Sep, 09:00–17:00 Oct–Mar, tel: 0365 296 511, www.vittoriale.it).

Toscolano-Maderno

The next town on the western shore is **Toscolano-Maderno**, an amalgamation of two villages built partially on the alluvial fan built up by the River Toscolano. This was the largest town on Lake Garda during Roman times and a 1st-century villa has been discovered here with some well-preserved mosaics. Toscolano had a famous printing press in the 15th century, and paper-making is still an important industry in the area. The elegant Romanesque **Church of Sant' Andrea** is worth a look for its paintings by Paolo Veneziano. Take a glance at the tourist office, which has two cannonballs embedded in its walls, relics of the naval bombardment by the Austrians in 1866. On the north side of the town is **Villa Feltrinelli**, the home of Mussolini during the short-lived Salò Republic. Lake Garda's only car ferry runs from Toscolano-Maderno to Torri del Bernaco on the eastern shore.

Gargnano

Gargnano, surrounded by old citrus terraces, is well known as a sailing centre. It is also the site of a 13th-century Franciscan monastery with some well-preserved cloisters. A popular excursion from Gargnano is inland via a tortuous mountain road to the Val Toscanino and Lake Valvestino, which has been dammed to provide hydroelectric power. The road continues, winding its way down to Lake Idro.

Limone sul Garda

After Gargnano the lake shore becomes steep and the road frequently tunnels into the mountains. The last notable town on the western shore is **Limone sul Garda**, a former fishing village which has expanded into a thriving resort that many consider has been ruined by tourism. Old citrus terraces with their concrete supporting posts line the hillside. Limone was the first place in Europe to grow lemons, but today many of the terraces have been converted into vineyards. There is a historic quarter behind the fishing port with a couple of interesting churches, but the ambience is overwhelmed by the stalls and shops selling cheap souvenirs.

Riva del Garda

Located at the northern tip of the lake, Riva has always been of strategic importance, being held at various times by Verona, Milan, Venice, the French and the Austrians. During the Austrian rule from 1813–1918 it became a popular resort and was described as the 'Southern Pearl on the Austro-Hungarian Riviera'. It continues, today, to be the most stylish resort on Lake Garda and attracts many German and Austrian tourists. Next to the shore is the moated **castle**, the Rocca, built in the 12th century by the Scaligeri to defend the town against waterborne pirates. The castle now houses the **Museo Civico**, which displays paintings, sculpture and finds from the Bronze-Age settlement at nearby Lake Ledro

---

LEMON GROWING

The town of **Limone** may have got its name from the lemons that once grew here. Lemons were introduced to the area by monks in the 13th century, but growing these and other citrus fruit was difficult because the crop is ruined if the temperature drops below -3°C. The trees, supported by pillars and sometimes covered with glass, were grown on terraced south-facing slopes. Stoves were lit if frost threatened. Lemon cultivation declined after the unification of Italy, as cheap lemons were available from frost-free Sicily, and today only a few lemon groves are found around Lake Garda.

Opposite: *The resort of Limone is backed by terraces of lemon trees and vines.*
Below: *Riva is the most stylish resort on Lake Garda and is popular with German visitors.*

GALLEONS ON LAKE GARDA

The size of Lake Garda has lent itself to waterborne battles, and none was more bizarre than the naval skirmish between Milan and the Venetians in the 13th century. Venice decided to bring a fleet of 26 ships overland to the town of Torbole at the north of the lake. The boats were hauled overland by ox carts and then rowed up the Adige River to Lago di Lappio. There they were dismantled and carted over the pass to Torbole – a journey that had taken three months. They were rebuilt, but were barely seaworthy, so it was hardly surprising that the fleet was defeated by the Milanese.

(see below). The museum is open 10:00–18:00 Tuesday–Sunday, 09:30–22:30 July and August. Joint ticket with the Torre. The castle butts on to Riva's main square, the Piazza III Novembre. Dominating the square is the 13th-century clock tower, the **Torre Apponale**, which can be entered using the museum ticket. Outstanding among the buildings in the main square are the **Palazzo Pretorio**, built in 1376, and the 15th-century **Palazzo Communale**. Among the churches in Riva, the best is undoubtedly the **Inviolata**, which was built in 1603 and has a number of fine frescoes and paintings. In Piazza Garibaldi is a museum you will either love or hate. This is **Reptiland**, which has a comprehensive collection of creepy crawlies including snakes, tarantulas, giant beetles and scorpions. Open daily 11:00–20:00, April–October.

The area around Riva is rich in interest. The large pipe on the mountainside behind the town is part of a hydro-electric scheme using water from Lake Ledro. More waterworks, this time of a natural kind, can be seen near the village of Tenno, where a waterfall, known as the **Cascata del Varonne**, crashes down 87m (287ft) in a dark, spray-filled gorge. An interesting excursion can be made by taking the mountain road west to **Lake Ledro**. The eastern end of the lake was the site of Bronze-Age pile dwellings, and many of the stakes can be seen when the demands of Riva's hydroelectric scheme lowers the level of water in the lake. One of the dwellings has been reconstructed near the village of **Molina di Ledro** at the eastern end of the lake, where the **Museo delle Palafitte** displays jewellery, pottery and weapons found at the site. Opening times vary according to the season. The road continues past the lake and the small resort of **Pieve de Ledro** and through the gorge of Valle d'Ampola before dropping down to Lake Idro.

Below: *Italian ice cream is widely acknowledged to be the best in the world.*

LAKE GARDA'S EASTERN SHORE

The **Gardesana Orientale** or Garda's eastern shore is entirely within the province of Verona. The shoreline is lower than the west side of the lake, but backed by the limestone massif of **Monte Baldo**, which rises to 2130m (6989ft). The eastern shore is often called the **Olive Riviera**, on account of the large number of olive groves to be seen.

Tòrbole

Only a few kilometres separates Riva from Tòrbole, a popular wind-surfing resort. The Sarca River, which is the main feeder of Lake Garda, runs through the town and provides the pass

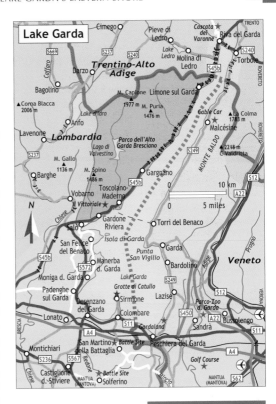

whereby the N240 runs east to the Adige Valley. Tòrbole is above all a young persons' resort, with the emphasis on outdoor activities of many kinds. The streets are full of roller bladers, joggers and mountain bikers – all in their specialist kits.

Further south is the beautifully situated town of **Malcésine**, distinguished by its 13th-century **Scaligeri castle**, which seems to rise directly out of the waters of the lake. With its tulip-like crenellations and battle-ments the castle is truly distinctive. Inside is a **museum** with natural history and archaeological sections. One room is devoted to the German writer, Goethe, who was briefly imprisoned here, being suspected of spying after he was seen sketching the lake! The old part of

LAKE GARDA'S MARKETS

One of the delights of taking a holiday in the Lake Garda region is to visit the weekly street markets on the following days:
Monday: Peschiera, Torri del Benaco.
Tuesday: Desenzano, Limone, Torbole.
Wednesday: Gargnano, Riva.
Thursday: Bardolino.
Friday: Garda, Sirmione.
Saturday: Malcésine, Salò.
Sunday: Bardolino.

Above: *Malcésine is a charming little resort on the eastern shore of Lake Garda.*

Malcésine is a maze of narrow streets backing the charming little harbour. The only building of real note is the **Palazzo dei Capitani del Lago**. Dating from the 15th century, it is now the town hall.

A wonderful excursion from Malcésine is by cable car to **Monte Baldo**. The journey takes 30 minutes and the top station is at 1650m (5410ft), March–October daily, every 30 minutes. From here there are a number of hiking trails, including one along the main ridge to the summit. The mountain is noted for its rare plants and it is a popular ski resort in the winter.

Torri del Benaco

Further south is Torri del Benaco, arguably the most attractive and least spoiled of Garda's lakeside villages. From here a car ferry crosses the lake to Maderno. Torri also has a **Scaligeri castle**. It dates from 1383 and is now a **museum** which has displays on the trades of the area such as the production of olive oil, wine, citrus fruits and fishing. South of Torri is the headland of **Punta San Vigilio**, with a little church of the same name. There are stunning views in all directions.

Garda

Sandwiched between the headlands of Punta San Vigilio and Rocca del Garda is the town of **Garda**. The name comes from the German *warten* or fortress, referring to the walls of the town, although few of these remain. Set back from the small port is an attractive tree-lined promenade, where a market is held on Fridays. Among the cobbled alleyways is the **Church of Santa Maria Maggiore**. Although the church dates largely from the 18th century, there is a well-preserved 15th-century cloister.

THE WORK OF GIANTS?

Just north of Torbole is the village of **Nago**, where there are some huge potholes near the old river bed. These are known as the **Marmitte dei Giganti** or the 'Pots of the Giants'. Some of these potholes are several metres across, but their origin had nothing to do with giants. We have to go back to the Ice Age, some 15,000 years ago, when torrents of glacial meltwater were pouring down from the Alps. Huge boulders were carried in the torrents and were swirled around on the bed of the river, wearing out the potholes by abrasion.

Bardolino

To the south of Garda is **Bardolino**, the centre of an area famous for the production of wine and olive oil. There are museums dedicated to both of these liquids. The **Museo del Vino**, at via Costabella 9, shows the methods of production and offers wine tasting (open daily 09:00–13:00 and 14:00–18:00, March–October). The **Museo dell'Olio d'Oliva** can be found at via Peschiera 54 (open 09:00–12:30 and 14:30–19:00, closed on Sunday and Wednesday afternoon). Bardolino is at its most lively during the *Fiesta del Uva*, the Festival of the Grape, which is held between mid-September and mid-October.

Bardolino has a number of churches, the most interesting of which are the 11th-century Romanesque **San Severo** with some good frescoes and an imposing campanile, and the 8th-century **San Zeno** with its cruciform structure and curious semicircular apses.

Lazise

The last town on the eastern shore is **Lazise**, with remains of the town walls and yet another Scaligeri castle. There has been a port here since the Venetian occupation and it is said that in those days a chain could be drawn from the castle across the harbour entrance. Next to the quay is the 12th-century **Church of San Niccolò**, with some highly regarded frescoes, and the arcaded medieval former **customs house**. Just outside Lazise is **Gardaland**, one of the largest theme parks in Italy. If you have bored children, this might be just the place to go (*see* panel, page 112). Open daily 09:30–18:00 from mid-March to September; longer hours in the height of summer; tel: 045 644 9777, www.gardaland.it

LAKE GARDA'S SOUTHERN SHORE

The southern shore of Lake Garda is low lying with a few rolling hills of glacial moraine. The towns of **Peschiera** and

OLIVE OIL

So many olive trees are grown on the southeast shores of Lake Garda that this has become known as the 'Olive Riviera'. The olive harvest begins around mid-November and continues until January. The milling of the olives is nowadays an industrial process. The quality of the oil depends on its acidity – the best oil has less than one per cent. This is known as 'Extra Virgin', which is green in colour. What better memento of a holiday in the Lake Garda area than a bottle of high-quality extra virgin olive oil? What's more, it contains no cholesterol and is an essential part of a healthy Mediterranean diet.

Below: *The attractive port of Garda.*

Opposite: *The town of Sirmione is protected by the Rocca Scaligeri.*
Below: *One of the many rides at the Gardaland Theme Park.*

Desenzano make good bases for visiting the lake. Between them is the remarkable town of **Sirmione**, which should be on every visitor's itinerary.

Peschiera del Garda

Located where the River Mincio drains Lake Garda, Peschiera has been a strategic town throughout its history. The Romans built the town's first defensive walls, which were extended and strengthened, first by the Scaligeri of Verona and later by the Venetians. Finally the Austrians, two centuries later, added two more towers. Today, it is possible to walk along part of the walls giving views over the town and the sizeable fishing harbour. There is not too much to see in the town itself apart from the 18th-century **Church of San Martino**, which has some impressive frescoes. The town hall clock in the main square is also of interest – two bronze eagles strike the bell with their beaks on the hour.

Sirmione

Positioned on a low 4km (2.5-mile) long peninsula, Sirmione has one of the most spectacular sites in Italy. The medieval core of the town occupies the rocky tip of the peninsula, protected by the **Rocca Scaligeri** built by the Verona dynasty in the 13th century, open Tuesday–Sunday 08:30–19:00, reduced hours in winter. Surrounded by a moat full of wildfowl and approached over a drawbridge, the castle is an imposing sight. Although there is not much to see inside the fortress, it is worth climbing up to the crenellated, tulip-shaped battlements and towers for a wonderful view over the roofs of the town to the point of the peninsula and the lake beyond. Next to the castle is the **Church of Santa Maria Maggiore**, with the usual set of frescoes. Note,

too, the Roman capital that has been set into the façade. Next to the church is the start of the *passegiatta panoramica* that runs along to the northern point of the peninsula.

Few tourists find their way to the end of the peninsula, but it is full of interest. There has been a spa here since Roman times, making use of the hot sulphurous water that originates beneath the lake bed. There is a large excavation site here, known as the **Grotte di Catullo**, named after the Roman poet Catullus. It was once thought that this was his villa, but such is the size of the area covered it can only have been a Roman spa. A small **museum** displays some of the artefacts and mosaics that have been recovered. The Grotte and the museum are open 08:30–19:00 Tuesday–Saturday, 09:00–18:00 Sunday from March to October; 08:30–16:30 Tuesday–Saturday, 09:00–16:30 Sunday from November to February. Nearby, occupying the highest point of the tip of the peninsula, is the **Church of San Pietro**. Romanesque in style, it was founded in the 8th century and has a good collection of frescoes dating from the 13th to the 16th centuries.

The old town of Sirmione is usually heaving with people, many of whom arrive by boat. Fortunately, traffic is not allowed past the castle. If arriving by car you will have to park and walk over the drawbridge.

Desenzano del Garda

At the southwest corner of the lake, Desenzano is the Lake Garda's largest town. As a transport centre, it is a good starting point for visiting the lake – close to the A4 *autostrada* and on the main railway line from Milan to Venice. Many of the lake steamers call at the attractive

THE FOUNDING OF THE RED CROSS

Perhaps the only good thing about the slaughter of thousands of soldiers at the battles of Solfarino and San Martino della Battaglia was the founding of the Red Cross organization. A Swiss gentleman, **Henry Dunant** from Geneva, was in the area trying to present a petition to Napoleon III. Dunant was appalled by the carnage of the battles and he helped local villagers to care for the wounded. On his return to Geneva, he wrote a book describing the battles and the large number of injured. Within two years the International Committee of the Red Cross was formed. Later Dunant was awarded the first **Nobel Peace Prize**, but sadly he became bankrupt and spent the last years of his life in a home for impoverished men.

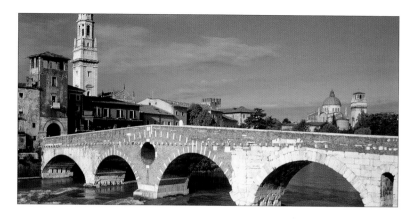

Above: *Peter's Bridge over the River Adige, Verona.*

little harbour. There are one or two items of interest in the town, including the Baroque **Church of Santa Maria Magdalena**, well known for Tiepolo's unusual version of the *Last Supper*. It features serving women and a dog, as well as the Apostles. Also worth a visit is the **Roman Villa** in Via Crocifisso. Dating from the 3rd century and excavated in 1921, it was obviously owned by a wealthy family and has some mosaics in excellent condition. Open 08:30–19:00 Tuesday–Saturday, March to October; 08:30–16:30 Tuesday–Saturday, November to February.

Notorious Battles

The plain south of Desenzano has been fought over by armies throughout history, but during the fight for Italian independence there occurred here, on the same day, two of the bloodiest battles ever. On 24 June 1859 at **San Martino della Battaglia**, Victor Emmanuel II and his Sardinian army defeated the Austrian right wing, while 11km (7 miles) to the southwest Napoleon III annihilated the main army of Emperor Franz Joseph at **Solferino**. Casualties were huge. At San Martino, a chapel contains the bones of over 2600 dead from both sides, while at Solferino over 7000 French and Austrian troops are buried. Both towns have museums and monuments to remember the dead.

SCALIGERI NICKNAMES

The Scaligeri dynasty were ruthless rulers of Verona and the Lake Garda area during the 13th and 14th centuries. The founder of the dynasty was **Mastino I**. Mastino means 'mastiff' and as a mark of respect all other male members of the family had some mention of dogs in their names. After **Mastino II**, all the male rulers had the prefix 'can' (or dog) added to their name. **Cangrande**, for example, was 'big dog' and **Cansignorio** was 'top dog'. Less endearing, however, was **Canrabbiaso** or 'mad dog'.

LAKE ISEO

Lying midway between lakes Como and Garda and situated just to the northwest of the town of Brescia, Lake Iseo is the fifth largest of the northern Italian lakes. It is, however, the least known outside Italy, although very popular with Italians. In the north of the lake around the town of **Lovere** are steep cliffs falling directly into the lake, giving it a fiord-like appearance. In the south the main town is the transport centre of **Iseo**.

Nearby is the village of **Zone**, which has some remarkable erosion features called the **Pyramidi di Zone**. These soft glacial deposits, known as erosion pyramids, have been worn away by erosion, leaving behind thin pillars topped by granite boulders.

Towards the southern end of Lake Iseo is **Monte Isola**, the largest island in the Italian lakes and indeed Europe. This island is essentially a huge mountain rising some 400m (1312ft) above the surface of the lake. It is capped by the **Church of the Madonna della Ceriola**, which is an important place of pilgrimage.

At the southern end of Lake Iseo is a large wetland area called the **Torbiere**, protected because of its wildlife and the remains of prehistoric pile dwellings.

LAKE ISEO FACTS

Lake Iseo is the fifth largest of the northern Italian lakes.
Length: 24km (15 miles).
Maximum width: 5km (3 miles).
Maximum depth: 250m (820ft).
Lake Iseo also has the largest island of any lake in Europe in Monte Isola.

VERONA

Most visitors to Lake Garda will probably land at Verona Airport and it is well worth spending a day or two in this ancient city before going on to the lake area. Verona is situated on a meander of the **River Adige**. This was a good defensive position to guard the routes coming south from the Alps and east–west across the Plain of Lombardy. Verona was an important

WHEREFORE ART THOU ROMEO?

During the 12th and 13th centuries in Verona there was an ongoing feud between the Cappelletti and Montechi families. The 16th-century Italian writer **Luigi da Porta** wrote a story based on this feud, which was adapted by Shakespeare, who changed the names to Capulet and Montague in his play *Romeo and Juliet*. A number of sites in Verona are associated with the play, such as Juliet's house, Romeo's house and Juliet's grave. Although the connections are dubious, this does not appear to worry tourists, who are happy to soak up the associations, particularly at the balcony of Juliet's house.

Below: *The Roman arena, site of Verona's famous summer opera festival.*

Roman city and a number of remains from this period have survived. Later it was an important city-state, typified by feuds amongst powerful local families. During the 13th and 14th centuries Verona came under the rule of the Scaligeri dynasty. Although fiercely authoritarian, they were also great benefactors of the arts. Verona was then briefly under the control of the Viscontis before having four centuries of Venetian rule. On the collapse of the Venetian Empire, Verona came successively under the rule of the French and the Austrians, before the unification of Italy.

Verona's Main Sights

The focal point of life in Verona is the elegant **Piazza Brà**, which is dominated by the immense **Roman Arena**. Built in the 1st century AD, it has an oval ground plan measuring 152m (498ft) by 123m (403ft). An earthquake in the 12th century destroyed much of the outer wall – that which remains is known as the wing. Over 20,000 spectators were able to watch gladiatorial contests, but today they flood in to watch the **opera festival** that takes place here during July and August. The Arena is open from 08:00–19:00 Tue–Sun, and during opera season from 08:15–15:30 Tue–Sun (www.arena.it).

Northeast of the Arena is the **Piazza dell'Erbe**, home of an ancient market selling vegetables and herbs. The market stalls remain today, but mostly sell tourist souvenirs and fast food. In the centre of the square almost concealed by the stalls is an old Roman fountain, while around the edge of the square are numerous fine houses and palaces. The Piazza dell'Erbe almost merges with the much quieter **Piazza dei Signori**. The square is also known as the Piazza Dante and there is a statue of the poet in the centre of the square. Dante settled in Verona after his exile from Florence. Good views of both squares and the rest of the town can be seen from the top of the **Torre dei Lamberti**, which fortunately has a lift. In front of the Romanesque **Church of Santa Maria Antica** are the **Arche Scaligeri**, the tombs of the Scaligeri family. Most imperious of all is the equestrian statue of Cangrande I, while the other tombs have elaborate wrought-iron grilles.

Above: *The balcony where Romeo and Juliet are supposed to have courted.*

A couple of blocks away from Piazza dell'Erbe, in Via Capello, is the **Casa di Giulietta** – Juliet's House. This is the Juliet of Shakespeare's *Romeo and Juliet* fame, and although the characters are largely fictional this does not deter the thousands of visitors that flock here annually to be photographed on the balcony. The 14th-century house is attractive enough, but a suitor would have to be extremely athletic to climb up to the balcony. 'Romeo's House' is situated close by and 'Juliet's Grave' is an empty sarcophagus in a nearby monastery. Open 08:30–19:30, Mondays 13:30–19:30. Combined ticket with Juliet's tomb.

The Castelvecchio Area

There is another collection of monuments southwest of the historic core of Verona. The **Porta dei Borsari** used to be the city's largest Roman gate and probably dates from the 1st century. The **Castelvecchio** (old castle), with a superb riverside position, was built by the Scaligeri in the mid-14th century and it formed their main stronghold. In later times it was a college, and the French and Austrians

> ### OPERA AT THE ARENA
>
> The opera festival at Verona runs through July and August and usually features many of the favourite Italian operas performed by world-famous singers. A visit to the Verona opera ought to be on everyone's itinerary, but a few words of advice are helpful. Remember that this is a Roman arena and the seats are extremely hard, so hire a cushion or bring one of your own. Seats are very expensive, but cheaper if bought on the day. Performances start at 21:00, when every member of the audience lights a small candle, giving the whole arena a marvellous atmosphere. However, opera-goers should be prepared for poor acoustics, noisy children and less than adequate toilets.

Above: *Verona's Ponte Scaligero, with the Castelvecchio to the left of the bridge.*

used it as a barracks. It was badly damaged in World War II, but has been fully restored and today houses the town **museum**. It has a fascinating collection of paintings, sculpture, jewellery and weapons (open 08:00–19:00, closed Mondays). Next to the Castelvecchio is a Roman Triumphal Arch, the **Arco dei Gavi**. It was destroyed by Napoleon's troops, but rebuilt in the 1930s. On the other side of the castle, spanning the River Adige, is the **Ponte Scaligero**, a bridge built by Cangrande II in the 14th century. It was blown up by the retreating Germans in 1945, but this too has been faithfully restored from the debris.

Northeast of the River

The Roman **Ponte Pietra** crosses the Adige to a group of monuments, museums and churches in the northeast of the town. The most important is the **Teatro Romano**, a Roman theatre dating back to the first century and probably older than the Arena. It is an amphitheatre with semicircular seating and it is used in the summer months for plays and concerts. At the back of the theatre is a lift that takes visitors up to the **Museo Archeologico**, which is based in an old convent. Both the theatre and the museum are open 09:00–15:00 Tuesday–Sunday, July and August; 09:00–18:30 September–June. There are two other mildly interesting museums on this side of the river – the **Museo Storico Naturale** at lungadige Porta Victoria 9, open 09:00–19:00 Monday–Saturday, and the **Museo Africano**, at vicolo Pozzo 1, open 09:00–12:00 and 15:00–18:00 Tuesday–Saturday.

NORTHERN ITALY'S MOTORWAYS

For the tourist motoring east–west across the Plain of Lombardy there is no need to experience the traffic snarl-ups in Verona, because the excellent *autostrada* bypasses the city. The *autostrada* system centres on Milan, making it easy to reach all parts of the region. The speed limit is 130kph (75mph), though this may be lowered during holiday periods. Remember, however, that the *autostradas* are toll roads and charges can mount up surprisingly quickly.

Verona's Churches

Verona has a wealth of interesting churches. Located at the most northerly bend of the river is the red and white striped **Duomo** or cathedral. It has a wonderful façade with elegantly carved portals. The lower part of the building is Romanesque, merging into Gothic at higher levels. The interior has some beautiful carving in the chapels. Look particularly in the first chapel on the left, where the altarpiece contains Titian's *Assumption*. More impressive than the Duomo, however, is the **Church of San Zeno Maggiore**, which is located just over a kilometre north-west of the Castelvecchio. It dates from the first half of the 12th century and has been described as the most significant Romanesque church in northern Italy. Of particular importance are the large rose window, the 48 relief panels on the bronze doors, and the triptych by Andrea Mantegna. San Zeno also has an imposing campanile and some elegant arcaded cloisters. Close to the Plaza dei Signori is the massive Gothic **Church of Sant'Anastasia**, Verona's largest church. Although rather plain on the outside, the interior is more interesting. Look for the fresco of *St George and the Princess* to the right of the main altar.

Other churches of note are **San Lorenzo**, near the Castelvecchio, which has an unusual women's gallery, and the 9th-century **Santa Elena** adjacent to the Duomo. It is possible to obtain a pass that allows admission to all the churches in Verona that belong to the *Chiese Vive* (Living Churches group). Better still is the **Verona Card**, which, for a remarkably cheap fee, gives admission to all the city's churches, museums and buses over a three-day period. Remember, however, that all the museums close on a Monday.

THE SHAKESPEARE CONNECTION

William Shakespeare, generally acknowledged to be the world's greatest playwright, wrote a number of dramas with northern Italian connections. His *Romeo and Juliet*, a love affair based on two feuding families in Verona, is well known, as is the *Merchant of Venice*. Less frequently performed is *The Two Gentlemen of Verona*, a comedy involving businessmen, their families and their love affairs. Surprisingly, there is no evidence that Shakespeare ever visited Italy.

Below: *San Zeno Maggiore – this basilica is claimed to be the most beautiful Romanesque church in northern Italy.*

Lake Garda and Verona at a Glance

BEST TIMES TO VISIT

Many attractions around Lake Garda close in winter, while Jul–Aug can be crowded and hot. Unless you're an opera fan, avoid Verona in August when hotels will be fully booked. **Spring** is the most pleasant season to visit Lake Garda, as the gardens will be in full flower and the higher mountains will still have a capping of snow. Sep–Oct, when the crowds have gone home, is also a good time.

GETTING THERE

The most convenient airport is Verona, just a 20-minute drive from the lake. The area is well served by *autostradas*: the A22 follows the Adige valley from the Alps and the A4 runs east–west along the Lombardy Plain to the south. **Railways** often closely follow the *autostrada* routes, with the Milan–Venice line calling at Verona, Peschiera and Desenzano. It is possible to travel from London to Verona by rail: use **Eurostar** to Paris and then take the over-night sleeper to Verona Porta Nuova (www.eurostar.com).

GETTING AROUND

Visitors with a **car** will find that You can drive around the lake in a day, although few would want to tour at this speed. A more leisurely way of seeing the lake is by **boat**, from speedy hydrofoils to traditional lake steamers. Most monuments, churches and museums can be reached on foot.

WHERE TO STAY

A variety of accommodation is available both around Lake Garda and in Verona. Many lakeside hotels, however, may be fully booked. It is essential to book ahead in the height of summer and especially in Verona during the opera season in July and August.

LUXURY

Grand Hotel Fasano, via Zanardelli 160, Gardone Riviera, tel: 0365 290 220, fax: 0365 290 221, www.ghf.it An 18th-century Habsburg hunting lodge converted into a hotel in 1900. In lakeside park with a range of sports facilities.
Du Lac et du Parc, viale Rovereto 44, Riva del Garda, tel: 0464 551 500, fax: 0464 555 200, www.hoteldulac-riva.it Lakeside hotel in large park. Well-appointed rooms. Closed Nov–Mar.
Palace Hotel, via Grotte 6, Sirmione, tel: 030 990 5890, fax: 030 916 390, www.dilos.com Neoclassical villa with gardens and elegant rooms.
Due Torre Baglioni, Piazza Sant'Anastasia 4, Verona, tel: 045 595 044, www.baglionihotels.com High-class traditional hotel in the historic core of the city.

MID-RANGE

Guilietta e Romeo, Vicolo Tre Marchetti 3, Verona, tel: 045 800 3554. Small, friendly hotel just off the Piazza Brà.
Flora, via Giorgione 27, Garda, tel: 045 725 5008,

www.hotelflora.net
On higher ground above the town, with gardens and pools.
Vega, Viale Roma, Malcésine, tel: 045 657 0355 fax: 045 740 1604, www.hotelvegamalcesine.it Modern hotel, well-equipped rooms; private beach.
Il Valiero, Via T. da Molin, Desenzano del Garda, tel: 030 914 1318 fax: 030 914 0322. Has its own beach close to the boat terminals.

BUDGET

Diana, lungolago d'Annunzio 30, Gardone Riviera, tel: 0365 21815, www.hotel dianagardone.it Simple rooms at small lakeside hotel.
Mercedes, via Nanzello 12, Limone, tel: 0365 954 073, www.hotelmercedes.com Bargain rates, pool and views.
Catullo, via Priori 11, Malcésine, tel: 045 740 0352, www.catullo.com Good value small hotel with a swimming pool.
Giardinetto, via G. Marconi 39, Riva del Garda, tel: 045 725 5051, fax: 045 627 8302. Comfortable small hotel. All rooms have lake views.

Youth Hostels

Lake Garda's only youth hostel is at **Riva**, Piazza Cavour 10, tel: 0464 554 911. Closed Nov–Mar. There is another hostel in **Verona** – Ostello Villa Francescatti, Salita Fontana del Ferro 15, tel: 045 590 360. Near the Teatro Romana. Take bus 73. Recommended evening meals.

Lake Garda and Verona at a Glance

Camp Sites

There are numerous camp sites around the lake and to the south. The following are recommended:

Rucc, via Rimenbranze 23, Gargnano, tel: 0365 71805.
Serenella, Riva, tel: 045 721 1333, fax: 045 721 1552.
La Rocca, Riva, tel: 045 721 1111, tel/fax: 045 721 1300.
Sirmione, via Sirmioncino 9, Sirmione, tel: 030 990 4665.
Verona, Campeggio Castel San Pietro, Via Castel San Pietro, Verona. Next to the youth hostel. Tel: 045 592 037.
Note that nearly all camp sites in the Garda area are closed from November to March.

WHERE TO EAT

There are plenty of eating options around Lake Garda and in Verona. The classiest restaurants are often in the large hotels, but rarely serve Italian regional dishes. For these, try the local trattorias.

LUXURY

La Rucola, Vicolo Strentelles, Simione, tel: 030 916 326, www.ristorantelarucola.it
Small refined restaurant close to the castle, specializing in lake fish and pizzas.
Al Caval, via Gardesana 186, Torri del Benaco, tel: 045 722 5666. Another restaurant famed for its lake fish.
Cavallino, via Gherla 30, Desenzano, tel: 030 912 0217, www.ristorantecavallino.it
Oustanding seafood, with lakeside terrace (closed Mon).

MID-RANGE

La Terrazza, via Pasubio 15, Torbole, tel: 0464 505 083. Taditional food, lake views.
Accademia, via Scala 10, Verona, tel: 045 800 6072. Attentive service at this homely city centre restaurant.
Trattoria Bicocca, via Molini 6, Desenzano, tel: 030 914 3658. Atmospheric trattoria serving a variety of lake fish.
Trattoria al Combattante, San Bernardetto, Via Sabino, Peschiera, tel: 045 755 3227. Lake fish and antipasti are the specialities of this trattoria on the road to Sirmione.

BUDGET

Belvedere, via Serafini 2, Arco, near Riva, tel: 0464 516 144. Specializes in meat and home-grown vegetables.
La Terraza, via Roma 53, Gardone. Cheap and cheerful snacks and pizzas
Gondoliere, Piazza Matteotti, Malcésine. Very reasonably priced seafood.
Taverna Fregosa, corso Vittorio Emanuele II 37, Riva. Large helpings at this taverna on the old town's main street.

SHOPPING

There are good opportunities for shopping in street markets in the towns around Lake Garda. Bargains can be had in leather goods, metalwork, carved wooden objects and ceramics. The area south and east of Lake Garda specializes in the production of wine and olive oil, and there are several outlets where these items can be bought directly from the producer. Verona is particularly good for high-quality shoes.

TOURS AND EXCURSIONS

Local tour operators offer excursions to historic towns such as **Bergamo**, **Mantua** and **Verona**. The most popular venues by the lake itself are the Gardaland theme park near Peschiera and **Il Vittoriale** at Gardone. With a comprehensive network of passenger boats on the lake, it is easy to plan your own tours.

USEFUL CONTACTS

Tourist Information Offices:
Sirmione, tel: 030 916 114.
Gardone, via Repubblica 39, tel: 0365 20347.
Gargnano, Palazzo Communale, tel: 0365 71222.
Riva del Garda, Giardini di Porta Orientale, tel: 0464 554 444, www.gardatrentino.it
Torbole, tel: 0464 505 177.
Malcésine, via Capitanato 6–8, tel: 045 740 0044.
Torri del Benaco, tel: 045 722 5120.
Garda, via Don Gnocchi 23, tel: 045 627 0384.
Verona, Piazza Brà, tel: 045 806 8680, www.verona.it

USEFUL WEBSITES

www.lagodigarda.it
www.tourism.verona.it

FERRY SERVICES

Navigazione Lago di Garda, tel: 030 914 511

Travel Tips

Tourist Information

The **Italian State Tourist Office** (ENIT) has offices abroad in USA (New York, Chicago and Los Angeles), Canada (Montreal and Toronto), Australia (Sydney) and the Republic of Ireland. The address of the UK office is: ENIT, 1 Princes Street, London, W1R 8AY, tel: 020 7408 1254, fax: 7493 6695. These offices are useful before departure, providing maps, brochures, transport details and lists of accommodation.

Within Italy itself there are regional and provincial tourist boards. All cities, towns and airports will have a tourist office usually known as an **APT** (*Azienda per il Turismo*) and shown with the standard 'i' symbol. The larger APTs are found in the following towns and cities:

Milan: Piazza Duomo 19a, tel: 02 7740 4343, open Mon–Sat 08:45–13:00 and 14:00–18:00, www.visitmilano.it
Bergamo: viale Vittorio Emanuele II 20, tel: 035 213 185, fax: 230 184, website: www.bergamo.it
Brescia: corso Zanadelli 38, tel: 030 45052, fax: 293 284, website: www.bresciaholiday.com
Como: piazza Cavour 17, tel: 031 269 712, fax: 261 152,

website: www.lakecomo.org
Cremona: Piazza del Comune (opposite the cathedral), tel: 0372 23233, website: www.aptcremona.it
Monza: Piazza Communale, tel: 039 323 222.
Pavia: via F. Filzi 2, tel: 0382 22156, fax: 32221.
Stresa: Via Principe Tomaso, tel: 0323 30150, fax: 32561, website: www.lagomaggiore.it
Varese: via Carrobio 2, tel: 0332 283 604.
Verona: Piazza Brà, tel: 045 806 8680, website: www.verona-apt.net

Entry Requirements

All visitors to Italy need a valid passport. Citizens of EU countries, including the UK and the Republic of Ireland, can stay as long as they like. Visitors from USA, Australia, Canada and New Zealand can stay for up to 3 months before requiring a visa. Visitors from other countries should consult their embassies regarding visas. It is a legal necessity to register with the police within three days of entering Italy – your hotel or camp site automatically do this for you. Anyone on holiday who decides to register with the local police station will probably be greeted with baffled amusement!

Customs

EU regulations apply, so that there is a free exchange of non-duty-free goods for personal use for citizens of these countries. There is little point in bringing in duty-paid goods as tobacco and alcohol are as cheap or cheaper here than in other European countries. Visitors from non-EU countries are subject to restrictions which vary from country to country. The age limit for importing alcohol and tobacco is 17. There is no limit on the amount of traveller's cheques that can be imported or exported.

Health Requirements

The standard of health care in northern Italy is generally on a par with the rest of Europe and travellers should encounter few problems. EU residents should have the EHIC card to obtain treatment on the same terms as residents. Australia also has a reciprocal health care agreement, but visitors from other countries should take out travel insurance that includes health benefits. For minor medical problems, go to the nearest *farmacia*, open during shopping hours. There is generally a duty pharmacy open at other times. In Milan there is a 24-hour *farmacia* at the Stazione Centrale.

Getting There

By air: Milan has two airports, Linate and Malpensa. **Linate** (tel: freephone 1673 37337, www.sea-aeroportimilano.it) is 8km (5 miles) east of the city centre. As it is near Milan, it is popular with business travellers, and two low-cost airlines, **EasyJet** (www.easyjet.com) and **Ryanair** (www.ryanair.com) run daily flights from Stansted to Linate. Ryanair uses Brescia airport as its northern Italian 'hub'. **Malpensa** (tel: freephone 7485 2200, www.sea-aeroporti milano.it) is 50km (31 miles) northwest of Milan. Terminal One deals with international flights and Terminal Two handles charters. Both **British Airways** (info tel: 0345 222 111, www.ba.com) and **Alitalia** (info tel: 020 760 2711, www.alitalia.it) offer daily flights to and from London and other British Airports. Alitalia also has connections from Boston, Chicago, Los Angeles, Miami and New York. There are also regional airports at Bergamo and Verona. All main international car hire firms have offices at Malpensa, but many visitors prefer to use public transport to Milan. A high-speed railway line connects the airport to the city, with trains at 30 minute intervals. There are two efficient coach lines. The Malpensa Shuttle drops passengers at the Stazione Centrale, and the Malpensa Express connects with both the Stazione Centrale and the more central Piazzale Cadorna. Both coach lines run at 20-minute intervals. Airline passengers visiting Lake Garda can also use EastJet and

British Airways daily flights to **Verona**.

By road: The UK is linked with Europe by car ferry and the Channel Tunnel. Once on the mainland you can drive all the way to Milan on the motorway system, but tolls can be expensive, particularly in Switzerland. At Italian frontier crossings it is possible to buy booklets for fuel coupons and vouchers for motorway tolls. Italian motorways are called *autostradas* – all are toll roads. The *autostrada* system in northern Italy focuses on Milan, with motorways leading off to all the major lakes. Traffic congestion in Milan can be awful and motorists are advised to leave their cars in the ATM car parks on the outskirts, thereby avoiding the city centre congestion charge. Sightseeing is easy using public transport: metro, buses, trams and trolleys. Motorists are advised to have comprehensive cover and an international green insurance card. In cases of breakdown, call tel: **116**. Milan can also be reached by **coach**. Eurolines run services from the UK and other European countries to Milan, Verona and Bergamo. For bookings and information in the UK, tel: 020 7730 8235.

By train: the quickest rail route to Milan from the UK is by Eurostar to Paris, then take the overnight service to Milan. Drivers can load their cars on the overnight **motorail** service at Bologna or Paris, arriving in Milan the next morning. Most trains arrive at Milan's **Stazione Centrale** (tel: freephone 1478 88088), from where buses and

metro go to the city centre. The station has a tourist office, banks, restaurants, a supermarket and a 24-hour pharmacy.

What to Pack

Strong walking shoes are advisable. You'll need a sweater for the evenings (except Jul–Aug). Rainwear is likely to be needed in spring and autumn. Do not wear shorts and beachwear when visiting churches. There are opportunities to swim from many of the lake shores and in the pools of the larger hotels – so pack a costume. The Milanese are formal in their dress – it is the fashion capital of Europe and designer gear features strongly in casual wear.

Money Matters

ATMs are found everywhere and accept all major cards. **Credit or debit cards** can be used at hotels, restaurants, petrol stations and most shops. American Express **travellers' cheques** are widely accepted. **The euro** replaced the lira on 1 January 2002. It is issued in notes of 5, 10, 50, 100, 200 and 500 euros, and the coins come in denominations of 1, 2, 5, 10, 20 and 50 cents and 1 and 2 euros.

Accommodation

Hotels or *alberghi* are rated from 1–5 stars (depending on facilities, not service standards). *Pensioni* are more modest. Most hotels have different rates in summer and winter, and some resort hotels in the lake region close in winter. Check if breakfast is included – you can usually get a cheaper, better meal in a bar. Lists of hotels and pensions are posted in tourist offices, but they are not obliged to make bookings. The decent hotels in Milan are often fully booked during trade fairs. Most hotels are in the city centre near Stazione Centrale and the Piazza della Repubblica. To book, contact Milano Hotels Central Booking, Piazza Missori, tel: 02 805 4242. Waterside hotels in the lake region can be expensive.

There are **youth Hostels** (*Ostelli per la gioventu*) in Bergamo, Como, Mantua, Menaggio, Riva del Garda and Verona. Milan's Piero Rotta hostel is at viale Salmoiraghi 2, tel: 02 3926 7095. Italy's Youth Hostel Association is the *Associazione Italiana Alberghi per la Gioventu* (or AIG), Pallazzo della Civilta del Lavoro, Quadrato della Concordia, 00144 EUR Roma, tel: 06 591 3702. An international membership card is needed, which can often be bought at the hostel. Hostels are closed during the day and may have a curfew at night. They are renowned for noisy school parties, particularly around the Easter period.

Camping is popular. The lakes have fine waterside sites, but they are crowded and noisy in August. Milan has two sites on the outskirts of the city. Unofficial camping is frowned on by the police, but tourist offices have lists of official sites. To obtain a camping carnet and details of all Italy's camp sites, contact *Centro Internazionale Prenotazioni Campeggio*,

Casella Postale 23, 50041, Calenzano, Firenze, tel: 055 882 382.

Eating Out

Milan's restaurants serve food from China, India, Mexico and Japan, with ubiquitous North American fast food, but do try some **Milanese specialities**. A *ristorante* offers antipasto, pasta, main course and dessert. Cheaper *trattorias* are more likely to serve regional dishes. Specialist restaurants include *spaghetterias* and *pizzerias*. For snacks, try a *tavola calde* or *panini* bar. **Vegetarians** are catered for at most eateries. Restaurants usually open from 12:00–15:00 and from 19:30 onwards. Many close on one day a week, typically Sunday, though in the lake area it is more likely to be on Monday.

Transport

Getting around poses few problems, apart from traffic congestion in central Milan. **Road:** Milan has an efficient public transport system, which is fortunate as driving a car in the city is very difficult. Outside

CONVERSION CHART		
FROM	**TO**	**MULTIPLY BY**
Millimetres	Inches	0.0394
Metres	Yards	1.0936
Metres	Feet	3.281
Kilometres	Miles	0.6214
Square kilometres	Square miles	0.386
Hectares	Acres	2.471
Litres	Pints	1.760
Kilograms	Pounds	2.205
Tonnes	Tons	0.984
To convert Celsius to Fahrenheit: x 9 ÷ 5 + 32		

WHSmith

Shop online at whsmith.co.uk

Sweet Dreams. Think

every year,
you tell 13 million
bedtime stories and
we love you for it

Milan, the *autostada* system allows you to reach all parts of the area more easily.

Car hire: Cars and camper vans (*autonoleggios*) can be hired at the main airports, where firms such as **Avis** (tel: 02 669 0280), **Hertz** (tel: 02 669 0061) and **Europcar** (tel: 02 8646 3454) have offices. It is cheaper to hire in advance in your own country. There is a minimum age limit of 21 and a credit card will be required.

Public transport: Milan's city transport system is operated by *Azienda Trasporti Municipali (ATM)*, with buses, trolley buses, trams and the metro. **Buses** and **trams** are orange, and their stops are marked with yellow signs. They are frequent but often crowded. Buy tickets before boarding. The green *Tram Turistico* departs from Piazza Castello on a two-hour tour with multilingual taped descriptions. Bus tours, run by Autostradale, depart from the cathedral square and last for three hours. Both tours are highly recommended. The **Metro** has four lines. Line one is shown on maps in red, line two in green, line three in yellow and line four (the latest) in blue. Trains run from 06:00 to midnight. ATM tickets can be used for all types of transport, though they cannot be used twice on the metro. As well as day tickets, weekly and monthly passes can be bought; 24- or 48-hour tourist tickets are good value. Tickets must be bought in advance (from automatic machines, tobacconists and newspaper kiosks).

Taxis: White in colour, taxis (expensive) cannot be hailed and must be boarded at the official taxi ranks scattered around the city. Make sure that the meter is switched on at the beginning of the ride. There will be surcharges for night-time journeys, luggage and trips to the airports.

Train: Italy's national railway, **FS** (*Ferrovie dello Stato*), is efficient and inexpensive. Routes link Milan with all the lakes. Tickets can be bought at the stations and at travel agents. A number of passes are available. For exploring northern Italy by train the 'Travel at Will' (*Biglietto Turistico Libera Circolazione*) ticket is useful. Other passes include Flexicard and the Kilometrico. Details can be obtained from the Stazione Centrale and travel agents.

Boat: All the larger lakes are served by watercraft such as steamers, hydrofoils, paddle steamers and motor boats. Some have timetabled ferries for foot passengers or vehicles, while others cruise the lakes. Contact local tourist offices about daily or weekly passes. Services are considerably curtailed in winter. See regional chapters for information.

Cycles and motorbikes: Cycling is popular and bikes can be hired in all major towns. It is not recommended in Milan, despite the existence of cycle lanes, as motorists can be ruthless. Cycling around the lakes or in the Alpine foothills can make a delightful holiday. Motorbikes, mopeds and scooters can also be hired. Helmets are compulsory and there are minimum age limits.

USEFUL WORDS AND PHRASES

Yes/No • *Si/No*
Please • *Per favore*
Thank you • *Grazie*
You're welcome • *Prego*
Good morning • *Buongiorno*
Good evening • *Buona sera*
Good night • *Buena Notte*
Excuse me • *Mi scusi*
Do you speak English? • *Parla inglese?*
I don't understand • *Non capisco*
Speak slowly • *Parla lentamente*
What/Who/Where? • *Che?/Chi?/Dove?*
How?/When?/Why? • *Come?/Quando?/Perché?*
Good • *Buono*
Bad • *Male*
Fast • *Rapido*
Slow • *Lento*
Big • *Grande*
Small • *Piccolo*
Hot • *Caldo*
Cold • *Freddo*

The Globetrotter Travel Map of Milan and the Italian Lakes is highly recommended. Free guides provided by the tourist offices are good for general purposes. The Touring Club of Italy's *Lombardia* is good, as is their street plan of Milan.

Business Hours

Unlike in the south of Italy, the afternoon siesta is becoming more rare in the north. Most businesses in Milan work a 09:00–17:00 day. Shops close on Saturday afternoons and Sundays and some may take a lengthy lunch break. Most museums and galleries close on Mondays, but may stay open until 20:00 in summer. Chemists (*farmacias*) usually open 09:30–19:30 Monday–Saturday. A rota for late and Sunday opening is posted in all chemists' windows.

Tipping

A service charge and VAT are added to most restaurant and hotel bills; no tipping is needed unless service is outstanding. It is customary to tip porters, usherettes in cinemas, bellboys and attendants. A gratuity of 10 per cent is usual for taxi drivers and tour guides.

Time Difference

Italy uses Central European time, normally 1hr ahead of GMT, 7hr ahead of US Eastern Standard Time. From the last weekend of March to the end of September clocks are put one hour ahead.

Communications

Although the Italian **postal system** has a poor reputation, most post offices in Milan and the north of the country work efficiently. They open 08:30–13:50 Mon–Fri and 08:30–12:00 Sat. There are post offices at Stazione

Centrale and at Milan's two airports. Stamps can be bought at tobacconists. Public **telephones** are run by *Telecom Italia* and there are plenty in Milan and around the lakes. Public phones take coins and cards (from tobacconists and newsstands). GSM mobile phones can be hired at the Euro Business Centre at Malpensa Airport. A Telecom Office at Stazione Centrale allows you to make international calls and send and receive faxes. Milan's area code is 02. When dialling abroad from Italy, use 0044 for the UK, 001 for the USA, 00353 for Ireland, 0061 for Australia. **Internet Cafés** are appearing widely in Milan and other cities in the north of Italy. Most large hotels catering for business customers have free Wi-Fi facilities in rooms.

Electricity

The supply is 220 volts and plugs have two or three round pins. Visitors should bring their own travel plug adapter from home.

Weights and Measures

Italy uses the metric system.

Health Precautions

Water is safe to drink and bottled water is available too. **Food** in restaurants is normally hygienically prepared, but shellfish can cause upset stomachs. Prevent **sunstroke** by using a hat and a high-factor sunscreen. **Mosquitoes** can be a problem in the summer, so take an insect repellent.

Personal Safety

Though the lake region sees little crime, Milan, like many cities, does have petty theft. A few sensible precautions reduce the risk considerably. Carry only minimal cash and keep valuables in the hotel safe. Beware of pickpockets on crowded trains, buses and in public places. Avoid poorly lit places at night. Lock your car and never leave valuables on view. If you are a victim, report to the local police station (*questura*). Larger stations have a tourist department and can issue a report for your insurance company. The police emergency number is **113**.

Etiquette

Wearing shorts or beachwear in **churches** is offensive. Do not disturb worshippers during a service, particularly with flash photography. Milan is fashion conscious; smart dress and formality are deemed important. **Smoking** is banned on public transport and in museums and many of the attractions, but may be tolerated in some restaurants). Reaction to **topless sunbathing** varies, but it is usually not acceptable at hotel pools or on lakeside beaches.

GOOD READING

Carluccio, Antonio *Carluccio's Complete Italian Food,* Quadrille.
da Vinci, Leonardo *Notebooks,* Oxford University Press.
David, Elizabeth *Italian Food,* Penguin.
Ginsborg, Paul *A History of Contemporary Italy,* Penguin.
Jepson, Tim *Wild Italy.* Aurum Press.
McCarthy, Patrick *The Crisis of the Italian State,* Palgrave.
Murray, Peter and Linda *Art of the Renaissance,* Thames & Hudson.
Peterson, Mountford & Hollom *Birds of Britain and Europe,* Collins.
Procacci, Guiliano *History of the Italian People,* Penguin.